BROOKINGS bw WHARTON

papers on URBAN AFFAIRS

2004

*William G. Gale and
Janet Rothenberg Pack
Editors*

BROOKINGS INSTITUTION PRESS
Washington, D.C.

BROOKINGS-WHARTON

papers on URBAN AFFAIRS

2004

| Purpose | *The Brookings Wharton Papers on Urban Affairs* is an annual publication containing articles and formal discussant remarks from a conference held at the Brookings Institution and arranged by the editors. The annual forum and journal are the products of a collaboration between the Brookings Institution Center on Urban and Metropolitan Policy and the Zell Lurie Real Estate Center at the Wharton School of the University of Pennsylvania. All of the papers and discussant remarks represent the views of the authors and not necessarily the views of the staff members, officers, or trustees of the Brookings Institution or the Wharton School of the University of Pennsylvania. |

William C. Strange   *University of Toronto*
Joseph Tracy   *Federal Reserve Bank of New York*
Jacob Vigdor   *Duke University*
Joel Waldfogel   *University of Pennsylvania*

Conference Participants

Patrick Bayer   *Yale University*
Alan Berube   *Brookings Institution*
Victor Calanog   *University of Pennsylvania*
Jerry Carlino   *Federal Reserve Bank of Philadelphia*
Sam Chandan   *University of Pennsylvania*
Anthony Downs   *Brookings Institution*
Ingrid Gould Ellen   *New York University*
Kathryn Engebretson   *William Penn Foundation*
Dennis Epple   *Carnegie-Mellon University*
Bengte Evenson   *Illinois State University*
William Gale   *Brookings Institution*
David Garrison   *Brookings Institution*
Andrew Haughwout   *Federal Reserve Bank of New York*
Vernon Henderson   *Brown University*
Brian Jacob   *Harvard University*
Pascale Joassart-Marcelli   *University of Massachusetts*
Helen F. Ladd   *Duke University*
Frank Levy   *Massachusetts Institute of Technology*
Amy Liu   *Brookings Institution*
Jens Ludwig   *Georgetown University*
Janice Madden   *University of Pennsylvania*
Therese McGuire   *Northwestern University*
Edwin S. Mills   *Northwestern University*
Dick Netzer   *New York University*
Carol O'Cleireacain   *Brookings Institution*
Katherine O'Regan   *New York University*
Robert Puentes   *Brookings Institution*
Martha Ross   *Brookings Institution*
Janet Rothenberg Pack   *University of Pennsylvania*
Amy E. Schwartz   *New York University*
Todd Sinai   *University of Pennsylvania*
Audrey Singer   *Brookings Institution*
Leanna Stiefel   *New York University*
Anita Summers   *University of Pennsylvania*
Jennifer Vey   *Brookings Institution*
Richard Voith   *Econsult Corporation*
Susan Wachter   *University of Pennsylvania*
Margy Waller   *Brookings Institution*
Tara Watson   *Princeton University*
William Wheaton   *MIT Center for Real Estate*
Cliff Winston   *Brookings Institution*

Preface

The *Brookings-Wharton Papers on Urban Affairs* is devoted to bringing forward-looking research to bear on urban policy issues in an accessible manner. The collaboration between the Wharton School and the Brookings Institution in this endeavor represents an effort to draw on resources and personnel in both academia and the policy community. We hope and expect that the journal itself will be of interest and use to an even wider audience that includes policymakers and their staffs, interested parties in the private sector, journalists, students, and others.

The existence of this journal owes much to the efforts of key people at Brookings and Wharton. At Brookings, President Strobe Talbott continues to support this project. Bruce Katz, director of the Center on Urban and Metropolitan Policy, has been a tireless and vocal supporter of the journal and its goals and provides major financial support.

At Wharton, Peter Linneman and Joseph Gyourko, former director and current director of the Samuel Zell and Robert Lurie Real Estate Center, have supported this undertaking intellectually and financially from its inception. The dean's office has made its contribution by freeing some of Janet Rothenberg Pack's time to organize the conference and edit the volume. The Department of Business and Public Policy has in numerous ways encouraged her participation in this endeavor.

Several people made vital contributions to the publication of this volume and the conference on which it is based. Saundra Honeysett at Brookings organized conference logistics and managed the paper flow with efficiency and good cheer. Amy Liu and Jamaine Fletcher provided valuable support at many stages. The authors and discussants deserve special thanks for making extra efforts to draft their arguments in a clear and accessible manner.

Editors' Summary

The *Brookings-Wharton Papers on Urban Affairs* presents new research to a broad audience of interested policy analysts and researchers. The papers and comments contained in this volume, the fifth in the series, were presented at a conference at the Brookings Institution on October 23 and 24, 2003. The conference amply displays the breadth of issues that fall under the rubric of urban economics and includes topics as diverse as the influence of the 1960s riots on long-term outcomes in urban labor markets, alternative explanations for the increasing attraction of people to cities with greater human capital, the role of educational policies in determining residential location choices, the effects of immigrants on the housing opportunities available to native renter households, the impact of states' parole practices, and the effects of larger urban markets on the diversity of television programming.

The Labor Market Effects of the 1960s Riots

William J. Collins and Robert A. Margo investigate the impact of the 1960s riots on long-term labor market outcomes. Although many studies have examined the determinants of race-related civil disturbances in the 1960s, few have explored the consequences.

Collins and Margo analyze riots as natural disasters with direct and indirect effects on the level and location of economic activity. While direct effects of destroyed physical capital may be small, the economic

We thank Brennan Kelly for outstanding assistance in the preparation of this introduction.

impact may be magnified by indirect effects felt over a long time. The authors envision a process of potential self-reinforcing decline as a result of a riot. For a business owner whose property is damaged, potential costs might rise because of higher security expenses and insurance premiums. Potential benefits of remaining in business may decline if customers avoid the area. As businesses decide to close, business revenues and personal income may fall; tax revenues and thus public services may decline; and falling rental and property values may increase poverty. For the population unable to relocate, a new labor market equilibrium may ensue with fewer employed workers, lower wages, and fewer residents with high human capital.

To identify the effects of riots, they cite the work of Seymour Spilerman, who shows that black population size and region were the two most important explanatory factors in predicting the incidence and severity of riots. They also use a two-stage approach, with the number of days of rain in April 1968 used as an instrument. The authors show that just 6 of 752 riots accounted for roughly 60 percent of the total fatalities.

Drawing from both city and individual-level data, the authors conclude that riots were associated with slower subsequent income growth for blacks and that cities that experienced riot-related relative declines in income during the 1960s did not catch up during the 1970s. Cities that had riots had relatively large subsequent increases in the share of the city population that was black. The onset of severe riots did not affect the likelihood of employment for black men between 1950 and 1970 but caused a 3 to 4 percentage point decline in the 1970s in the employment rate of black men in cities affected by severe riots.

Several hypotheses may explain the relative declines in income. The riots may have hurt the labor market outcomes of people living in the riot cities during the 1960s and 1970s; relatively high-income individuals may have moved out, leading to a decline in average income; and family units may have disintegrated faster in cities stricken by riots than elsewhere.

The Rise of the Skilled City

Between 1980 and 2000, the population of metropolitan areas where less than 10 percent of adults had college degrees in 1980 grew on average by 13 percent. In areas where more than 25 percent of adults in 1980 had college degrees, average population growth was 45 percent. Similar trends have occurred during the past one hundred years in both Britain and the United States. Edward L. Glaeser and Albert Saiz explore alternative explanations of these trends.

The first question is whether the relationship demonstrates that growth causes increases in skills or that increases in skills cause growth. The authors test for causation using a panel of metropolitan areas and cities during the past three decades. They find generally that increases in skills cause growth but also acknowledge that there is at least some potential for reverse causality.

The second question is whether skills cause growth by raising consumption or production. To examine this question, the authors show that production-led growth raises population and increases wages and house prices, whereas consumption-led growth raises population but reduces real wages. When Glaeser and Saiz return to their panel of metropolitan areas and cities, they find that an increase in the share of the population that is college educated is associated with an increase in housing prices during the following decade. That is, they conclude that the connection between education and growth at the metropolitan level is driven primarily by productivity growth rather than amenity growth.

The third question, then, is why more skills lead to productivity growth. One hypothesis is that higher skills lead to more rapid technological change. The authors reject this hypothesis, however, by showing that variations in patenting activity do not explain the relationship between human capital and growth across cities. They develop an alternative explanation, namely, that more educated cities are better able to respond to changing economic events. To support this view, they show that among cold, Rust Belt manufacturing cities, those with high human capital made greater shifts out of manufacturing during the past several decades than those with lower human capital.

School Funding Equalization and Residential Location for the Young and the Elderly

Christian A. L. Hilber and Christopher J. Mayer investigate the impact of school funding equalization (SFE) policies on the location choices of households. Using census data from 1970 to 2000, the authors show that the concentration of households with children and the elderly has changed little across states, but low-income households have become increasingly concentrated in a few states. Within states, the elderly, non-whites, and households with children have experienced the most deconcentration. This evidence supports the idea of the weakening importance of Tiebout sorting at the local level.

They find that households with children tend to locate in states with higher spending levels and where local revenues fund a greater percentage of total school spending relative to state sources of revenue. The SFE indicators like maximum inverted tax price and minimum foundation tax rate have little impact on location of households with children across states. For poor households with children, however, a high minimum foundation tax rate—a high floor on spending of local schools—proves attractive to households as they choose where to live.

As the share of elderly households is expected to grow in the United States during the next decades, research suggests spending on local public schools will suffer. This effect is likely to vary depending on the nature of state-level policies. States with local control and little redistribution are attractive to middle- and high-income households but not to low-income households. In states with considerable redistribution, wealthier households with children and elderly households have fewer reasons to avoid low-income places, resulting in less concentration of poor households and less separation of young and elderly population. They conclude that school services play an important role in residential location choices, and Tiebout sorting may partially mitigate the risk that a growing elderly population poses to support for public schools.

The authors find that Tiebout sorting by many household characteristics has been decreasing over time, but local public schools are an important element in residential location decisions. Since many states have passed school finance equalization packages, which seem to lead to reduced concentrations of households with children and poor households with children, school funding may help to explain the apparent reduction in Tiebout sorting in the past few decades.

The Anatomy of Rent Burdens: Immigration, Growth, and Rental Housing

Since 1970, immigration has accounted for roughly one-quarter of U.S. population growth in the United States, and the foreign-born population rose from 5 percent of the resident population then to more than 10 percent in 2000. During the same period, median rent burdens rose in the United States, especially among the lowest-income households. Erica Greulich, John M. Quigley, and Steven Raphael examine the relation between these trends.

Several factors suggest that immigrants may put pressure on low-income rental housing markets. Immigrants are disproportionately concentrated in a small number of states and a handful of metropolitan areas, they tend to have less education and lower income than natives, and are more likely to reside in rental housing.

Despite all of these factors, the authors find little evidence that immigration raises rent burdens. This conclusion is drawn from a series of tests that examine changes in immigration and rental burdens within metropolitan statistical areas, across metropolitan areas, and over time. The somewhat surprising finding may be caused by factors such as declining poverty rates and increasing incomes for the poor during the 1990s. It may also be a result of the ability of native households to move in response to housing price changes or to the fact that immigrant populations tend to move from renter to homeowner status fairly quickly.

The Effect of Prison Releases on Regional Crime Rates

Between 1980 and 2000, the U.S. prison population increased from 300,000 to more than 1.2 million. During the same period, the number of exoffenders residing in the community increased from 1.8 to 4.3 million. Annually, there are large flows into and out of the state and federal prison systems. For example, in 1999 approximately 550,000 inmates were released from prison, 75 percent being conditionally released into state parole systems. Steven Raphael and Michael A. Stoll examine how the presence of parolees affects the incidence of violent and property felony crime.

They find increases in crime associated with increases in the parole population. The net increase in the population of exoffenders caused by prison releases during the previous year accounts for approximately 14 percent of murders and 7 percent of robberies in 1994, and about 2 percent of property crime in a typical year during the 1990s.

They also find that postrelease criminal behavior of paroled offenders is likely to be affected by the correction policies of individual states. For both violent and property crime rates, the marginal effect of an increase in parole rates is higher in states with weak or no parole boards than in those in which parole boards have power over parole decisions.

The analysis indicates that higher prison incarcerations reduce violent offenses. In comparing new prison admits and prison releases, the authors find that the groups have similar educational, gender, and racial characteristics, commit comparable offenses, and have similar sentence length distributions. But they also find that having a felony record and acculturating to the prison environment are likely to increase criminality after prison, while participation in prison programs and the aging of inmates are likely to reduce criminality.

Who Benefits Whom in Local Television Markets?

When production carries substantial fixed costs, the larger local markets afforded by urban areas can support more, more varied, and higher-quality products, which increases consumer welfare. Joel Waldfogel examines these issues in the context of the market for television programming, which is a mixed local and national medium.

The author draws from the Scarborough Prime Next dataset of product consumption patterns for 180,000 individuals surveyed in the second half of 1999 and second half of 2000 in sixty-six large U.S. markets. Viewers in all markets face the same prime-time national programming options and the same national cable options, but within each market, viewers face a range of locally controlled programs.

The data appear to show that preferences in media products divide sharply along racial lines and that local television programming is an equilibrating force. Local markets have large numbers of shows with overwhelmingly minority audiences compared with prime-time shows that attract national audiences that are, at most, a third black. Thus the local data seem to indicate the distance between black and white preferences and that local programming, far more than national programming, caters to those preferences. Waldfogel concludes that areas with higher shares of black or Hispanic populations have substantially more black- and Hispanic-targeted programming outside of prime time.

These results have implications for the welfare of urban consumers. When preferences differ across audience groups, the welfare of local media consumers depends on the size of the group in the local population. Waldfogel concludes overall that different racial groups prefer different television programming; that markets with a higher percentage of minorities have larger amounts of minority-targeted programming; minorities have a greater tendency to watch, and presumably derive more satisfaction from, television in markets with more minority-targeted programming. His conclusion is that increasing the minority share of a local population will raise the welfare of local minorities.

WILLIAM J. COLLINS
Vanderbilt University

ROBERT A. MARGO
Vanderbilt University

The Labor Market Effects of the 1960s Riots

ALTHOUGH THE UNITED STATES has experienced race-related civil disturbances throughout its history, those that occurred in the 1960s were unprecedented in frequency and scope. Between 1964 and 1971, hundreds of riots erupted in American cities, resulting in large numbers of injuries, deaths, and arrests, as well as considerable property damage concentrated in predominantly black neighborhoods. Law enforcement authorities took extraordinary measures to end the riots, sometimes including the mobilization of National Guard units. In retrospect, the riots marked a turning point in American racial politics, as the carefully orchestrated demonstrations of the early civil rights movement gave way to violent, chaotic civil disturbances.

At the time of their occurrence, the riots prompted congressional investigations into their proximate and underlying causes and into their immediate consequences in the form of looting, property damage, injuries, and deaths.[1] Subsequently, a large sociology literature developed that attempted to identify city-level correlates of the occurrence and

The authors thank Gregg Carter, Michael Haines and Justin McCrary for sharing their data with us. Brett Austin, Hannah Moon, Stephanie Schacht, and Dustin Worley provided excellent research assistance. Portions of this research are supported by the National Science Foundation. Suggestions from William Dickens, Lawrence Katz, Ilyana Kuziemko, Deirdre McCloskey, Daniel Myers, Martha Olney, Jasmin Sethi, Seymour Spilerman, Jacob Vigdor, and seminar participants at the National Bureau of Economic Research, Harvard University's Kennedy School of Government and Department of Economics, the Federal Reserve Bank of New York, Indiana University, Northwestern University, and Tufts University are gratefully acknowledged.
    1. U.S. Senate (1967).

1

severity of riots.[2] But there have been comparatively few studies of a systematic, econometric nature that examine the impact of the riots on the relative economic status of African Americans or on the cities and neighborhoods in which the riots took place.[3]

In this paper we study the impact of the 1960s riots in the context of long-term racial disparities in labor market outcomes. Among full-time male workers, the racial gap in average earnings narrowed up to 1975, with periods of sharp convergence (for example, the 1940s) alternating with periods of relative stasis (for example, the 1950s and early 1960s). Since 1970, racial convergence in earnings has slowed markedly, and a substantial part of the observed convergence has been driven by the selection of low-income black males out of the full-time labor force.[4] Over the same period, the proportion of blacks living in "high poverty" urban neighborhoods increased sharply, and black ghettos turned increasingly "bad" in the sense that residential segregation led to increasingly poor socioeconomic outcomes among young blacks.[5]

The post-1970 rise in concentrated poverty in black central-city neighborhoods has received a great deal of scholarly attention. One prominent view, associated with the work of William Julius Wilson, is that the underlying causes of this adverse trend are essentially macroeconomic in nature.[6] Technological change and the relative decline of manufacturing employment may have reduced relatively high-wage job openings for urban, unskilled workers. The geographic concentration of poverty was then reinforced by the movement of relatively well-off blacks from central-city neighborhoods to suburbs and the proliferation of single-parent

2. See, among others, Wanderer (1969); Spilerman (1971); Lieske (1978); Carter (1986); Myers (1997).

3. Aldrich and Reiss (1970); Frey (1979); Kelly and Snyder (1980); King (2001). Aldrich and Reiss (1970) examined the impact of riots in Boston, Chicago, and Washington, D.C., on small businesses, primarily retail establishments. They find a direct negative impact of the riots through property damage and an indirect effect through higher insurance rates, which created incentives to move or close up shop. Frey (1979) examined the causes of "white flight" in the 1960s in a sample of thirty-nine metropolitan areas. He used the number of riots per 100,000 central city population as an explanatory variable for the city-to-suburb net mobility rate; the estimated effects are positive but weak. Kelly and Snyder (1980) are closest in spirit to our paper. Using city-level data, they regress nonwhite family income in 1970 on income in 1960, measures of riot frequency and severity, and other controls. The results are small and statistically insignificant.

4. Brown (1984); Chandra (2000).

5. Wilson (1987); Cutler and Glaeser (1997); Collins and Margo (2000).

6. Wilson (1987).

households. Another prominent view, associated primarily with the work of Massey and Denton, emphasizes that preexisting residential segregation and ongoing racial discrimination in housing allowed for the potent endogenous magnification of adverse economic shocks. Feedback among macroeconomic forces, residential segregation, and social norms may have pushed entire neighborhoods into a downward socioeconomic spiral.[7] The hypothesis we are pursuing is that the riots may be examples of such negative shocks.

Like any shock, some of a riot's impact will be felt directly—in this case, by individuals who were immediately affected by the event. To some extent, these effects may be offset by private sector responses (for example, insurance payments) or changes in government policies (subsidies or loans to riot-afflicted businesses or infrastructure investment in riot areas). But other, and potentially much larger, effects may be indirect. A riot might alter the course of a city's economy by influencing the economic decisions of individuals who were not directly affected by the event. In essence, the hypothesis under investigation has two parts: that a riot's effect on African Americans' labor market outcomes was, on net, negative; and that the magnitude of the local effect increased with the severity of the local riot.

We present two complementary empirical analyses. The first uses aggregate, city-level data on income, employment, unemployment, and the area's racial composition from the published volumes of the federal censuses.[8] After constructing an index of riot severity, we estimate the "riot effect" by both ordinary least squares (OLS) and two-stage least squares (2SLS). The second empirical approach uses individual-level census data from the Integrated Public Use Microdata series for 1950, 1970, and 1980.[9] We adopt a difference-in-difference framework to compare blacks' labor market outcomes in cities that had severe riots with blacks' outcomes in cities that did not have severe riots, after controlling for a variety of relevant individual characteristics.

The findings, which are broadly consistent across different types of data and estimation techniques, suggest that the riots had negative effects

---

7. See, among others, Murray (1984); Wilson (1987); Jencks (1993); Massey and Denton (1993); Sugrue (1996).

8. To use 1960 as a starting point, we have to proceed at the city-level because the 1960 public use microdata samples do not identify city of residence.

9. IPUMS, Ruggles, Sobek, and others (1997).

on blacks' income and employment that were economically significant and that seem to have been larger in the long run (1960–80) than in the short run (1960–70). We view these findings as suggestive rather than definitive for two reasons. First, the data are not detailed enough to identify the precise mechanisms at work. Second, the wave of riots may have had negative spillover effects to cities that did not experience severe riots; if so, we would tend to underestimate the riots' overall effect.

The 1960s Riots in Historical Perspective

The United States has a long and terrible history of race-related riots. Gilje documents scores of riots including antebellum attacks on free blacks, Civil War draft riots in the North that targeted blacks for abuse, Reconstruction and post-Reconstruction collective violence against southern blacks, and inner-city eruptions during World War I, the Great Depression, and World War II when blacks competed with whites for jobs and housing.[10]

The riots of the summer of 1943 provide the closest parallel to those of the 1960s. There were close to fifty riots in that year, including one in Detroit in which thirty-four people were killed (twenty-five of them black). Harlem also erupted in violence, and although the riot was not as severe as Detroit's in fatalities, looting and property destruction occurred on a large and possibly unprecedented scale. One thousand and five hundred stores were looted or damaged, virtually all in predominantly black neighborhoods.[11] The riots during the 1960s were not unprecedented in their individual severity (measured by number of deaths), but as a group, their high frequency, wide geographic distribution, and destructiveness were unique. The 1960s riots were historically unusual in that they were characterized by what sociologists called "black aggression" (though the aggression was rarely directed toward physically harming white civilians), in contrast to most previous significant race-related riots, which were characterized by whites attacking blacks.[12]

10. Gilje (1996).

11. Gilje (1996, p. 158).

12. There were, of course, instances of violence against white bystanders, police, and shop owners. Nonetheless, the Kerner Commission report asserts: "While the civil disorders of 1967 were racial in character, they were not interracial. The 1967 disorders, as well as earlier disorders of the recent period, involved action within Negro neighborhoods

Measuring the incidence and severity of "race-related riots" requires that one define such an event. Spilerman posited an operational definition that has stood as the literature's standard for years.[13] To enter his sample, a riot had to involve at least thirty participants, some of whom were African Americans engaged in "aggressive" behavior (for instance, looting or property damage); had to occur outside a school setting; and had to be "spontaneous" in the sense that it was not the adjunct of an organized civil rights protest. Spilerman drew on the Congressional Quarterly's *Civil Disorder Chronology*, the Kerner Commission report, an index prepared by the *New York Times*, and the "Riot Data Review" prepared by the Lemberg Center for the Study of Violence at Brandeis University.[14] Each of these primary sources used somewhat different definitions of a riot, collected different dimensions of data, and covered different time frames.[15] However, with some margin of error, the sources can be combined to document the date and location of each significant disturbance and to construct measures of riot severity.

Carter extended the Spilerman data to 1971, cross-checked the data with other sources, added new information, and, in general, refined the database for subsequent studies.[16] For 1964 to 1971, the data set includes the dates and location of each riot, and the number of arrests, injuries,

---

against symbols of white American society—authority and property—rather than against white persons" (1968, p. 110).

13. Spilerman (1970; 1971).

14. The Kerner Commission report (National Advisory Commission on Civil Disorders [1968]) was preceded by hearings before the Senate Permanent Subcommittee on Investigations headed by John L. McClellan. U.S. Senate (1967). The subcommittee's staff identified cities that had experienced riots and then surveyed the mayors of those cities seeking information about the proximate causes and severity of the event. The McClellan data cover the years 1965 to 1967 and, therefore, do not include riots occurring in 1968 (such as those following the assassination of Martin Luther King). It is not clear from the testimony of Robert Emmet Dunne and Crichton Jones, who collected and organized the subcommittee's statistics, exactly how the cities were identified, or what criteria were used to determine whether the disturbance was "major" and therefore worthy of inclusion in the study. See part 1 of the hearings for the testimony, data, and the survey instrument sent to the mayors.

15. The McClellan report (see note 14) appears to use the most stringent criteria, with an emphasis on high levels of violence (number of deaths), involvement of law enforcement (number of arrests), and destruction of physical property (looting, arson), while the Lemberg Center used the loosest criteria. Unfortunately, the data collected by the Lemberg Center do not overlap (in timing) those collected by McClellan or Kerner, since they start in 1968 and end in 1971. The *Times* index essentially replicates the material found in the other sources.

16. Carter (1986).

occurrences of arson, and deaths. We use Carter's data to construct an index of riot severity that is central to our measurement of the riots' effects. Each riot (indexed by j) is assigned a value $S_j = \Sigma_i (X_{ij}/X_{iT})$ where X_{ij} is a component of severity (deaths, injuries, arrests, arsons, and days of rioting) and X_{iT} is the sum of component X_{ij} across all riots. That is, S_j is the proportion of all riot deaths that occurred during riot j, plus the proportion of all riot injuries that occurred during riot j, plus the proportion of all arrests, and so on. Summed over all riots, there are five total index points (a reflection of the five components that enter the index). We add the index values for each riot within a city to form a cumulative city-level riot severity measure.

The potential shortcomings of the index are clear. Counts of destructive events do not necessarily correspond to economic damage, let alone to a riot's impact on economic agents' expectations. One might argue, for example, that potentially important components are missing from the index, or that given the existing components, some should weigh more heavily than others.[17] Nonetheless, we believe that the index is a useful measure of riot severity for several reasons. First, the individual components of the index are highly positively correlated, and so in practice it matters little if, for example, we treat the proportion of deaths as "more important" than the proportion of injuries.[18] Given the rather high correlations among observable measures of severity, one might reasonably expect that they are well correlated with unobservable components as well. Second, any alternative choice of weights would necessarily be as ad hoc as our choice of equal weights.[19] Third, to conserve degrees of freedom, to facilitate instrumental variable estimation, and given the

17. Unfortunately, consistent value-based measures of property damage do not exist.

18. Nonetheless, we do note some results from regressions run using deaths as the only measure of severity. The correlations among deaths, arsons, arrests, and injuries across riots are high: at least 0.64 (deaths and injuries) and as high as 0.87 (deaths and arsons). Correlations of these variables with days of riots are somewhat lower, ranging from 0.32 to 0.48. All correlations are statistically significant at the 1 percent level. Later in the paper, we sum S_j over riots within cities for the city-level measures of riot severity. To test the robustness of this index, we created five alternative indexes, each of which omitted one of the observed severity components. The resulting indexes were highly correlated with one another and with the base index used here, with a correlation coefficient ranging from 0.96 to 0.99.

19. Our measure of riot severity is "absolute" in the sense that we do not scale severity by population; however, our city-level regressions control for population directly or indirectly in the IPUMS regressions when we include area fixed effects.

components' positive correlation, the use of an index is far more practical than entering each component separately in the regressions.

Table 1 summarizes each component of the index by year and reports the overall index by year and census region. The most obvious aspect of the data is the strong concentration of riot activity in 1967 and 1968, which together account for 3.3 out of the 5.0 total index points. When the index numbers are arrayed by census region, there seems to be a comparatively even geographic spread of riot activity, with the Midwest (1.57) and South (1.53) outpacing the Northeast (1.11) and West (0.79).[20] This impression is true in the sense that major riots occurred in every region, but it is misleading because the "severity" was heavily concentrated in a relatively small number of events (and cities), not spread evenly over them. For example, no deaths occurred in 91 percent of the 752 riots underlying table 1, and just six riots account for nearly 60 percent of the fatalities (228). By far the most deadly riots were in Detroit in July 1967 (43 deaths), Los Angeles in August 1965 (34 deaths), and Newark in July 1967 (24 deaths).[21] Using the index as a broader measure of severity, the riot in Washington following Martin Luther King's assassination ($S = 0.34$) would join Los Angeles in 1965 (0.48), Detroit in 1967 (0.44), and Newark in 1967 (0.23) as the most severe events on record. Fully 90 percent of the riots receive index values of less than 0.01. As we discuss, the intercity variation in riot severity will play a key role in our empirical strategy for measuring the riots' effects on labor market outcomes.

Causes of the Riots

The occurrence of the riots at a time when, at the national level, blacks' economic prospects were improving belies any simple causal connection running from economic status to riot severity. Although postriot government reports and journalistic accounts are replete with speculation and anecdotal evidence, the causes of the 1960s riots became a major research topic in sociology in the early 1970s. The point of departure for nearly all subsequent academic work was a series of papers

20. Washington, D.C., and Baltimore, which had sizable riots, are counted in the census South.

21. The other three were in Washington, D.C., in April 1968 (11 deaths); Cleveland, July 1968 (10 deaths); and Chicago, April 1968 (9 deaths).

Table 1. The Riots of the 1960s: Frequency and Severity

Item	1964	1965	1966	1967	1968	1969	1970	1971	Total
Riots	11	11	53	158	289	124	68	38	752
Days of riots	34	20	109	408	739	284	126	82	1,802
Killed	2	35	11	83	66	13	13	5	228
Injured	996	1,132	525	2,801	5,302	861	710	414	12,741
Arrested	2,917	4,219	5,107	17,011	31,680	4,730	2,027	1,408	69,099
Occurrences of arson	238	3,006	812	4,627	6,041	369	283	459	15,835
Index value	0.163	0.504	0.275	1.349	1.956	0.374	0.230	0.149	5.000
Northeast	0.145	0.003	0.027	0.419	0.288	0.125	0.078	0.023	1.107
Midwest	0.008	0.011	0.180	0.750	0.501	0.079	0.042	0.004	1.574
South	0.010	0.001	0.019	0.107	1.055	0.115	0.104	0.121	1.532
West	0.000	0.489	0.050	0.073	0.112	0.056	0.006	0.001	0.786

Source: Carter (1986).
Note: See text for definition of a riot. Each riot (I) is assigned a value $S_I = \Sigma_i(X_{ij}/X_{ri})$ where X_{ij} is a component of severity (days of rioting, injuries, arrests, deaths, and arsons) and X_{ri} is the sum of X_{ij} across all riots. Summed over all riots in the data set, there are five total index points (a reflection of the five components that enter the index).

by Spilerman, which estimated multivariate models of riot incidence and severity.[22] In this work, the unit of observation was the city, and the independent variables were drawn from the 1950 and 1960 federal censuses and related government documents. Spilerman's principal finding was simple: the absolute size of the black population (positively correlated with riots) and southern location (negatively correlated with riots) were the best predictors (in a statistical sense) of the incidence and severity of the riots. He found little support for many other seemingly plausible explanatory factors, including a variety of indicators of blacks' absolute and relative (to whites) economic status.[23]

Thus, taken literally, Spilerman found that conditional on black population size and region, severe riots were essentially idiosyncratic events. The chronologies of specific riots suggest this is not as far-fetched an interpretation as it might at first sound. In many (perhaps most) cases, there were identifiable, idiosyncratic "sparks" that, through a series of unforeseen complications, turned a minor altercation into a full-blown riot. The spark might be an encounter gone wrong between a black motorist and the police (as in Watts), or an impromptu, incendiary speech by activist H. Rap Brown (as noted in a congressional report).[24] The most incendiary event was surely the assassination of Martin Luther King in April 1968, after which more than one hundred riots erupted.

Subsequent research has modified Spilerman's work by improving the quality of the riot data, using event history analysis, introducing covariates that were not available to (or not considered by) Spilerman, and extending the time frame under study.[25] But nearly all of the "second-generation" studies confirm Spilerman's original finding that black population size and region are the most consistent and quantita-

22. Spilerman (1970, 1971, 1976).

23. Spilerman and subsequent authors relate riots to socioeconomic conditions in 1950 or 1960 census data. It is unknown whether short-term movements in socioeconomic conditions (for example, between 1960 and 1965) would be more useful predictors of riot activity. Recently, Chandra and Foster (forthcoming) reported state-level evidence suggesting a complex relationship between riot occurrence and the residual wage gap between blacks and whites (after accounting for observable differences in human capital). Spilerman (1976) argues that, on average, riot severity was higher for early riots in a city than for later riots.

24. The Senate Hearings on Riots, Civil, and Criminal Disorders (1967, part 1) contain a table describing "major riots," including their "triggering incident."

25. Lieske (1978); Carter (1986, 1990); Olzak and others (1996); Myers (1997; 2000); DiPasquale and Glaeser (1998); Chandra and Foster (forthcoming).

tively important explanatory variables for riot incidence and severity in the 1960s.[26]

Most recently, Myers has found that contagion played a role in determining the geographic pattern of riots.[27] Riots were given extensive television news coverage, suggesting one mechanism (not the only one) by which an outbreak of violence in one city might spill over to another, especially if they shared the same media outlets. This contagion effect seems to have waned quickly over time. The occurrence of a second (or higher-order) riot also seems to have been more likely following an initial disturbance, though within cities, riots declined in severity over time.[28] The sociological studies cannot rule out the possibility of underlying city-specific causes, but it is clear that matching the events to observable city-level correlates, beyond location, black population size, and proximity to other riots, is extremely difficult.

How Might Riots Affect Labor Markets?

Our model supposes that people and businesses choose locations that maximize utility and profits respectively. Household utility is a function of the benefits and costs associated with inhabiting a particular space. The benefits come in many forms: access to local public goods (schools, churches, entertainment, and so on), proximity to one's place of work, and proximity to one's friends and family. The costs include rent or mortgage interest payments, property upkeep and insurance, and taxes. For businesses, the benefits derive from the flow of revenue associated with the location, which might depend on demand from local residents or on proximity to other businesses. The costs derive from rent or mortgage interest payments, labor costs, property upkeep and insurance, and taxes. We suppose that in the short run, movement is inhibited by fixed costs associated with "starting over" in new locations.

---

26. As we point out, the form of local government may have mattered in determining the occurrence and severity of riots, along with weather. Spilerman considered the former, finding some evidence of effects, but he did not consider the latter, at least not in his published work.

27. Myers (1997, 2000).

28. Spilerman (1976).

The occurrence of a riot may have direct and indirect effects on the level and location of economic activity. The direct effects are experienced by individuals whose connection to the riot is immediate: an injured rioter, a resident whose home is in the line of fire, a business owner whose establishment is torched or looted, and so on. For some individuals, the direct effects are irreversible (obviously, for anyone who is killed), but for others, the effect may be transitory, depending on subsequent decisions made in light of changed perceptions of the economic environment.

Consider, for example, a business owner whose establishment is damaged or looted and, therefore, is temporarily shut down. Whether or not the business reopens depends on the expected benefits and costs of doing so at that location relative to all others (and relative to staying permanently closed and putting the remaining capital to some other use).[29] For some, the costs of rebuilding or restocking may be covered by insurance or public subsidies, but others may be uninsured or ineligible for assistance. Looking forward, the expected costs of operation in that location may increase after the riots. There may be higher insurance costs, expenses from the installation of additional security features (fire and burglar alarms), higher interest rates on small business loans, and higher taxes to pay for redistribution programs or an increased police presence.[30] At the same time, the expected benefits of being in that location might fall, especially if the firm's revenue depends heavily on business from nearby firms or residents.

If only direct effects come into play, the labor market implications of a riot might be small and short-lived, especially when viewed at the city

29. A business may be viable in the short run—that is, with its capital stock fixed—but only because it can cover variable costs, not because the rate of profit is "normal" in the long run. Even if the costs of rebuilding are covered by insurance or other means and the costs of operation do not rise, it may not pay to reopen if, before the riot, the business was not economically viable in the long-run sense. Some such owners may relocate elsewhere in the city, but others may leave entirely, taking whatever capital remains with them.

30. On higher insurance costs see Aldrich and Reiss (1970); Bean (2000). There were reasonable grounds for expectations of higher taxes for redistribution and police. For example, the Governor's Commission report on the Watts riot made three "high-priority" recommendations: "cooperative programs" with businesses for the training and employment of blacks, "a new and costly approach to educating the Negro child," and increased police efforts on crime prevention and community relations (1965, p. 8). Systematic evidence on the extent to which such programs were actually undertaken is scarce. See Hahn (1970) for some discussion of the issue.

level. Even at their worst, the 1960s riots never directly involved vast numbers of people or vast amounts of capital. For example, property damage during the Detroit riot in July 1967 was approximately $50 million, a small share of total property value in the city. The great majority of Detroit's 500,000 black residents at the time had no direct involvement in the riot.[31] The worst of the direct effects were borne by the residents and businesses located in the general vicinity of 12th Street, where the riot originated after a police raid on a "blind pig" (an after-hours drinking establishment).

However, even if the direct effects are limited, a riot's ultimate economic impact may be magnified through endogenously propagated indirect effects that unfold over a longer period. After a riot, firms and residents might revise their expectations of the benefits, costs, and risks of locating in or near a particular central-city neighborhood even if they were not directly affected by the riot. If some residents leave and firms close because of the initial shock (and are not replaced instantaneously), local economic activity and employment may slacken. The web of potential knock-on effects is extensive: personal income and local business revenues may fall, local sources of tax revenue may diminish, the area may experience a rise in crime and a decline in publicly provided services, and declining rents and property values (and perhaps the outmigration of the relatively well-off) may exacerbate the concentration of poverty in inner-city neighborhoods. Along the lines of Wilson and Massey and Denton, the idea is that a process of negative decline may reinforce itself and may be concentrated in predominantly black neighborhoods.[32]

The downward spiral could continue, in theory, until the location is entirely abandoned, with all workers and capital relocating elsewhere. In practice, owing to the large stock of immobile residential capital, nontrivial relocation costs, and perhaps government efforts at revitalization, the spiral may eventually arrest itself.[33] But the new labor market equilibrium may differ significantly from the initial equilibrium. The central city may have fewer employed workers who earn lower wages than before (essentially reflecting a leftward shift of labor demand), and it may have fewer high human-capital residents (reflecting relocation to the

31. Widick (1989, p. 167).
32. Wilson (1987); Massey and Denton (1993).
33. Glaeser and Gyourko (2001).

suburbs or other cities).[34] Relatively poor central city blacks may be especially unlikely to relocate from adversely affected areas because of a variety of labor, housing, and credit market imperfections, including, but not limited to, racial discrimination.

In sum, a riot could lead to a decline in economic activity because of the destruction of physical capital, a rise in costs of production, and a decline in perceived security. Although it is difficult to be precise about the nature of the link, it seems reasonable to hypothesize that the net effects, if any, are increasing with the severity of the riot. Because the riots were concentrated in central-city black neighborhoods, it also seems reasonable to hypothesize that the effects, if any, were felt most strongly by central-city black residents. In predominantly black neighborhoods, those with the most capital at stake and those facing the highest potential tax burdens would have the greatest incentive (and ability) to relocate. White central-city neighborhoods might lose residents and businesses as well, not because of direct physical destruction of property, but because of changes in expected taxes, security costs, and public services. Again, those with the most capital at stake and those with the most taxable resources would have the greatest incentive to depart for the suburbs or, perhaps, other cities.

Empirical Framework

We use variation across cities in the severity of the riots to estimate their impact on African Americans' labor market outcomes. The validity of this strategy depends on two assumptions. First, we assume that the riots' effects were concentrated in the cities that experienced riots. In the-

---

34. With perfectly mobile labor, a leftward demand shift in the central city would be followed immediately by outmigration such that wages would equalize across locations. With imperfectly mobile labor, any such response would take time, and wages would be depressed during the period of adjustment. If the skill mix of the central city changes (because of selective outmigration), observed wages will be lower in the new equilibrium. Blanchard and Katz (1992) explore the dynamics of adjustments to labor demand shocks at the state-level in the 1978–90 period. In their model, a decline in wages in one location (relative to wages elsewhere) attracts firms seeking to minimize labor costs. If so, wages and employment tend to move back toward their initial levels. Empirically, they find that this job-creation mechanism is not strong and that outmigration plays a key role in adjusting to the shock.

ory, however, it is possible that very well-integrated labor markets could dissipate adverse shocks quickly, leaving no trace of a wage effect in cross-city comparisons (though possibly leaving evidence of migration). And if the riots had strong intercity spillover effects on perceptions of the benefits and costs associated with central-city locations, then cross-city comparisons would tend to understate the riots' impact. The second major assumption is that the geographic distribution of riots was exogenous to blacks' economic status before the riots. We have already discussed the sociology literature's findings about this idea. If the riot variation is essentially random, then estimation by ordinary least squares is straightforward. Nevertheless, we report estimates for specifications that control directly for pre-1960 trends in labor market outcomes. We also relax the riot exogeneity assumption by pursuing two-stage least squares estimates.

Our analysis draws on two sources of information about labor market outcomes: city-level data from the published census volumes and individual-level data for metropolitan areas from the IPUMS.[35] The published city-level data are particularly useful in this case because the IPUMS sample for 1960 does not identify cities and because, in the 1970 and 1980 samples, metropolitan area or central city status is undisclosed for some households. The main advantage of the individual-level data is that one can observe and control for a variety of individual and household characteristics. For now, we restrict our attention to changes in income, employment, unemployment, and the racial composition of city populations.

City-Level Approach

We focus on cities with total populations of at least 100,000 and black populations of at least 1,000 in 1960, providing a base sample of 130 cities.[36] We also exclude cities that, according to the relevant issues of the *County and City Data Book,* had large changes in boundaries during the period under study.[37] For each city, we summed the index values for each

35. Ruggles, Sobek, and others (1997). In future work, we intend to examine the CPS samples, which contain data on an annual basis, though for a comparatively small set of cities. We also have begun to match maps of the riot areas to maps of census tracts for a handful of cities, which will allow us to follow specific neighborhoods over time.

36. In 1960, 83 percent of blacks in cities with at least 25,000 residents lived in cities with at least 100,000 residents.

37. U.S. Department of Commerce (various years).

riot (as already defined) that occurred between 1964 and 1971. In the following regressions, the index is first entered in quadratic form as an explanatory variable for changes in black labor market outcomes. Then, to simplify the analysis, we split cities into two groups, "severe" and "not severe" on the basis of the index values.[38] A relatively small number of cities fall into the "severe" group, but they account for the overwhelming majority of deaths, injuries, arrests, and arsons in the sample. For example, 77 percent of the deaths in the base sample occurred in the "severe" riot cities. On the basis of the index, the severe riot cities are Los Angeles, Detroit, Washington, Newark, Baltimore, Chicago, Cleveland, New York, Mobile, and San Francisco.

In the simple "severe dummy variable" specification, let y stand for an economic outcome and S stand for the severity of the 1960s riots ($S = 1$ if riots were "severe"), and consider the following two regression equations:

(1) $$\Delta y_{1970-1960} = X\beta + \gamma S + e$$

(2) $$\Delta y_{1980-1960} = X\beta + \gamma S + e$$

The X vector includes a set of city-level characteristics such as region indicators, the manufacturing proportion of employment in 1960, black population size in 1960, and total population size in 1960. The treatment group consists of blacks living in cities for which $S = 1$, and the control group consists of blacks living in cities for which $S = 0$.[39] Essentially, this is a difference-in-difference (DD) estimator in which time-invariant city-specific effects, region-specific trends, and city-invariant period-specific effects are differenced out, and identification comes from differences in changes in y across the two groups of cities (conditional on X).[40] In equa-

---

38. A city's index is considered "severe" (= 1) if the index value falls into approximately ninetieth percentile (or higher) of the distribution of severity. See the text for a list of the severe riot cities

39. Data are not reported for black income and unemployment for 1960. Rather, the data pertain to the nonwhite population. For most cities, the black and nonwhite proportions of the population in 1960 are very similar. The results are similar if we exclude cities with substantial fractions of nonblack nonwhites.

40. In principle, using white outcomes as an additional level of control, one could pursue a difference-in-difference-in-difference (DDD) estimator. One might hope that this third "difference" would absorb race-invariant city-specific shocks and trends, but because

tion 1, γ is a rough measure of the "short-run" impact of a severe riot; that is, the effect (if any) in the census closest in time to the period of the riots (1970) relative to the "preriot" census (1960). Equation 2 measures the "long-run" impact. Since many of the "not severe" cities did have small riots, γ should be interpreted as the effect of severe riots over and above any effects associated with small riots (as opposed to the effect of a severe riot relative to a no-riot counterfactual).

In general, unobserved trends and shocks that are correlated with the occurrence of "treatment" threaten the credibility of difference-in-difference estimators. Controlling for observable economic characteristics, perhaps including the 1950 to 1960 trend in labor market outcomes, may reduce the scope for bias from unobserved shocks and trends—the idea being that cities similar on observables may be similar on unobservables as well. Alternatively, instrumental variables may help isolate variation in riot severity that is plausibly exogenous to unobserved labor market shocks and trends.

One possible set of instrumental variables derives from differences in city government structure. The sociology literature suggests that differences in governmental form may have implied differences in responsiveness to the political interests of the local black population and therefore differences in the likelihood and severity of riots.[41] Along these lines, many riots were preceded by a series of racial incidents spread over a period of weeks, and it is possible that some governmental forms responded more effectively to alleviate the building tension. We use a dummy variable indicating the presence of a city manager to help predict the incidence of riots even after controlling for black population size and region.[42] We take the position that the government's structure is unlikely

---

it is highly plausible that whites in riot-cities responded in some way to the "treatment" event, it is difficult to justify using whites as an additional control group. Moreover, the 1960 census volumes do not report white-specific outcomes at the city level. We can measure black outcomes relative to the overall city outcomes, but this is highly imperfect because blacks were a substantial proportion of many cities' populations. Backing out figures for whites would be possible if (for example) citywide and nonwhite average incomes were reported, but in fact, the tables report medians. In the following pages, we do report some DDD estimators using the IPUMS data.

41. See Lieberson and Silverman (1965); Spilerman (1971, 1976).

42. Additional governmental characteristics such as the use of nonpartisan elections and the proportion of the city council that is elected at large made little contribution in the implicit first stage of the instrumental variable procedure. The sociology literature tends to argue that, in theory, mayors may be more responsive to minority needs than city man-

to alter black economic outcomes directly and, therefore, is a legitimate instrument. There is no evidence of significant correlations between the city-manager variable and preexisting trends (1950–60) in nonwhite income, employment, or unemployment.[43]

Our second instrumental variable strategy is to make use of weather data for April of 1968. The idea is that a specific, identifiable event—the assassination of Martin Luther King—greatly increased the likelihood of a riot during the month. However, in places where the weather was unfavorable, and especially in places where it rained, riots may have been less likely or less severe.[44] Although, as far as we know, rainfall has not been considered in the sociology literature on the 1960s riots, there is anecdotal evidence that rain has dampened or precluded political protests and civil disturbances at various times and places. For example, in his discussion of "the riot that didn't happen," Sidney Fine notes that rainfall played a key role in defusing an emerging riot in Detroit in August 1966.[45] Most recently, after two nights of riots, a CNN.com headline on June 19, 2003, read "Rain, curfew help bring quiet night to Benton Harbor."[46] The instruments hold up well in the implicit first stage of our two-

---

agers, but the evidence does not support that hypothesis. Spilerman (1976) finds a positive correlation between mayors and riots; Eisinger (1973) finds a positive correlation between mayors and black protest activity, and we find a significant negative correlation between riot severity and city managers. The negative correlation is consistent with the view that use of city managers led to greater "professionalism" in local government in general and police who are better prepared to deal with civil disturbances in particular, but we admit that this is pure speculation.

43. Regressing the 1950–60 change in nonwhite family income, change in nonwhite unemployment rate, and change in nonwhite employment rate on the city manager variable yields the following coefficients: –0.047 (t-stat = 0.58) for income; –0.004 (t-stat = 0.46) for unemployment; 0.003 (t-stat = 0.21) for employment. The samples are similar to those in tables 2A, 3A, and 4A and control for region, black and total population size, and manufacturing employment.

44. Riot activity was very high in the two weeks after the assassination, but even later in the month, riot activity was substantially higher than in previous Aprils (1964–67). So we used rainfall for the entire month. When we limit the "rain window" to ten days after the assassination, we get broadly similar results. The Kerner Commission did note that several cities with substantial riots in 1967 seemed to have relatively high temperatures around the time of the riots (1968, p. 123). This observation has been supported in statistical analyses by Baron and Ransberger (1978) and Carlsmith and Anderson (1979). There is a more general criminology literature that links temperature and violent crime (for example, see Field [1992]). We may attempt to use temperature variation as a second weather instrument in future work.

45. Fine (1989, p. 4).

46. www.cnn.com/2003/US/Midwest/06/18/michigan.unrest/.

stage least squares estimates: city managers and more rainfall in April of 1968 are consistently associated with a lower values of S.[47]

City-level Results

To estimate the effect on median family income, we use a "broad" and a "narrow" sample. The broad sample includes all available cities for comparison. The narrow sample uses a smaller set of comparison cities for which the 1950 IPUMS can be used to establish a pre-1960 trend in nonwhite income. Table 2A reports estimates of the riots' effect on the change in median black family income between 1960 and 1970. The first three columns all use the raw index numbers for severity (in quadratic form), whereas the last six columns use a dummy variable for severe riot cities. The last three columns are two-stage least square estimates of the riot impact, relying on the instrumental variables discussed above. Columns 3, 6, and 9 include controls for the 1950–60 trend in black family incomes for a reduced set of cities. To help distinguish the influence of changing sample composition from that of changing specification, columns 2, 5, and 8 exclude the trend variable but use the reduced sample of cities.

Column 1's results indicate that riots were associated with slower income growth for blacks through the relevant range of the riot index (0 to 0.5). The coefficients suggest a maximum negative impact around a riot index value of 0.3 (approximately the center of the "severe riot" range). At that point, the estimated negative riot effect on median black family income is greater than 12 percent. Moving to the smaller sample (column 2) and adding the 1950–60 trend (column 3) has a small impact on the estimated riot effect—the profile becomes steeper but still reaches a maximum impact around 0.3, at which point the riot effect on income is almost negative 16 percent. The significant positive coefficient on the *South* dummy variable reflects the convergence of southern blacks' incomes on the incomes of blacks elsewhere.

---

47. In the implicit first stage of IV estimates below (with 102 cities), the April 1968 rainfall coefficient is –0.033 (t-stat = 2.35), and the city manager coefficient is –0.12 (t-stat = 2.13). The regression also includes region dummies, black population size, total population size, and manufacturing proportion of employment 1960. The F statistic for the joint significance of rainfall and city manager is 3.7. Key results are similar when estimated using limited-information maximum likelihood.

Qualitatively, the results are similar in columns 4 to 6, which replace the quadratic severity index with a simple dummy variable for cities that had the most severe riot experiences. In each column, the estimated riot effect on black income is about –0.09 and statistically significant. The 2SLS point estimates for the riot effect (columns 7 to 9) are larger in magnitude and somewhat weaker in terms of statistical significance (though still significant at the 10 percent level at least). All of the results in table 2A are consistent with a nontrivial negative effect of riots on black income.

Table 2B reports results for similar regressions, run for the 1960 to 1980 period. The results suggest that the riots' effects were not transitory. Cities that experienced riot-associated relative declines in income during the 1960s did not catch up during the 1970s. The coefficients in columns 1 to 6 are roughly similar in magnitude to those from table 2A, but the estimated riot-effect profile is somewhat steeper in the quadratic specifications of columns 1 to 3 (reaching an impact of –0.22 in column 1 at a riot index value of 0.3). Similarly, column 4 estimates an average "severe riot city" effect of about 12 percent (compared with 9 percent in table 2A), and again, the 2SLS coefficients increase in magnitude, as do the associated standard errors.

We have checked the robustness of the basic income results (columns 1 and 4 of tables 2A and 2B) in several ways: we limited the sample to cities with at least 50,000 black residents in 1960 (essentially, a large city sample); we split the sample into southern and nonsouthern cities and ran separate regressions; and we replaced the quadratic severity index with a quadratic in the number of persons killed in riots. In each case, the negative and statistically significant (or nearly so) association of riots with declines in median black family income persists.[48]

The true nature of these apparent relative income declines is difficult to discern from the city-level data. Two distinct, but not necessarily exclusive, hypotheses suggest themselves. First, the riots could have negatively affected the labor market outcomes of people residing in the riot cities throughout the 1960s and 1970s. Second, relatively high-income blacks could have moved out of riot cities after their occurrence, leading to a decline in average income of those remaining (a compositional change). Though imperfect, we can use measures of median schooling

---

48. These results are available from the authors on request.

Table 2A. Riots and Change in Log Median Family Income for Blacks, 1960–70

Item	1: OLS	2: OLS	3: OLS	4: OLS	5: OLS	6: OLS	7: 2SLS	8: 2SLS	9: 2SLS
Riot index	-0.8330 (3.17)	-1.179 (3.07)	-1.121 (2.67)	...	...	...	...	...	...
Riot index^2	1.391 (2.41)	2.101 (2.92)	1.983 (2.63)	...	...	...	...	...	...
Severe riot	...	...	...	-0.09168 (4.27)	-0.08522 (2.78)	-0.08560 (2.51)	-0.2688 (1.96)	-0.1792 (1.80)	-0.1878 (1.76)
Black 60	4.28 e-07 (2.75)	4.44 e-07 (2.39)	4.29 e-07 (2.22)	3.62 e-07 (2.66)	3.33 e-07 (2.15)	3.28 e-07 (2.07)	7.09 e-07 (2.14)	5.18 e-07 (1.88)	5.29 e-07 (1.83)
Population 60	-5.33 e-08 (2.43)	-5.22 e-08 (2.13)	-5.08 e-08 (2.02)	-3.99 e-08 (2.04)	-3.30 e-08 (1.61)	-3.26 e-08 (1.61)	-6.33 e-08 (1.87)	-4.49 e-08 (1.56)	-4.54 e-08 (1.55)
Proportion manufacturing 60	0.002458 (2.53)	0.001699 (1.00)	0.001516 (0.97)	0.002419 (2.55)	0.001917 (1.18)	0.001650 (1.16)	0.002578 (2.50)	0.002104 (1.23)	0.001851 (1.16)
Trend 1950–60	...	...	-0.07050 (1.25)	...	...	-0.09621 (1.72)	...	...	-0.09741 (1.58)
Midwest	0.05313 (2.47)	0.05390 (1.86)	0.05653 (2.18)	0.05888 (2.71)	0.06525 (2.21)	0.06884 (2.59)	0.06180 (2.51)	0.08305 (2.16)	0.08823 (2.44)
South	0.1089 (4.30)	0.1147 (3.16)	0.1058 (2.93)	0.1193 (4.74)	0.1450 (4.12)	0.1316 (3.86)	0.1192 (4.11)	0.1635 (3.79)	0.1515 (3.49)
West	0.007036 (0.21)	-0.02873 (0.70)	-0.03629 (0.88)	0.01943 (0.59)	0.01124 (0.31)	0.0002322 (0.01)	0.04133 (1.01)	0.07007 (0.93)	0.06403 (0.77)
Constant	0.4048 (11.96)	0.4345 (7.07)	0.4843 (6.79)	0.3889 (11.69)	0.3856 (6.67)	0.4561 (7.14)	0.3804 (9.97)	0.3609 (5.12)	0.4301 (5.52)
N	102	41	41	102	41	41	102	41	41
R^2	0.28	0.53	0.54	0.31	0.48	0.51	0.16	0.40	0.41
Mean change	0.5103	0.5327	0.5327	0.5103	0.5327	0.5327	0.5103	0.5327	0.5327

Source: Manufacturing and population variables are from issues of the *County and City Data Book* (tabulated in ICPSR 7735). The city manager instrumental variable is from the Governmental Units Analysis Data (Aiken and Alford [1998]; ICPSR 28). Rainfall data are from the National Climatic Data Center website (www.ncdc.noaa.gov). See table 1 and text for discussion of riot severity data.
Note: t statistics are in parentheses. Median family income figures for 1960 and 1970 are from the published census volumes. A family income measure for 1950 is constructed using the IPUMS (excluding households of one person). Regional designations follow census convention.

Table 2B. Riots and Change in Log Median Family Income for Blacks, 1960–80

Item	1: OLS	2: OLS	3: OLS	4: OLS	5: OLS	6: OLS	7: 2SLS	8: 2SLS	9: 2SLS
Riot index	-1.415 (3.12)	-1.626 (2.83)	-1.333 (3.15)	...	...	...	...	...	...
Riot index²	2.290 (2.42)	2.853 (2.55)	2.160 (2.70)	...	...	...	...	...	...
Severe riot	...	...	...	-0.1178 (2.42)	-0.07175 (1.19)	-0.08307 (2.07)	-0.5133 (1.91)	-0.3641 (1.22)	-0.3916 (1.49)
Black 60	3.54 e-07 (1.68)	4.23 e-07 (1.95)	5.13 e-07 (2.56)	1.50 e-07 (0.83)	2.00 e-07 (0.98)	3.38 e-07 (2.01)	9.25 e-07 (1.46)	7.65 e-07 (1.07)	9.49 e-07 (1.48)
Population 60	-4.08 e-08 (1.25)	-5.05 e-08 (1.69)	-6.33 e-08 (2.32)	-1.12 e-08 (0.37)	-2.16 e-08 (0.71)	-3.83 e-08 (1.48)	-6.30 e-08 (1.00)	-5.69 e-08 (0.84)	-7.74 e-08 (1.21)
Proportion manufacturing 60	0.001467 (0.85)	-0.0007769 (0.35)	0.0006385 (0.21)	0.001343 (0.78)	-0.0002467 (0.09)	0.001092 (0.34)	0.001749 (0.93)	0.0009615 (0.23)	0.002528 (0.54)
Trend 1950–60	...	...	-0.3520 (1.89)	...	...	-0.4104 (2.30)	...	...	-0.4614 (2.01)
Midwest	0.1460 (4.16)	0.06738 (1.32)	0.0440 (0.63)	0.1544 (4.31)	0.06816 (1.30)	0.04231 (0.58)	0.1622 (3.78)	0.1230 (1.32)	0.09676 (0.92)
South	0.2714 (5.50)	0.2131 (3.07)	0.1931 (2.94)	0.2866 (5.74)	0.2413 (3.24)	0.2126 (3.23)	0.2976 (4.80)	0.3178 (2.61)	0.2894 (2.73)
West	0.1239 (1.95)	0.03368 (0.37)	0.06182 (0.82)	0.1399 (2.20)	0.06199 (0.66)	0.08159 (1.19)	0.1961 (2.48)	0.2903 (1.13)	0.3239 (1.37)
Constant	0.9780 (15.31)	1.085 (11.76)	1.246 (10.19)	0.9538 (14.94)	1.019 (10.44)	1.227 (9.80)	0.9325 (12.79)	0.9217 (5.02)	1.1505 (5.25)
N	85	31	31	85	31	31	85	31	31
R²	0.39	0.61	0.69	0.37	0.53	0.65	0.07	0.15	0.23
Mean change	1.119	1.138	1.138	1.119	1.138	1.138	1.119	1.138	1.138

Note: t statistics are in parentheses. See table 2A for discussion of variables.

levels for adult black (or nonwhite) males in 1960 and 1970 to see if a compositional change drives the observed results. Adding this change in average schooling to the regressions of columns 1 or 4 in table 2A (not shown) does not undercut the estimated riot effect, though it does have a positive, independent relation to income changes. Furthermore, regressing the change in education on measures of riot severity, region dummies, and so on suggests that there was no significant difference in the change in education levels between the severe riot cities and others. Thus the compositional story does not seem to drive the negative income results, at least for the 1960s. A third potential avenue would be for family units (over which median income is measured) to disintegrate faster in the riot cities than elsewhere; in particular, a relative increase in the proportion of female-headed households could drive a relative decline in the census measure of median family income. The published city-level data are not consistently detailed enough to test this hypothesis, but we intend to explore the issue in future research.

Tables 3A and 3B report estimates of the effect of riots on male unemployment rates. Since black (or nonwhite) unemployment figures are available for 1950 for all the cities, there is no change in sample composition across the columns. Columns 1, 4, and 7 control only for region; columns 2, 5, and 8 add variables for total and black population size and the proportion of employment in manufacturing; and columns 3, 6, and 9 include the 1950–60 unemployment trend as an independent variable. There is no strong evidence that riot severity affected black male unemployment rates, and in fact, most of the point estimates suggest a relative decline in measured unemployment rates (though not statistically significant).

Tables 4A and 4B repeat the exercise for male employment ratios (defined as the ratio of employed males over the male population above a particular age).[49] Here, we find little evidence of a short-run effect (between 1960 and 1970), especially when we include a preexisting trend. However, the long-run effect is strongly negative even when con-

49. The 1960 published census data reports the number of men over age 14 (the denominator for the employment rate), whereas the 1970 and 1980 censuses report the number over age 16. Since most 15- and 16-year-olds are not employed, the shift in the denominator's definition tends to cause an understatement of the magnitude of the decline in black male employment over time. There is no reason to believe that this biases the estimated riot effect.

trolling for the preexisting trend: measuring between 4 and 8 percentage points in columns 4 to 6. Like the results for median income, the 2SLS coefficients are larger (but less precisely estimated) than the OLS coefficients. Thus, even though variation in the city-level black male unemployment rate is weakly correlated with riot severity (table 3B), it seems that between 1960 and 1980 there were especially large declines in black male employment rates in cities with severe riots (table 4B). Further evidence on the riots' effect on employment is gleaned from the IPUMS data in the following pages.

Table 5A reports estimates of the riots's impact on the black share of total city population during the 1960s. Controlling only for region (columns 1, 4, and 7), it is clear that cities that had riots had comparatively large increases in the share of the city population that was black. The differences are large and statistically significant, reaching a maximum impact of about 0.11 in column 1 and an average "severe riot city" effect of 0.07 in column 4. As more variables are added to the regressions, however, the estimated riot effects diminish in magnitude: the maximum impact suggested by column 3 (after accounting for 1950–60 trend) is only about 0.03, and in column 6 is smaller yet. After accounting for the 1950–60 trend in black population share, the 2SLS estimate in column 9 yields a very small (and imprecise) point estimate. Qualitatively, the results from table 5B, which cover 1960 to 1980, are quite similar to those in table 5A: severe riots were strongly positively correlated with increases in black population share, but those increases were apparently well under way before the riots occurred.[50]

Microlevel IPUMS Data

Our second empirical analysis uses individual-level data for men living in metropolitan areas from the 1950, 1970, and 1980 IPUMS. Unfortunately, metropolitan areas are not disclosed in the 1960 sample, and it is not possible to observe both metropolitan area and central-city status simultaneously in the available 1970 samples. Together, these limitations

---

50. Similar regressions run for the size of city population return somewhat similar results. Cities with severe riots lost population relative to those that did not (by about 8 percent during the 1960s, controlling only for region), but as more control variables are added, the negative population effect tends to diminish. Because cities change geographic size in nontrivial ways over time, we view the "total population" results as highly speculative.

Table 3A. Riots and Change in Black Male Unemployment Rate, 1960–70

Item	1: OLS	2: OLS	3: OLS	4: OLS	5: OLS	6: OLS	7: 2SLS	8: 2SLS	9: 2SLS
Riot index	−0.1274 (1.50)	−0.09022 (0.86)	−0.1459 (1.61)	…	…	…	…	…	…
Riot index^2	0.1868 (0.87)	0.1476 (0.65)	0.2709 (1.45)	…	…	…	…	…	…
Severe riot	…	…	…	−0.007919 (0.94)	0.0008385 (0.10)	−0.005686 (0.64)	0.005244 (0.22)	0.04014 (0.88)	0.04477 (0.92)
Black 60	…	−5.60 e-08 (1.31)	−3.82 e-08 (1.00)	…	−8.51 e-08 (2.20)	−6.34 e-08 (1.78)	…	−1.62 e-07 (1.54)	−1.63 e-07 (1.44)
Population 60	…	1.01 e-08 (1.66)	7.81 e-09 (1.45)	…	1.31 e-08 (2.36)	1.08 e-09 (2.19)	…	1.82 e-08 (1.89)	1.76 e-08 (1.73)
Proportion manufacturing 60	…	−0.0009548 (2.93)	−0.0009579 (3.43)	…	−0.0009697 (2.99)	−0.0009666 (3.47)	…	−0.001006 (3.01)	−0.001013 (3.48)
Trend 1950–60	…	…	−0.3222 (3.72)	…	…	−0.3177 (3.67)	…	…	−0.2854 (3.06)
Midwest	0.01398 (1.65)	0.01398 (1.65)	0.02874 (3.04)	0.01409 (1.54)	0.01441 (1.68)	0.02947 (3.05)	0.01349 (1.45)	0.01375 (1.54)	0.02711 (2.65)
South	0.002360 (0.27)	0.002360 (0.27)	0.01338 (1.53)	0.01695 (2.36)	0.003489 (0.40)	0.01503 (1.73)	0.01670 (2.36)	0.003474 (0.38)	0.01384 (1.47)
West	0.01877 (1.80)	0.01877 (1.80)	0.02189 (2.41)	0.03707 (3.91)	0.01871 (1.82)	0.02337 (2.56)	0.03658 (3.91)	0.01384 (1.15)	0.01673 (1.46)
Constant	−0.003094 (0.25)	−0.003094 (0.25)	−0.01405 (1.27)	−0.03742 (5.85)	−0.004244 (0.34)	−0.01646 (1.47)	−0.03840 (5.91)	−0.002314 (0.18)	−0.01277 (1.06)
N	102	102	102	102	102	102	102	102	102
R^2	0.26	0.26	0.42	0.16	0.25	0.41	0.14	0.18	0.29
Mean change	−0.02288	−0.02288	−0.02288	−0.02288	−0.02288	−0.02288	−0.02288	−0.02288	−0.02288

Note: t statistics are in parentheses. See table 2A for discussion of variables.

Table 3B. Riots and Change in Black Male Unemployment Rate, 1960–80

Item	1: OLS	2: OLS	3: OLS	4: OLS	5: OLS	6: OLS	7: 2SLS	8: 2SLS	9: 2SLS
Riot index	-0.0009105 (0.01)	-0.09153 (0.78)	-0.1266 (1.12)	...	...	...	...	...	...
Riot index^2	0.05026 (0.27)	0.1705 (0.79)	0.2456 (1.17)	...	...	...	...	...	...
Severe riot	...	...	...	0.002970 (0.40)	-0.006324 (0.64)	-0.01191 (1.15)	0.04237 (1.67)	0.05818 (1.27)	0.06028 (1.23)
Black 60	...	8.52 e-08 (1.65)	1.01 e-07 (1.86)	...	7.54 e-08 (1.74)	9.65 e-08 (1.97)	...	-5.09 e-08 (0.47)	-4.71 e-08 (0.40)
Population 60	...	-1.18 e-08 (1.54)	-1.41 e-08 (1.79)	...	-1.03 e-08 (1.55)	-1.28 e-08 (1.79)	...	-1.91 e-09 (0.17)	-3.03 e-09 (0.25)
Proportion manufacturing 60	...	0.0004629 (1.01)	0.0004458 (0.93)	...	0.0004608 (1.02)	0.000449 (0.95)	...	0.0003947 (0.83)	0.0003789 (0.77)
Trend 1950–60	...	...	-0.2531 (1.81)	...	...	-0.2555 (1.84)	...	...	-0.2000 (1.42)
Midwest	0.02104 (1.86)	0.01948 (1.71)	0.03197 (2.43)	0.02136 (1.92)	0.02009 (1.79)	0.03304 (2.51)	0.01913 (1.61)	0.01883 (1.55)	0.02883 (2.04)
South	-0.02282 (2.45)	-0.01893 (1.51)	-0.01257 (0.90)	-0.02276 (2.48)	-0.01798 (1.47)	-0.01112 (0.80)	-0.02575 (2.65)	-0.01977 (1.47)	-0.01457 (0.99)
West	-0.02509 (2.19)	-0.01608 (1.16)	-0.01120 (0.86)	-0.02454 (2.27)	-0.01462 (1.08)	-0.008409 (0.65)	-0.02688 (2.33)	-0.02376 (1.57)	-0.01981 (1.30)
Constant	0.04876 (5.80)	0.03449 (1.95)	0.03450 (1.95)	0.04872 (6.62)	0.03271 (1.92)	0.02350 (1.34)	0.04580 (6.11)	0.03617 (2.02)	0.02931 (1.60)
N	85	85	85	85	85	85	85	85	85
R^2	0.23	0.25	0.32	0.23	0.25	0.32	0.12	0.10	0.13
Mean change	0.04516	0.04516	0.04516	0.04516	0.04516	0.04516	0.04516	0.04516	0.04629

Note: t statistics are in parentheses. See table 2A for discussion of variables.

Table 4A. Riots and Change in Black Male Employment Rate 1960–70

Item	1: OLS	2: OLS	3: OLS	4: OLS	5: OLS	6: OLS	7: 2SLS	8: 2SLS	9: 2SLS
Riot index	−0.1135 (0.93)	−0.1625 (1.27)	0.05298 (0.46)	...	...	...	...	...	...
Riot index^2	0.2348 (0.74)	0.2923 (1.04)	−0.1482 (0.67)	...	...	...	...	...	...
Severe riot	...	...	...	−0.01618 (1.38)	−0.02288 (1.96)	−0.007996 (0.84)	0.002276 (0.06)	0.006213 (0.10)	−0.02016 (0.35)
Black 60	...	9.33 e-08 (1.37)	8.14 e-08 (1.52)	...	9.54 e-08 (1.56)	9.69 e-08 (2.13)	...	3.84 e-08 (0.27)	1.20 e-07 (0.97)
Population 60	...	−1.78 e-08 (1.79)	−1.56 e-08 (1.97)	...	−1.64 e-08 (1.89)	−1.66 e-08 (2.42)	...	−1.26 e-08 (0.97)	−1.82 e-08 (1.63)
Proportion manufacturing 60	...	0.0006636 (1.23)	0.0006523 (1.44)	...	0.0006663 (1.24)	0.0006508 (1.45)	...	0.0006397 (1.16)	0.0006619 (1.45)
Trend 1950–60	...	...	−0.4921 (4.79)	...	...	−0.4828 (4.75)	...	...	−0.4768 (4.29)
Midwest	−0.000124 (0.01)	−0.001476 (0.14)	−0.03088 (2.83)	0.0009914 (0.10)	−0.0001849 (0.02)	−0.03069 (2.79)	0.0001437 (0.01)	−0.000671 (0.07)	−0.03011 (2.69)
South	−0.00764 (0.61)	−0.001139 (0.08)	−0.03528 (3.16)	−0.006432 (0.52)	0.0008964 (0.07)	−0.03522 (3.14)	−0.006795 (0.54)	0.0008851 (0.06)	−0.03477 (3.02)
West	−0.02334 (1.38)	−0.01097 (0.58)	−0.01739 (1.10)	−0.02075 (1.28)	−0.007430 (0.40)	−0.01773 (1.12)	−0.02143 (1.27)	−0.01103 (0.51)	−0.01612 (0.86)
Constant	−0.004008 (0.43)	−0.02368 (1.19)	−0.01438 (0.88)	−0.005622 (0.69)	−0.02726 (1.40)	−0.01360 (0.84)	−0.006989 (0.78)	−0.02583 (1.29)	−0.01436 (0.86)
N	102	102	102	102	102	102	102	102	102
R^2	0.03	0.06	0.37	0.05	0.07	0.37	0.03	0.05	0.36
Mean change	−0.01264	−0.01264	−0.01264	−0.01264	−0.01264	−0.01264	−0.01264	−0.01264	−0.01264

Source: See table 2A.

Note: The employment rate is calculated using published census data. It is the ratio of employed males over total males over age 14 (in 1960) or age 16 (in 1970). Since a comparatively high proportion of 15- and 16-year-olds are not employed, the change in definition tends to understate the decline in employment over time, but we have no reason to believe that it biases the regression results. t statistics are in parentheses.

Table 4B. Riots and Black Male Employment Rates, 1960–80

Item	1: OLS	2: OLS	3: OLS	4: OLS	5: OLS	6: OLS	7: 2SLS	8: 2SLS	9: 2SLS
Riot index	-0.6087 (3.25)	-0.5621 (2.23)	-0.3566 (1.50)	...	...	...	...	...	...
Riot index^2	0.8864 (2.29)	0.8400 (1.78)	0.4393 (1.04)	...	...	...	...	...	...
Severe riot	...	...	...	-0.07231 (4.19)	-0.06167 (2.31)	-0.04398 (1.87)	-0.1373 (2.94)	-0.1620 (1.81)	-0.1625 (1.74)
Black 60	...	-4.54 e-08 (0.44)	-6.63 e-08 (0.73)	...	-1.16 e-07 (1.27)	-1.26 e-07 (1.66)	...	8.10 e-08 (0.36)	1.02 e-07 (0.47)
Population 60	...	6.08 e-09 (0.43)	9.89 e-09 (0.80)	...	1.79 e-08 (1.46)	1.94 e-08 (1.89)	...	4.76 e-09 (0.22)	4.09 e-09 (0.19)
Proportion manufacturing 60	...	-0.001448 (1.69)	-0.001383 (1.68)	...	-0.001504 (1.73)	-0.001444 (1.74)	...	-0.001401 (1.53)	-0.001337 (1.52)
Trend 1950–60	...	...	-0.4789 (3.36)	...	...	-0.4749 (3.41)	...	...	-0.3909 (2.30)
Midwest	0.01599 (0.95)	0.01663 (1.05)	-0.01505 (0.84)	0.01769 (1.03)	0.01996 (1.23)	-0.01297 (0.72)	0.02136 (1.14)	0.02193 (1.24)	-0.004884 (0.23)
South	0.04709 (2.83)	0.02436 (1.17)	-0.005024 (0.25)	0.05104 (2.95)	0.03084 (1.45)	-0.000489 (0.02)	0.05598 (3.06)	0.03361 (1.46)	0.008239 (0.36)
West	0.07288 (2.91)	0.04825 (1.52)	0.03651 (1.33)	0.08258 (3.44)	0.05485 (1.78)	0.03895 (1.43)	0.08644 (3.55)	0.06907 (1.93)	0.05812 (1.70)
Constant	-0.1149 (10.97)	-0.06503 (2.09)	-0.05876 (1.95)	-0.1262 (13.17)	-0.07454 (2.42)	-0.06391 (2.14)	-0.1214 (12.54)	-0.07992 (2.43)	-0.07199 (2.22)
N	85	85	85	85	85	85	85	85	85
R^2	0.27	0.30	0.42	0.26	0.30	0.41	0.18	0.19	0.28
Mean change	-0.1033	-0.1033	-0.1033	-0.1033	-0.1033	-0.1033	-0.1033	-0.1033	-0.1033

Source: See table 2A.

Note: The employment rate is calculated using published census data. It is the ratio of employed males over total males over age 14 (in 1960) or age 16 (in 1980). Since a comparatively high proportion of 15- and 16-year-olds are not employed, the change in definition tends to understate the decline in employment over time, but we have no reason to believe that it biases the regression results. t statistics are in parentheses.

Table 5A. Change in Black Proportion of City Population, 1960–70

Item	1: OLS	2: OLS	3: OLS	4: OLS	5: OLS	6: OLS	7: 2SLS	8: 2SLS	9: 2SLS
Riot index	0.6673 (5.59)	0.4520 (2.85)	0.1732 (1.30)	…	…	…	…	…	…
Riot index^2	-0.9851 (3.45)	-0.6946 (2.65)	-0.2674 (1.18)	…	…	…	…	…	…
Severe riot	…	…	…	0.06668 (3.86)	0.03457 (1.69)	0.01156 (0.75)	0.09825 (3.92)	0.05277 (0.91)	-0.005251 (0.09)
Black 60	…	2.65 e-07 (2.58)	1.16 e-07 (1.44)	…	3.46 e-07 (3.71)	1.38 e-07 (1.79)	…	3.10 e-07 (2.26)	1.59 e-07 (1.48)
Population 60	…	-4.36 e-08 (3.16)	-1.86 e-08 (1.66)	…	-5.46 e-08 (4.51)	-2.13 e-08 (2.03)	…	-5.22 e-08 (3.90)	-2.19 e-08 (1.95)
Proportion manufacturing 60	…	0.0006529 (1.50)	0.0004573 (1.41)	…	0.0007046 (1.58)	0.000466 (1.45)	…	0.0006883 (1.52)	0.0004693 (1.49)
Trend 1950–60	…	…	0.5559 (4.24)	…	…	0.5835 (4.61)	…	…	0.6100 (3.68)
Midwest	-0.01795 (1.72)	-0.02271 (2.21)	-0.01622 (2.37)	-0.01968 (1.72)	-0.02529 (2.31)	-0.01681 (2.45)	-0.02113 (1.81)	-0.02560 (2.37)	-0.01616 (2.20)
South	-0.03787 (3.46)	-0.03939 (2.69)	-0.01464 (1.08)	-0.04360 (3.62)	-0.04509 (2.95)	-0.01543 (1.13)	-0.04422 (3.66)	-0.04509 (3.02)	-0.01409 (0.95)
West	-0.03436 (3.17)	-0.01947 (1.68)	-0.01791 (2.27)	-0.04406 (3.77)	-0.02288 (1.86)	-0.01899 (2.37)	-0.04523 (3.55)	-0.02513 (1.74)	-0.01686 (1.62)
Constant	0.04905 (5.81)	0.03448 (2.14)	0.01787 (1.44)	0.06232 (6.97)	0.04165 (2.42)	0.01955 (1.56)	0.05998 (6.70)	0.04253 (2.44)	0.01779 (1.31)
N	102	102	102	102	102	102	102	102	102
R^2	0.41	0.50	0.64	0.31	0.47	0.63	0.27	0.47	0.63
Mean change	0.04258	0.04258	0.04258	0.04258	0.04258	0.04258	0.04258	0.04258	0.04258

Note: t statistics are in parentheses. See table 2A for discussion of variables.

Table 5B. Change in Black Proportion of City Population, 1960–80

Item	1: OLS	2: OLS	3: OLS	4: OLS	5: OLS	6: OLS	7: 2SLS	8: 2SLS	9: 2SLS
Riot index	0.8514 (2.86)	0.3560 (1.08)	-0.08810 (0.27)	...	...	...	...	...	...
Riot index^2	-1.212 (1.58)	-0.5559 (0.86)	0.1366 (0.21)	...	...	...	...	...	...
Severe riot	...	...	...	0.08079 (2.36)	0.01222 (0.32)	-0.02119 (0.66)	0.1442 (3.30)	0.04331 (0.48)	0.003883 (0.05)
Black 60	...	5.46 e-07 (2.60)	2.96 e-07 (1.65)	...	6.36 e-07 (3.20)	3.05 e-07 (1.62)	...	5.75 e-07 (2.43)	2.74 e-07 (1.44)
Population 60	...	-8.28 e-08 (2.89)	-4.06 e-08 (1.57)	...	-9.31 e-08 (3.57)	-3.98 e-08 (1.48)	...	-8.90 e-08 (3.38)	-3.92 e-08 (1.53)
Proportion manufacturing 60	...	0.001985 (2.03)	0.001720 (1.98)	...	0.002041 (2.13)	0.001721 (2.02)	...	0.002009 (2.08)	0.001711 (1.98)
Trend 1950–60	...	...	0.8758 (3.39)	...	...	0.8854 (3.63)	...	...	0.8444 (3.08)
Midwest	-0.01195 (0.61)	-0.02289 (1.16)	-0.01255 (0.76)	-0.01291 (0.61)	-0.02457 (1.21)	-0.01164 (0.70)	-0.01649 (0.77)	-0.02518 (1.25)	-0.01271 (0.73)
South	-0.01598 (0.71)	-0.009839 (0.36)	0.03133 (1.18)	-0.01980 (0.84)	-0.01319 (0.49)	0.03316 (1.23)	-0.02462 (1.00)	-0.01405 (0.53)	0.03036 (1.07)
West	-0.06028 (2.64)	-0.01888 (0.78)	-0.01829 (0.91)	-0.07225 (3.22)	-0.01990 (0.84)	-0.01549 (0.82)	-0.07601 (2.97)	-0.02431 (0.86)	-0.01903 (0.78)
Constant	0.09028 (5.98)	0.03519 (1.07)	0.007285 (0.24)	0.1077 (7.69)	0.04009 (1.22)	0.004749 (0.16)	0.1030 (7.28)	0.04176 (1.26)	0.007651 (0.24)
N	85	85	85	85	85	85	85	85	85
R^2	0.27	0.42	0.54	0.18	0.41	0.54	0.12	0.40	0.54
Mean change	0.09631	0.09631	0.09631	0.09631	0.09631	0.09631	0.09631	0.09631	0.09631

Note: t statistics are in parentheses. See table 2A for discussion of variables.

imply that we cannot make microlevel comparisons between 1960 and other years, and we cannot limit the scope to central-city black residents. Despite several differences between this second analysis and that of the previous section, the basic identification strategy is the same: to compare changes in labor market outcomes in areas that had severe riots with areas that did not.

The regressions are estimated by OLS and take the following basic form, where Y is an individual's labor market outcome (income or employment) and S is a dummy variable equal to one for metro areas that had severe riots.[51]

(3) $$Y = \alpha + \beta_1 X + \beta_2 S + \beta_3 Year + \beta_4 (S \times Year)$$

In this specification, β_4 measures the average change in Y for black workers in the severe riot cities relative to blacks in nonsevere riot cities, after accounting for differences in personal and regional characteristics (X). The X variables include age (quartic), education (quadratic), marital status, migrant status (dummy for those residing in state that is different from birth state, dummy for foreign born), region or residence indicators (four regions), and region interacted with the year dummy (allowing for region-specific trends). We compare 1950 with 1970 in one set of regressions, and we compare 1970 and 1980 in a second set (*Year* = 1 in the later year of the comparison). It is possible to include metro-area fixed effects in these regressions. Doing so makes it impossible to identify coefficients on any time-invariant city characteristics, but β_4 is still identifiable.

We also report difference-in-difference-in-difference (DDD) estimates, which use white workers to provide another layer of comparison. We do not rely heavily on the DDD estimates because whites might not form an effective control group to the extent that they too were affected by or responded to the riots, but the perspective is nevertheless still of interest. The DDD estimates indicate whether blacks in severe riot cities

---

51. The lists of "severe" cities in the previous section and "severe" metro areas in this section match up in a straightforward way (though obviously metro areas are larger than cities). One exception is that Philadelphia ranked high in the metro-area summation of the riot index even though the city proper did not rank high in the city-level summation. We treat the Philadelphia metro area as a "severe riot" area. Excluding Philadelphia from subsequent regressions has little effect on the results.

fared worse relative to whites in severe riot cities than blacks in nonsevere riot cities fared relative to whites in nonsevere riot cities.

Panel A of table 6 reports results for log annual income among male workers who were between 18 and 64 years of age, were not in school, and worked at least forty weeks in the relevant year. Column 1 suggests that blacks in severe riot cities lost some ground (about 2 percent) relative to blacks living in other cities between 1950 and 1970, though the decline is not statistically significant. The addition of city fixed effects in column 2 has little impact on the coefficient, indicating that unobserved city-specific fixed factors did not drive the result. The estimates in columns 3 and 4, using a DDD approach, are nearly identical to those in columns 1 and 2, suggesting that the relative decline of blacks in severe riot cities (relative to blacks elsewhere) was not matched by a similar decline among whites (relative to whites elsewhere). The point estimates for the 1970s (columns 5 and 6) are similar in magnitude, but more precisely estimated, suggesting a relative decline of 2.5 to 3.0 percent in blacks' annual income in the riot cities. These losses are smaller, but still negative, when differenced by white income trends in columns 7 and 8.

Conditioning the sample on those who worked at least forty weeks makes a significant difference to the magnitude of the estimates for income changes in the 1970s.[52] Removing the "working" condition entirely and rerunning the regression in column 5 with all men 18 to 64 (and not in school) results in a severe-riot coefficient of –0.085 (t-stat = 5.12). Including only men who were in the labor force (regardless of weeks worked) results in a severe-riot coefficient estimate of –0.065 (t-stat = 4.04). (Regressions are not in table.) These findings suggest that there were relatively poor employment prospects in severe riots during the 1970s, and we explore this possibility directly in panel B of table 6.

The employment regressions show no decline in the likelihood of employment for black men between 1950 and 1970 in severe riot states; if anything, the likelihood appears to have risen. There is evidence, however, of a 3 to 4 percentage point decline in the employment rate of black men in severe riot cities during the 1970s. This decline is consistent and statistically significant across columns 5 through 8. Moreover, the decline seems to be stronger among younger black workers: the coeffi-

---

52. The condition does not seem to make a significant difference for the 1950 to 1970 income results.

Table 6. Riots, Income, and Employment in the IPUMS Data

	1: 1950–70 DD black only	2: 1950–70 DD black only	3: 1950–70 DDD black and white	4: 1950–70 DDD black and white	5: 1970–80 DD black only	6: 1970–80 DD black only	7: 1970–80 DDD black and white	8: 1970–80 DDD black and white
				Panel A: Annual income				
Severe × Year	-0.02309	-0.02175	...	...	-0.02539	-0.02983	...	...
	(0.97)	(0.96)			(1.97)	(2.23)		
Severe × Year × black	...	...	-0.02830	-0.02228	...	...	-0.01537	-0.01741
			(0.81)	(1.05)			(1.15)	(1.41)
N	24,245	24,245	258,131	258,131	48,194	48,194	501,620	501,620
MSA fixed effects	No	Yes	No	Yes	No	Yes	No	Yes
				Panel B: Employment				
Severe × Year	0.02698	0.03352	...	...	-0.03514	-0.03327	...	...
	(1.56)	(2.95)			(3.15)	(4.88)		
Severe × Year × black	...	...	0.03073	0.03380	...	...	-0.03844	-0.03896
			(1.71)	(3.65)			(4.15)	(6.91)
N	33,057	33,057	311,477	311,477	71,291	71,291	619,716	619,716
MSA fixed effects	No	Yes	No	Yes	No	Yes	No	Yes

Source: Microdata are from Ruggles, Sobek, and others (1997). Riot data are from Carter (1986) and discussed in table 1.
Note: Each coefficient is from a separate regression. t statistics are in parentheses. All regressions include males, 18 to 64 years old, who are not in school. The income regressions only include those employed for at least 40 weeks in the preceding year. Standard errors are clustered by metropolitan area in regressions without fixed effects. All regressions control for age (quartic), education level (quadratic), marital status, migrant status (dummies for foreign born and those born in a state different from residence), region of residence, year dummy, interactions of region and year dummies, dummy for severe riot areas, interaction of severe riot areas and year dummies. All of these control variables are interacted with a black dummy variable in the DDD regressions.

cient in column 5 increases in magnitude to 4.5 percentage points when the sample is limited to men under 40 years of age, and to 6 percentage points when limited to men under 30.

The declining employment rate reflects both a decline in labor force participation and a rise in unemployment relative to blacks elsewhere. Regressing labor force participation (=1 if in labor force) on the same set of variables as in column 5 returns a riot coefficient of –0.021 (t-stat = 2.83). Limiting the sample to those in the labor force and using unemployed status as the dependent variable yields a coefficient of 0.022 (t-stat = 2.69).

Conclusion

In the 1960s, the United States experienced a large number of race-related civil disturbances. Although social scientists have long studied the riots' causes, the riots' consequences have received much less attention. The riots were concentrated in neighborhoods that were predominantly African American, and in theory, they may have depressed the relative economic status of some African Americans through a downward spiral in neighborhood employment opportunities, property values, and peer quality. Measuring such effects is difficult, in large part because the riots may have been responses to unobserved forces that also simultaneously influenced labor markets. Nonetheless, given Spilerman's contention that the distribution and severity of riots were essentially random (conditional on black population size and region), and alternatively, given the scope for instrumental variable estimation that isolates plausibly exogenous variation in riot severity, we believe that a solid measurement of riot treatment effects is within reach.[53]

Thus far, the empirical evidence on the riots' effects on African Americans' labor market outcomes is mixed but highly suggestive and worthy of further exploration. Our examination of data from the published census volumes and the IPUMS samples suggests the existence of adverse riot effects on family income and male employment. For example, controlling for region and city characteristics, median family income declined significantly after 1960 in the cities that had severe riots relative

---

53. Spilerman (1970, 1971, 1976).

to those that did not. A relative decline in annual income for males is also apparent in the microlevel data spanning the 1970s, especially when the sample is widened to include men who worked relatively few weeks. The microlevel data also reveal a relative decline in the likelihood of male employment and labor force participation during the 1970s in the riot cities. Since all of these effects are measured by comparing blacks' outcomes across cities, and since it is possible that there were negative spillovers from the severe riots to other cities, our estimates of the riots' effects might be understated.

At this stage, our empirical results should be viewed as highly tentative. Besides considerable refinement to the data and analysis presented in this paper, we plan to extend our analysis to other economic outcomes, especially those related to housing markets, such as housing values and residential segregation.[54] We also intend to explore other sources of data. In particular, the analysis in this paper has looked for effects using city-level measures of riot severity on rather widely spaced (in a temporal sense) census data. It seems clear from our preliminary analysis that riot effects exist, but they are difficult to tease out of the data. To do so, one extension would be to explore the public use samples of the March Current Population Survey (CPS), which became available annually in the mid-1960s. While the CPS does not identify the city of residence for all individuals, it does identify the major cities, some of which had severe riots. Another strategy is to look for effects at a smaller geographic scale. We are in the process of matching maps of riot activity in cities with census tract maps to facilitate an "up close" look at the neighborhoods in which the riots occurred. Further work with the CPS and census tract data may provide a better sense of where and when the effects of riots took hold.

54. See Collins and Margo (2003).

Comments

Jacob Vigdor: Unfortunately, race riots are not a thing of the past. From Benton Harbor, Michigan, to Sydney, Australia, violent and destructive outbreaks in minority neighborhoods continue to make headlines in the twenty-first century. As William J. Collins and Robert A. Margo note, a considerable amount of social science research has sought to determine the causes of riots, perhaps in the hope that public policy offers some remedy that can prevent future events. Any such remedy, whether in the guise of governmental reform or redistributive policy, is likely to impose significant costs on society. To determine whether these costs are worth bearing, a complete accounting of the social costs of riots is indispensable. Collins and Margo make an important point: that the social costs of riots are likely to extend far beyond the bricks-and-mortar costs of rebuilding and revitalizing individual neighborhoods. As the authors' analysis and my comments should make clear, the costs identified in this paper are likely to represent only a fraction of the total. As Collins and Margo note, however, this work is but the beginning of an extensive, well-planned, and important research agenda.

Riots, by altering the risk perceptions of firms and households, should make certain neighborhoods less attractive places to live and work. Collins and Margo note the labor demand impact of this change—indeed, it serves as the central motivation for this study—but there are several other noteworthy implications. Demand for residential location in high-risk neighborhoods should decline as well: property destruction is presumably a disamenity to both firms and consumers. It is thus a straight-

35

Table 7. Long-Term Trends in Census Tract 185, Detroit, Michigan

Variable	1940	1950	1960	1970
Population	4,869	4,439	4,112	3,633
Percent black	0.6	34.0	91.3	97.7
Vacancy rate relative to city average (percentage points)	0.8 above	0.5 below	0.5 below	0.1 above
Median rent premium relative to city average (percent)	17	8.5	9.4	−6.3
Male unemployment rate relative to city average (percentage points)	Identical	0.4 below	6.4 above	4.8 above
Median household income relative to city average (percent)	n.a.	−8.1	−11.4	−0.3

n.a. Not available.

forward prediction that rents will decline in riot-prone neighborhoods.[55] Owners of property will experience negative wealth effects; renters will witness a reduction in housing costs to offset some or all (or even more than all) of the utility loss associated with increased risk.

Table 7 presents some basic evidence consistent with these implications. The table tracks basic census statistics for a single census tract in Detroit Michigan—sixteen blocks incorporating the epicenter of the 1967 riots. The neighborhood at the heart of the riot had within the past generation "tipped" from an ethnic enclave populated largely by Russian and Polish immigrants and their children to an overwhelmingly black neighborhood. Through this transition, the population was trending gradually downward, while vacancy rates remained stable and average rents maintained some premium over the citywide average. Three years after the riot, the census recorded an accelerating population decline, a significant relative drop in rents, and a noteworthy uptick in vacancy rates. Changes in census tract boundaries preclude the further tracking of this neighborhood through time, but the immediate response of the local property market to the riot seems consistent with basic economic logic.

What of the labor market implications of riots? As Collins and Margo point out, there are reasons to think any such impact would be muted. In the long run, we expect people to move out of a geographic area rather than stay perpetually unemployed. Moreover, if households are more averse to riot-prone neighborhoods than firms, remaining households

55. Roback (1982).

might witness a relative increase in job prospects. To believe that riots have long-term labor market effects, one must believe that residents of affected neighborhoods face obstacles to relocation and to taking jobs in areas outside their own neighborhood. Theoretical arguments in favor of such barriers have been made for many years, but empirical evidence on the spatial mismatch hypothesis, and of the influence of neighborhood on labor market outcomes in general, has been quite mixed.

Table 7 confirms the notion that the impact of riots on labor market outcomes is more ambiguous than the impact on property markets. As the neighborhood surrounding the epicenter of the 1967 riot transitioned from white to black between 1940 and 1960, residents' labor market outcomes tracked downwards. As of 1960, the unemployment rate of tract residents was significantly higher, and median income significantly lower, than the citywide average. The 1960s did not witness an acceleration of this trend; if anything, labor market outcomes of tract residents improved relative to the city as a whole. While this very basic analysis can be faulted on numerous grounds, it confirms basic economic intuition: riots may be harmful to locations (and those who own property in those locations) in the long run, but they are less harmful to people.

Of course, calling riots "less harmful" to individual labor market outcomes does not imply that no harm is done. Collins and Margo present some fairly convincing evidence of a negative impact of severe riots on black labor market outcomes. Not all of this evidence passes the threshold of statistical significance, but across data sets and empirical specifications there is a clear consistency to the findings. There are two major empirical concerns with the evidence, and the authors focus considerable attention on each. The first is a concern about reverse causality: the propensity to riot could be a function of declining economic fortunes in a community. Collins and Margo present evidence that riot severity is not linked to preexisting trends, as well as specifications utilizing instrumental variables based on weather and city government structure. The second concern is that observed changes in labor market outcomes among black residents of a particular city might reflect selective migration rather than any true causal impact of riots. To address this concern, Collins and Margo control for some basic measures of changes in the composition of the population and use census microdata to control for a broader array of individual characteristics.

Concerns about the economic fortunes of central-city black neighborhoods certainly predate the spate of riots analyzed in this paper. John Kain's seminal article on the spatial mismatch between black neighborhoods and centers of employment growth, published one month after Martin Luther King's assassination, makes no mention of riots or civic unrest.[56] The role of riots in the decline of the American inner city will surely be debated for decades to come. Collins and Margo, by providing evidence of a long-term cost associated with riots that almost certainly underestimates the full economic cost, have contributed significantly to this debate.

Daniel Myers: Civil disorders, or "riots" in the common parlance, can be very destructive events. A riot that directly causes severe damage is rare, but the ensuing social psychological effects of civil violence can be far more destructive. Especially when a series of riots occur that are similar in character or location, danger and fear build and become associated with the places and people connected to the riots, and the behaviors present in the most dramatic events are then assumed to have occurred in other civil disturbances and other neighborhoods. When we think, for example, of the riots of the 1960s, the images that dominate are those of Watts in 1965, Newark and Detroit in 1967, and Washington in 1968—four of the most destructive and deadly riots in American history. Who, in their right mind, would be attracted to these areas to open a business, find employees, or live? And, assuming that our images of these riots reflect rioting that occurred elsewhere, businesses and individuals would by repelled by rioting no matter where it occurred. This is the logic behind an analysis that asks the important question: do riots lead to long-term economic deterioration for the areas where the riots occurred and for the people associated with them?

Linking collective violence and economic conditions is not new, of course, but scholars have mainly used economic conditions as predictors of riots, expecting that riots were most likely to break out where economic conditions were poor and grievances about living conditions plentiful.[57] But William J. Collins and Robert A. Margo take a different tactic and attempt to show that, whether or not economic conditions cause riots,

56. Kain (1968).
57. Spilerman (1970; 1976); Carter (1986); Jiobu (1971); Myers (1997); Olzak and Shanahan (1996).

riots end up having an effect on economic conditions. Although they are not alone in examining this question, their analysis adds a sophistication and thoroughness that moves us toward some less equivocal conclusions about this relationship.[58]

The project is a difficult one, however, and it produces some trying challenges for the researchers—challenges that give one pause as one assesses the ideas and results in this study. As someone who is intimately familiar with these data and the characteristics of these civil disorders, my immediate reaction is to question whether it is even reasonable to suspect that the overwhelming majority of these riots could have any discernible economic impact at all. It is not hard to accept that Watts 1965 or Detroit 1967 could have had such effects, but these are extreme and rare cases. Most riots were, in fact, minor skirmishes compared with what happened in Watts, and the chances of a more typical riot having an economic impact on an entire city fifteen or more years later seems remote.

Consider the severity of riots in Gregg Carter's outstanding data set.[59] Suppose we separated these riots into quintiles and examine the line that separates the most severe quintile from the other 80 percent of the riots. A riot at this level would be relatively severe, although not among the most severe. One riot at this level was characterized by thirty-one arrests, at least one fire or arson attempt, four days of activity, five injured, and no one killed. Another at this level had forty-two arrests, one or more fires, fifty-one injured, no one killed, and lasted one day. It is hard to imagine that these riots could produce any effect that would linger for twenty years. In fact, one could probably find a more severe compilation of activity on many large college campuses the night after a home football game. Even if we move up to the ninetieth percentile, that activity is not stunning: seventy arrests, no fire, ten days of activity, nineteen injured, and no one killed. This is probably a newsworthy event, but how could it have a long-term effect on labor market outcomes? A challenge then exists for the researchers to develop a plausible mechanism that could theoretically and practically produce such an effect.

A second difficulty with such analysis is determining whether or not the relationships the analysts find have a causal connection—riots and bad economic conditions may be related, but does the former really cause

58. See, for example, Aldrich and Reiss (1970); Kelly and Snyder (1980).
59. Carter (1983).

the latter? The authors dutifully address this problem, and they recognize the possibility that some unobserved exogenous factor could be driving the link shown between riots and economic outcomes. They approach the problem in several ways, one of which is inserting some very reasonably selected control into the models. Given that the effects hold up, they have a stronger claim that there is a nonspurious relationship here.

The problem is, however, that one can never be certain the model is adequately specified and that something important has not been left out. It is a particularly difficult quandary in the present study because past attempts to find predictors of riots have been such a dismal failure. It is possible, as Spilerman concluded more than thirty years ago, that nothing really matters other than city size and regional location. But one wonders if for some reasons related to available data and variable specification, we have not just collectively missed some important processes that produce rioting, and also in this case, poor economic outcomes. Collins and Margo make a reasonable attempt to include some important controls, but as the effects are not overwhelming and are reduced through collinearity with some of the controls, one wonders whether adding a few more variables would eliminate the observed effects.

If that did occur, we could apply a quite different and plausible interpretation to the whole situation: riots are simply an indicator of another ongoing social and economic process. That is, riots are an endogenous outcome and do not really contribute anything to the trajectory of economic outcome on their own. They are, in essence, a bellwether of problems, but not a cause of them. Just as one example of an important variable that might be missing, consider policing. Police presence and behavior have much to do with both escalating and controlling riots—and at the same time, police density reflects the fiscal health of the city government, which might in turn provide greater or fewer resources to deal with the problems driving riots. Or municipal spending on policing compared with other social programs and services may belie an underlying orientation toward social control versus community development—which has implications for both rioting and economic outcomes in poor black neighborhoods.

These caveats are important and remind us to maintain reasonable vigilance when reading Collins and Margo, but despite the misgivings raised, one ultimately finds Collins and Margo convincing or at least provocative. It is true that the effects reported are not overpowering, and they might weaken further if the authors were able to make certain shifts in the analysis, but there are other reasons, some of them hinted at by the authors, to believe that the effects are very much understated.

First, we must recognize that as the riots of the 1960s not only reacted to economic and social problems and may have contributed to further problems, they also called attention to those problems and were viewed by many as a call for help. When a call for help is issued, help is sometimes delivered—often too little, too late, and too fleeting to rectify the situation, but help that nonetheless may offset some of the negative effects of the riots that are identified by Collins and Margo. The model cities program, no matter how short-lived, is an obvious example of a response designed to address the supposed sources and outcomes of riots.[60] More recently, the riot in Benton Harbor, Michigan, led Governor Jennifer M. Granholm to appoint a community task force charged with studying the problems faced by the city. It remains to be seen if substantial change will emerge from the seeds planted by the task force, but at least there is work being done, commitments being made, and energy being developed and expended that may offset some of the negative effects of that riot.

Given this reaction, the negative effects the authors detect would be even more pronounced when the "call for help" that emanates from a riot falls on deaf ears. We might speculate, for example, that under the current administration and economic conditions, the effects of riots will be more detrimental than in the past. In the report of the Benton Harbor Task Force, the authors make it clear on the first page of the executive summary that no resources to support their recommendations are going to be provided by the state.[61] Michigan, like many states, is facing a massive deficit and cannot afford to pour resources into addressing the problems in Benton Harbor.

A second reason that effects are probably understated is that the measurement is rather blunt. In some sense this is unavoidable because the data necessary to do the analyses are often not available on the level we would prefer—which in this case is the neighborhood or the area where riots did their damage. Riots should be expected to have stronger effects where they occur than on the city as a whole. Areas that are farther away

60. Gale (1996).
61. Governor's Task Force (2003).

from riots, dominated by whites, well-to-do, and rather suburban in character are not likely to feel much of an impact from racial civil disorders. In fact, they may benefit if businesses and residents move away from riot-prone areas. Unfortunately, conducting an analysis on the city level (the unit for which most data are available) combines these two types of areas and necessarily dilutes the apparent effects of riots. The solution to this problem is to reduce the size of the units of analysis. The problem, of course, is that moving to that size of unit also means losing important control variables.

The third source of understated effects, and perhaps the most consequential, is a different issue related to the unit of analysis. Collins and Margo are attempting to show local differences in economic conditions based on local occurrence of riots. But what if the effect of local riots is not really local in character? The authors mention this possibility when they are discussing the assumptions of the study, but it warrants a bit more attention. What if the wave of riots as a group had an effect on all poor black neighborhoods—whether those neighborhoods had a riot or not?

Returning to Spilerman's classic studies for a moment, it is true that once he controlled for black population size and region, the effects of economic variables he tested were insubstantial. This did not mean that economic conditions did not have any effects on rioting, though. It meant that *local variation* in economic conditions did not produce *local differences* in riot occurrence. In his discussion of the finding, he does not disavow economic conditions or grievances; instead, he suggests that the poor conditions that afflicted the black community were so widespread, prevalent, and well understood as grievances particular to the black community that they increased the chances of rioting in a similar way everywhere.[62] In effect, such conditions produced a blanket effect across the United States. This is a very different understanding of the connection between economic conditions and rioting than is typically recounted by readers of Spilerman's work.[63]

The idea driving Spilerman's discussion can be extended easily to the chapter by Collins and Margor as well. What the authors have found is that local riots damage local economic outcomes, but rather weakly. What if the effects of riots are not limited to the local environment? What

62. Spilerman (1970).
63. See McPhail (1994).

if, for example, riots cause flight from, and reluctance to invest in, poor black areas that have *not* experienced riots? The idea is that riots give these *kinds* of neighborhoods a bad name—not just the specific neighborhoods themselves.

This kind of outcome becomes even more likely when a wave or string of riots is clustered in time and relatively widespread. Isolated riots are more likely to become associated with their immediate locale, but a large number of riots lose that specificity. When this happens, they are more likely to contribute to the general impression that certain neighborhoods are poor prospects for development and investment of human capital.

As in Spilerman's study, a widespread effect will seem to dilute the apparent impact of riots on their local environments because the riot is making things worse in nonriot communities as well. Thus, when we compare riot and nonriot areas, the difference between the two is less than it would be if the riots had a more localized effect. This leads to underestimation of the effects in two ways: the difference between riot and nonriot areas is diminished, and the negative effect of riots on nonriot areas is completely invisible to the analysis.

In the end, then, I am making two recommendations for future study: We should both restrict and expand the scope of the study. First, we should restrict it by reducing the size of the units whenever possible so that we are combining poor black neighborhoods with rich white ones. Second, we should expand by recognizing that effects might have an impact beyond the immediate local environment. The latter aim is a bit trickier to accomplish, but considerations of distance decay between units or measure of structural equivalence could produce more nuance in hypotheses about where these riots could have effects.

References

Aldrich, Howard, and Albert J. Reiss. 1970. "The Effect of Civil Disorders on Small Business in the Inner City." *Journal of Social Issues* 26 (Winter): 187–206.

Aiken, Michael, and Robert Alford. 1998. *Governmental Units Analysis Data.* Inter-University Consortium for Political Research Study 0028.

Baron, Robert A., and Victoria A. Ransberger. 1978. "Ambient Temperature and the Occurrence of Collective Violence: The "Long Hot Summer" Revisited." *Journal of Personality and Social Psychology* 36 (2): 351–60.

Bean, Jonathan J. 2000. "'Burn, Baby, Burn': Small Business in the Urban Riots of the 1960s." *Independent Review* 5: 165–87.

Blanchard, Olivier Jean, and Lawrence F. Katz. 1992. "Regional Evolutions." *Brookings Papers on Economic Activity* 1: 1–75.

Brown, Charles. 1984. "Black-White Earnings Ratios since the Civil Rights Act of 1964: The Importance of Labor Market Dropouts." *Quarterly Journal of Economics* 99 (February): 31–44.

Carlsmith, J. Merrill, and Craig A. Anderson. 1979. "Ambient Temperature and the Occurrence of Collective Violence: A New Analysis." *Journal of Personality and Social Psychology* 37 (3): 337–44.

Carter, Gregg Lee. 1983. "Explaining the Severity of the 1960's Black Rioting." Ph.D. dissertation, Columbia University.

———. 1986. "The 1960s Black Riots Revisited: City Level Explanations of Their Severity." *Sociological Inquiry* 56: 210–28.

———. 1990. "Collective Violence and the Problem of Group Size in Aggregate-Level Studies." *Sociological Focus* 23: 287–300.

Chandra, Amitabh. 2000. "Labor Market Dropouts and the Racial Wage Gap: 1940-1990." *American Economic Review* 9 (May): 333–38.

Chandra, Siddharth, and Angela Williams Foster. Forthcoming. "The Revolution of Rising Expectations." *Social Science History.*

Collins, William J., and Robert A. Margo. 2000. "Residential Segregation and Socioeconomic Outcomes: When Did Ghettos Go Bad?" *Economics Letters* 69: 239–43.

———. 2003. "Race and the Value of Owner-Occupied Housing, 1940–1990." *Regional Science and Urban Economics* 33: 255–86.

Congressional Quarterly Service. 1967. *Urban Problems and Civil Disorder: Special Report No. 36.* Washington.

Cutler, David M., and Edward L. Glaeser. 1997. "Are Ghettos Good or Bad?" *Quarterly Journal of Economics* 112 (August): 827–72.

DiPasquale, Denise, and Edward L. Glaeser. 1998. "The Los Angeles Riot and the Economics of Urban Unrest." *Journal of Urban Economics* 43 (January): 52–78.

Eisinger, Peter K. 1973. "The Conditions of Protest Behavior in American Cities." *American Political Science Review* 67 (March): 11–28.

Field, Simon. 1992. "The Effect of Temperature on Crime." *British Journal of Criminology* 32 (3): 340–51.

Fine, Sidney. 1989. *Violence in the Model City: The Cavanagh Administration, Race Relations, and the Detroit Riot of 1967.* University of Michigan Press.

Frey, William H. 1979. "Central City White Flight: Racial and Nonracial Causes." *American Sociological Review* 44: 425–48.

Gale, Dennis. 1996. *Understanding Urban Unrest: From Reverend King to Rodney King.* Sage.

Gilje, Paul. 1996. *Rioting in America.* Indiana University Press.

Glaeser, Edward L., and Joseph Gyourko. 2001. "Urban Decline and Durable Housing." Working Paper 8598. Cambridge, Mass.: National Bureau of Economic Research.

Governor's Benton Harbor Task Force. 2003. *A Plan for Positive Change: Final Report of the Governor's Benton Harbor Task Force.* Benton Harbor.

Governor's Commission on the Los Angeles Riots. 1965. *Violence in the City: An End or a Beginning?* Los Angeles.

Hahn, Harlan. 1970. "Civic Responses to Riots: A Reappraisal of Kerner Commission Data." *Public Opinion Quarterly* 34 (Spring): 101–07.

Jencks, Christopher. 1993. *Rethinking Social Policy: Race, Poverty, and the Underclass.* Harper Perennial edition.

Jiobu, Robert M. 1971. "City Characteristics and Racial Violence." *Social Science Quarterly* 55 (1): 52–64.

Kain, John. 1968. "Housing Segregation, Negro Employment, and Metropolitan Decentralization." *Quarterly Journal of Economics* 82 (May): 175–97.

Kelly, William R., and David Snyder. 1980. "Racial Violence and Socioeconomic Changes among Blacks in the United States." *Social Forces* 58 (3): 739–60.

Kerner, Otto, and others. 1968. *Report of the National Advisory Commission on Civil Disorders.* New York: New York Times Company.

King, Mary C. 2001. "'Race Riots' and Black Economic Progress." Working Paper. Portland State University, Economics Department.

Lieberson, Stanley, and Arnold R. Silverman. 1965. "The Precipitants and Underlying Conditions of Race Riots." *American Sociological Review* 30 (December): 887–98.

Lieske, Joel A. 1978. "The Conditions of Racial Violence in American Cities." *American Political Science Review* 72 (December): 1324–40.

Massey, Douglas S., and Nancy A. Denton. 1993. *American Apartheid: Segregation and the Making of the Underclass.* Harvard University Press.

McPhail, Clark. 1994. "Presidential Address—The Dark Side of Purpose: Individual and Collective Violence in Riots." *Sociological Quarterly* 35 (1): 1–32.

Murray, Charles A. 1984. *Losing Ground: American Social Policy, 1950-1980.* Basic Books.

Myers, Daniel J. 1997. "Racial Rioting in the 1960s: An Event History Analysis of Local Conditions." *American Sociological Review* 62 (February): 94–112.

————. 2000. "The Diffusion of Collective Violence: Infectiousness, Suscepti- bility, and Mass Media Networks." *American Journal of Sociology* 106 (July): 173-208.

Olzak, Susan, and Suzanne Shanahan. 1996. "Deprivation Race Riots: An Exten- sion of Spilerman's Analysis." *Social Forces* 74 (3): 931–61.

Olzak, Susan, Suzanne Shanahan, and Elizabeth H. McEneaney. 1996. "Poverty, Segregation, and Race Riots: 1960 to 1993." *American Sociological Review* 61 (August): 590–613.

Roback, Jennifer. 1982. "Wages, Rents and the Quality of Life." *Journal of Political Economy* 90 (December): 1257–78

Ruggles, Steven, Matthew Sobek, and others. 1997. *Integrated Public Use Micro- data Series: Version 2.0.* Historical Census Projects. University of Minnesota.

Spilerman, Seymour. 1970. "The Causes of Racial Disturbances: A Comparison of Alternative Explanations." *American Sociological Review* 35 (August): 627–49.

————. 1971. "The Causes of Racial Disturbances: Test of an Explanation." *American Sociological Review* 36 (June): 427–42.

————. 1976. "Structural Characteristics of Cities and the Severity of Racial Disorders." *American Sociological Review* 41 (October): 771–93.

Sugrue, Thomas J. 1996. *The Origins of the Urban Crisis: Race and Inequality in Postwar Detroit.* Princeton University Press.

U.S. Department of Commerce. Bureau of the Census. Various years. *County and City Data Book.*

U.S. Senate Committee on Government Operations, Permanent Subcommittee on Investigations. 1967. *Riots, Civil, and Criminal Disorders.* 90 Cong. 1 sess., part 1.

Wanderer, Jules J. 1969. "An Index of Riot Severity and Some Correlates." *American Journal of Sociology* 74 (March): 500–05.

Widick, B. J. 1989. *Detroit: City of Race and Class Violence.* Wayne State Uni- versity Press.

Wilson, William Julius. 1987. *The Truly Disadvantaged: The Inner City, The Underclass, and Public Policy.* University of Chicago Press.

EDWARD L. GLAESER
Harvard University and National Bureau of Economic Research

ALBERT SAIZ
University of Pennsylvania

The Rise of the Skilled City

BETWEEN 1980 AND 2000, the population of metropolitan areas where less than 10 percent of adults had college degrees in 1980, grew on average by 13 percent. Among metropolitan areas where more than 25 percent of adults had college degrees, the average population growth rate was 45 percent. For more than a century, in both the United States and Great Britain, cities with more educated residents have grown faster than comparable cities with less human capital.[1] There is no consensus, however, on the causes or implications of this relationship.

Why have people increasingly crowded around the most skilled? Why does education seem to be a more and more important ingredient in agglomeration economies? Three disparate, but not incompatible, visions of the modern city offer different answers to these questions. The Consumer City view—cities are increasingly oriented around consumption amenities, not productivity—tells us that skills predict growth because skilled neighbors are an attractive consumption amenity. The Information City view—cities exist to facilitate the flow of ideas—tells us that we should expect cities to be increasingly oriented around the skilled because the skilled specialize in ideas. The Reinvention City view— cities survive only by adapting their economies to new technologies—

Glaeser thanks the National Science Foundation and the Taubman Center for State and Local Government for financial support. Shannon Mail provided superb research assistance.

1. Glaeser (1994); Glaeser, Scheinkman, and Shleifer (1995); Simon (1998); Black and Henderson (1999); Nardinelli and Simon (1996, 2002).

tells us that human capital predicts city growth because human capital enables people to adapt well to change.[2] Understanding why skills predict city growth will help us determine if cities thrive because of consumption, information, or reinvention.

We use four approaches to address the possibility that the rise of the skilled city is the result of a spurious correlation between local skills and other urban characteristics. First, we show that controlling for a wide range of other factors makes little difference to the impact of local skills on subsequent city growth and that local human capital is essentially unrelated to many of the most important local amenities such as weather variables. Second, we show that the metropolitan-area human capital effect is robust to including metropolitan-area fixed effects. Third, we examine the connection between the number of colleges per capita in 1940 and growth between 1970 and 2000. The pre–World War II number of colleges seems considerably more exogenous than current skill levels, and it still correlates strongly with growth in the modern era.[3]

Fourth, we examine the timing of skills and growth and test whether skilled workers flock to cities that are growing. Individuals with low education are particularly prone to live in declining cities, but exogenous differences in positive growth rates do not predict changes in the percentage of the population with a college education.[4] Reverse causation from growth to education seems to be present only in a handful of declining metropolitan areas and cannot account for much of the relevant effect. Overall, the evidence supports the view that skills induce growth.

Following Jesse Shapiro, we present a framework for understanding the connection between skills and growth.[5] The framework tells us that production-led growth should increase *nominal* wages and housing prices, while consumption-led growth should cause *real* wages to fall. Rising nominal wages are a sufficient condition for productivity growth, and declining real wages are necessary for the amenity story to be of relevance.

---

2. For the Consumer City view see, for example, Glaeser, Kolko, and Saiz (2001); for the Information City view see Jacobs (1969); and for the Reinvention City view see Glaeser (2003). For adaptation to change see Shultz (1964); Welch (1970).

3. In this we follow Moretti (forthcoming). Card (1995) uses proximity to college as an instrumental variable for the level of education of an individual.

4. Glaeser and Gyourko (2001).

5. Shapiro (2003).

Our empirical work shows that productivity drives the connection between skills and growth. At the metropolitan level, we find that education *levels* have a positive impact on future wage and housing price growth. With almost any reasonable set of parameter values, the connection between education and population growth is the exclusive result of rising productivity and has less to do with rising amenity levels. Indeed, real wages may be rising in high-education metropolitan areas, which suggests that consumer amenities are declining—in relative terms in high-skill areas.

At the city level, the results are less clear. In small municipalities within metropolitan areas, low levels of human capital predict urban decline and falling housing prices. At the city level (not at the metropolitan-area level), it is the bottom end of the human capital distribution that matters. The prevalence of high school dropouts predicts urban decline. Moreover, this decline seems driven, at least in part, through consumption-related effects. Perhaps, unfortunately, poverty has become perceived as an increasingly negative amenity because of social problems or a higher tax burden.

That skills increase the growth of a metropolitan area through productivity increases is compatible with the Information City and the Reinvention City hypotheses. We try to distinguish between these two interpretations of the connection between growth and skills. To test the Information City hypothesis, we turn to patent data. Previous research shows that areas with more human capital have higher rates of patenting per capita.[6] We find that controlling for patenting rates does not explain any portion of the effect of human capital on growth. This certainly does not disprove the Information City hypothesis, but it does not support it either.

One test of the reinvention hypothesis is to look at the cross effect between skills and factors that have an independent effect on city growth. The Information City view predicts that skills should predict growth among all types of cities. The Reinvention City hypothesis predicts that skills should only matter among those cities that have received negative shocks. We test this implication by looking at the cross effect between skills and the weather, and skills and immigration. Warm weather and immigration have been two of the most important drivers of contempora-

6. Carlino, Chatterjee, and Hunt (2001).

neous metropolitan population growth in the United States. We find that there is a strong negative cross-effect between skills and either warmth or immigration, which means that human capital really only matters in potentially declining places. This supports the reinvention hypothesis.

We further test the reinvention hypothesis by seeing whether skilled places shifted out of manufacturing more quickly. In the first part of the twentieth century, urban success generally meant specialization in manufacturing. Declining transport costs and declining importance of manufacturing have meant that at the beginning of the twenty-first century, successful cities have moved from manufacturing into other industries. If the reinvention hypothesis is right, then it should predict the speed at which cities reinvent themselves. Indeed, we find that metropolitan areas with high levels of education and significant manufacturing as of 1940 switched from manufacturing to other industries faster than high-manufacturing areas with less human capital. These results suggest that skills are valuable because they help cities adapt and change their activities in response to negative economic shocks.

Is the Skills-Growth Connection Spurious?

In this section, we confirm the empirical relationship between education and metropolitan statistical area (MSA) growth. We test whether the connection between skills and city growth is spurious, reflecting omitted variables. We use both cities and MSAs as our unit of analysis, because there are advantages and disadvantages to both. The MSAs are more natural labor markets, but cities are smaller and a better unit of analysis for understanding either amenities or real estate prices. We use the 1999 county-based boundaries (New England county metropolitan area [NECMA]) definitions in New England and primary metropolitan statistical area (PMSA) definitions in the rest of the country.[7] Using county-level data, we obtain a complete and consistent panel for 1970, 1980, 1990, and 2000. We select those cities with population over 30,000 in 1970. Table A-1 in appendix A to this chapter details the sources of all variables.

7. Using the most recent boundaries helps us avoid the endogeneity of current definitions to growth.

Figure 1. Growth of Metropolitan Statistical Area (1980–2000) and Human Capital (1980)

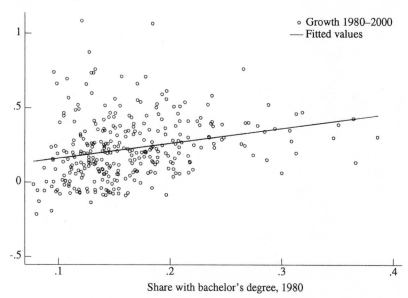

Share with bachelor's degree, 1980

Fitted line from the regression: log(pop2000/pop1980) = 0.0611 + 1.001 × share with bachelor's degree in 1980.
(0.036) (0.209)

R squared: 0.067, N: 318.

Figure 1 shows the correlation between the growth of the logarithm of population between 1980 and 2000 and the share of adults in 1980 with college degrees among metropolitan statistical areas. Table 1 (panel a) shows the correlation between metropolitan-area growth and the primary independent variables over the entire 1970–2000 period. Table 1 (panel b) shows similar correlations at the city level. In both cases, there is a significant association between initial education and later growth. The correlation between the share of college graduates and population growth is 18 percent for cities and 30 percent for metropolitan areas. Descriptive statistics on all variables are presented in appendix table A-2.

While we focus primarily on the share of the adult population with college degrees, an alternative measure of human capital, the share of adults who dropped out of high school, is a stronger (that is, more nega-tive) correlate of city growth but a weaker correlate of MSA growth. This suggests that the impact of higher education may be more important at the MSA level (maybe because of a productivity effect), whereas the

Table 1. 1970–2000 Population Growth and 1970 Variables: Correlations

	Log(population 2000) – log(population 1970)
Panel A: Metropolitan statistical areas (MSA)	
Share with bachelor's degree (age 25+) in 1970	0.30
Log population in 1970	–0.13
Log average heating degree days (1961–90)	–0.56
Log average annual precipitation (1961–90)	–0.31
Share of workers in manufacturing in 1970	–0.56
Share of workers in professional services in 1970	0.22
Share of workers in trade in 1970	0.29
Unemployment rate in 1970	0.15
Share of high school dropouts (age 25+) in 1970	–0.18
Log colleges per capita in 1940	0.25
Log family income in 1970	–0.28
Log home value in 1970	0.02
Panel B: Cities	
Share with bachelor's degree (age 25+) in 1970	0.18
Log population in 1970	–0.08
Log average heating degree days (1961–90)	–0.44
Log average annual precipitation (1961–90)	–0.45
Share of workers in manufacturing in 1970	–0.33
Share of workers in professional services in 1970	0.13
Share of workers in trade in 1970	0.21
Unemployment rate in 1970	0.11
Share of high school dropouts (age 25+) in 1970	–0.28
Log colleges per capita in 1940	0.25
Log family income in 1970	–0.08
Log home value in 1970	0.07

impact of low education is more important at the city level (maybe because of localized social interactions). Although these correlations are large, other variables such as heating degree days, annual precipitation, and the share of labor force in manufacturing have stronger correlations with population growth than the human capital variables.

Our baseline regressions use a panel of metropolitan areas (in table 2) and cities (in table 3) over three periods (the 1970s, the 1980s and the 1990s).[8] The dependent variable is the difference in the log of population between census years. We focus on the coefficient on the share of the

8. We have data for four years: 1970, 1980, 1990, and 2000. Since we are using population growth (the first difference in the log of population) we end up with three time periods.

population with a college education.[9] All regressions include decade-specific fixed effects and allow each geographic unit's standard errors to be correlated over time. More precisely, we estimate the coefficients β and γ_j in regressions of the form:

$$(1) \quad \log\left(\frac{\text{Population}_{i,t}}{\text{Population}_{i,t-10}}\right) = \beta \times \frac{\text{College}_{i,t-10}}{\text{Population}_{i,t-10}} + \sum_j \gamma_j Z_{i,j,t-10} + Y_t + \varepsilon_{i,t}$$

where $(\text{College}_{i,t-10}/\text{Population}_{i,t-10})$ is the share of the population with a college degree in the initial year, $Z_{i,j,t-10}$ is the value of independent variable j in the initial year, U_t is a decade-specific fixed effect, and $\varepsilon_{i,t}$ is the city-year error term, which we allow to be correlated across decades.

Regression 1 in tables 2 and 3 shows the raw impact of percent college educated on later growth for MSAs and cities respectively. For the MSA-level regressions, a 1 percentage point increase in the share of the adult population with college degrees increases the decadal growth rate by, approximately, almost one-half of 1 percent. The standard deviation of metropolitan-area growth is approximately .1, and the standard deviation of the college graduation variable is approximately .05: a one-standard-deviation increase in percent college graduates increases the expected growth rate by one-quarter of a standard deviation.

In the city-level regressions reported in table 3, the basic effect of college education is weaker. A 1 percent increase in college graduates increases the expected growth rate by one-fifth of 1 percent. At the city level the standard deviation of the percent college-educated variable is approximately .1, and the standard deviation of decadal growth rates is about .15. This means that a one-standard-deviation increase in the percent college educated at the city level is associated with approximately a one-seventh of a standard deviation increase in the expected growth rate. As suggested by the raw correlations, college education is a more powerful predictor of growth at the MSA level than growth at the city level.

In regression 2 of both tables, we include initial population, the log of heating degree days, the log of average precipitation, the share of labor force in manufacturing, trade and professional services,[10] and controls for

9. This corresponds to individuals with a bachelor's degree.
10. These are the three major occupations in our sample, representing 63 percent of total MSA employment in 1990.

Table 2. MSA Growth and Education

			Δlog(population)			
	(1)	(2)	(3)	(4)	(5)	(6)
Share with bachelor's degree (age 25+) at t-10	0.47 (0.096)***	0.582 (0.113)***	0.456 (0.117)***	0.508 (0.215)**	0.414 (0.153)***	
Log of population at t-10		-0.015 (0.004)***	-0.011 (0.005)**	-0.316 (0.030)***	-0.014 (0.004)***	0.003 (0.005)
Log average heating degree days (1961–90)		-0.082 (0.011)***	-0.075 (0.020)***		-0.084 (0.011)***	-0.07 (0.011)***
Log average annual precipitation (1961–90)		-0.026 (0.015)*	-0.001 (0.014)		-0.026 (0.015)*	-0.024 (0.015)
Share of workers in manufacturing at t-10		-0.173 (0.088)*	-0.167 (0.073)**	0.255 (0.125)**	-0.162 (0.085)*	-0.174 (0.084)**
Share of workers in professional services at t-10		-0.328 (0.145)**	-0.166 (0.132)	0.148 (0.203)	-0.238 (0.142)*	0.082 (0.117)
Share of workers in trade at t-10		0.034 (0.260)	0.113 (0.215)	0.229 (0.281)	0.007 (0.279)	-0.129 (0.219)
Unemployment rate at t-10					-0.427 (0.235)*	
Share of high school dropouts (age 25+) at t-10					-0.06 (0.089)	
Log colleges per capita in 1940						0.035 (0.008)***
Year fixed effects	Yes	Yes	Yes	Yes	Yes	Yes
Region fixed effects	No	Yes	No	No	Yes	Yes
State fixed effects	No	No	Yes	No	No	No
MSA fixed effects	No	No	No	Yes	No	No
Observations	918	918	918	954	918	816
R squared	0.56	0.51	0.6	0.89	0.51	0.5

Note: Robust standard errors in parentheses
*Significant at 10 percent level. **Significant at 5 percent level. ***Significant at 1 percent level.

Table 3. City Growth and Education

			Δlog(population)			
	(1)	(2)	(3)	(4)	(5)	(6)
Share with bachelor's degree (age 25+) at t-10	0.202 (0.044)***	0.217 (0.053)***	0.166 (0.050)***	0.121 (0.086)	0.061 (0.078)	
Log of population at t-10		-0.009 (0.004)**	-0.017 (0.005)***	-0.512 (0.017)***	-0.007 (0.004)	-0.010 (0.004)**
Log average heating degree days (1961–90)		-0.021 (0.009)**	0.000 (0.015)		-0.023 (0.009)***	-0.028 (0.009)***
Log average annual precipitation (1961–90)		-0.097 (0.018)***	-0.071 (0.025)***		-0.097 (0.019)***	-0.087 (0.021)***
Share of workers in manufacturing at t-10		-0.032 (0.060)	-0.023 (0.059)	0.327 (0.091)***	0.014 (0.063)	-0.042 (0.055)
Share of workers in professional services at t-10		-0.113 (0.090)	-0.095 (0.087)	-0.851 (0.144)***	-0.048 (0.102)	0.029 (0.077)
Share of workers in trade at t-10		0.276 (0.151)*	0.122 (0.154)	-0.393 (0.164)**	0.181 (0.154)	0.200 (0.149)
Unemployment rate at t-10					-0.043 (0.200)	
Share of high school dropouts (age 25+) at t-10					-0.163 (0.060)***	
Log colleges per capita in 1940						0.033 (0.007)***
Year fixed effects	Yes	Yes	Yes	Yes	Yes	Yes
Region fixed effects	No	Yes	No	No	Yes	Yes
State fixed effects	No	No	Yes	No	No	No
City fixed effects	No	No	No	Yes	No	No
Observations	2160	2160	2160	2169	2160	2070
R squared	0.11	0.26	0.36	0.8	0.27	0.26

Note: Robust standard errors in parentheses
*Significant at 10 percent level. **Significant at 5 percent level. ***Significant at 1 percent level.

the four census regions. Warm and dry weather has been shown to be among the important predictors of population growth in the United States at the end of the twentieth century. Heating degree days is a measure of cold weather severity (roughly proportional to how many days a household would need to use heating to keep warm). Initial population is usually unrelated to later city growth, but it remains a natural control.[11] The employment share variables capture aspects of industrial orientation, and we know from table 1 that specializing in manufacturing is a strong correlate of later decline.

For both cities and metropolitan areas we find that warm, dry places grow much more quickly than cold, wet places. There is a modest amount of mean reversion: bigger cities and metropolitan areas grow somewhat more slowly. Metropolitan areas with substantial manufacturing grow more slowly. Although these correlations are interesting, we do not discuss them further because they have been considered at length elsewhere.[12] Our focus is the extent that controlling for these variables changes the impact of college education on later city growth.

Including these controls has little impact on the coefficient on the college educated. Education does not predict growth because educated metropolitan areas have more employment in the service sector or better weather. In metropolitan areas, including these factors actually causes the coefficient on percent college educated to rise. That controlling for these major potential *omitted* variables causes the impact of college to rise should not surprise us, because skilled workers are less likely to live in warm, dry places. Since more educated people have tended to live in the areas of the country with less desirable climates, controlling for the weather variables makes the impact of education stronger, not weaker.

In specification three, we include state-specific fixed effects. In principle, these fixed effects should capture all time-invariant weather or geographic variables, as well as those state-level policies that change only slowly over time. In tables 2 and 3, controlling for state-specific effects has only a modest impact. For metropolitan areas, the state fixed-effects regressions have almost exactly the same coefficient as the regression with no controls. For cities, the state fixed effects cause the coefficient on

11. Glaeser, Kolko, and Saiz (2001); Glaeser and Shapiro (2003); Glaeser, Scheinkman, and Shleifer (1995); Eaton and Eckstein (1997).

12. Glaeser, Scheinkman and Shleifer (1995); Glaeser and Shapiro (2003).

education to drop 18 percent relative to the no control specification. We generally prefer not to work with state-specific fixed effects, especially for metropolitan-area regressions, since many states have only a small number of metropolitan areas.

In the fourth regression, we include a city or metropolitan-area fixed effect. This control is meant to address the possibility that skilled workers are just proxying for omitted variables that are pushing the area ahead. In this case, all of our identification comes from changes in the share of college educated over time within the city. In other words, during decades in which the city began with more college graduates (relative to its historical mean) did that city have a higher subsequent growth rate? For metropolitan areas, these fixed effects have little impact on the coefficient, although the standard errors rise significantly.[13] For cities, the coefficient drops by 40 percent (relative to the no control benchmark) and becomes statistically insignificant, but the difference between the coefficient in regression 4 and the coefficient in regression 1 is not statistically significant.

Including city-specific fixed effects is asking a great deal of the data, given the extremely high degree of persistence in human capital over time. The correlation coefficient in the share of the college educated in 1980 and 1990 is 97.3 percent across cities and 97.5 percent across metropolitan areas. As the fixed effects eliminate most of the variation in skills across space, we are amazed that we continue to find a positive effect, and we are not troubled that the effect gets somewhat weaker in the city specification.

In the fifth regressions of the two tables, we add two further controls to the specification in regression 2: share of the adult population without high school degree and the unemployment rate. We see both of these variables as added measures of human capital, but these measures capture the lower end of the human capital distribution. While high-frequency changes in the unemployment rate over time generally reflect time-varying labor market conditions, *differences* in the unemployment rate across cities (less so across metropolitan areas) are generally time

13. We understand that we cannot estimate the coefficient on the lagged dependent variable consistently in the fixed-effects specification. However, the results on the other coefficients would not change very much if we omitted the lag of population in the fixed-effects specification.

invariant and reflect characteristics of the labor force and the industry structure in the city.[14] The correlation coefficient between city-level unemployment rates in 1980 and 1990 is .75; the correlation coefficient between MSA-level unemployment rates in 1980 and 1990 is .5.

For metropolitan areas, the effect of the dropout rate is insignificant, and the unemployment rate is marginally significant. Together these variables reduce the coefficient on percent college educated by 15 percent relative to regression 1. In table 3, controlling for these other variables severely reduces the impact of higher education on city growth. The natural interpretation of table 2 and table 3 is that an abundance of college graduates drives the success of a *regional* labor market, but a *local* neighborhood succeeds by avoiding large numbers of low-educated workers. It seems that having high human capital matters most for the metropolitan area, but avoiding low human capital matters more for smaller units of geography.

Finally, in regression 6, we drop our measure of college graduation entirely and follow Moretti, using instead the presence of colleges in the area before 1940.[15] As seen in figure 2, there is a remarkably strong relationship between the number of colleges per capita before World War II and the level of people with higher education in 2000. This variable has the advantage of being predetermined and not a function of recent events that might attract the well educated to a metropolitan area.

Although we believe that this variable is less likely to reflect reverse causality or omitted factors than our share of college-educated variable, we are not confident that it is completely orthogonal to the error term. As such, using the variable as an instrument (as in Moretti) may give us quite misleading results because in instrumental variables regression, the correlation with the error term is essentially multiplied by the inverse of the first-stage R squared.[16] Instead, we present results by using this variable directly instead of using it to instrument for the share of college graduates. In fact, both as an instrument and as a right-hand-side variable, the variable has a strong, significant impact on population growth.

---

14. Thus most of the time-series variation in unemployment rates is common to all cities, whereas the relative differentials between cities are quite stable.

15. Moretti (forthcoming).

16. Moretti (forthcoming). Technically, this statement is only true in a univariate regression. Still, the basic point that correlation with the error term explodes in magnitude in instrumental variables regressions holds in all cases.

Figure 2. Colleges in the pre-WWII Era and the Share of College Educated in 2000

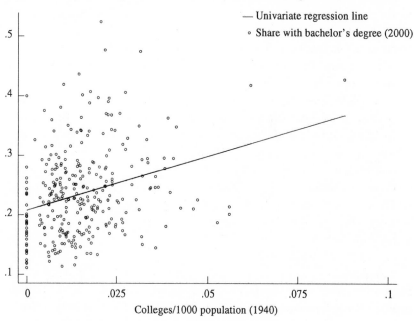

Share with bachelor's degree in 2000 = 0.207 + 1.816 × colleges per 1,000 population in 1940.
                                                (0.006) (0.337)
R squared: 0.085, N: 313.

The coefficient in table 2 implies that as the number of colleges per capita doubles, the expected growth rate during the decade rises by roughly 4 percent for both MSAs and cities.[17]

In appendix table A-3 we run similar regressions at the MSA level with a set of controls for other variables that may be correlated with initial high levels of education and find that the impact of education on growth is not driven by these *omitted* variables either.[18]

17. We have also experimented with college enrollment over population in 1970 as an exogenous proxy for human capital with qualitatively similar results (see table A-3, column 1).

18. In table A-3 we control for the possibility that the share of the highly educated may simply be capturing attributes of the age distribution in a city (for example, younger cities will tend to be more educated because of a cohort effect: younger cohorts are attaining higher education levels, or cities with lower education may be cities with elderly retired people). To address that issue we have augmented the MSA regression to control for the initial age distribution of the metropolitan area (variables for the shares of population in the following categories: age 0-21, 22-34, 35-44, 45-54, and 54-65). We also include in

In table 4 we look at reverse causality. In regression 1 we examine the relationship between population growth and the change in the share of the population with bachelor's degrees at the city level. Glaeser and Gyourko argue that durable housing causes unskilled people to move into declining cities for the cheap housing.[19] As such, the relationship between population change and human capital change should be much weaker among growing cities than among declining cities. This asymmetry occurs because durable housing means that housing prices fall sharply in declining cities, and this event attracts the unskilled. We estimate our regression with a spline at zero population growth.

Regression 1 does indeed find a strong relationship between growth and human capital among declining cities and little relationship among growing cities. In regression 4 we repeat this exercise with metropolitan areas and find similar results. Regressions 2 and 5 repeat regressions 1 and 4 with initial population and industry share controls and find little change in the coefficients on growth.

Although these regressions point to a connection between decline and human capital change, the fact that we are regressing change in human capital on contemporaneous population growth is problematic. Obviously, the causal link is hard to determine from this regression. To address this issue, we instrument for growth using the omitted climate variables (heating days and annual precipitation). As already shown,

---

appendix table A-3 other variables that are generally considered city amenities or disamenities. We control for the murder rate. Higher education levels have been shown to reduce crime (Lochner [1999]; Lochner and Moretti [2001]). Crime is a very salient disamenity. For instance, Berry-Cullen and Levitt (1999) show a causal link between crime and city depopulation. Murder rates are a good indicator of crime, because other crimes are not always reported, and reporting rates for other crimes may vary according to education levels. The number of museums, eating and drinking establishments per capita, health establishments per capita, the number of amusement and recreational service establishments, and the teacher-pupil ratio (a proxy for the quality of primary and secondary education in the metropolitan area) are included as local public goods or amenities that are likely to be provided in high human capital areas. We also include the number of membership organizations as a proxy for social capital. An alternative hypothesis to explain why the presence of highly educated people fosters growth hinges on the propensity of the highly educated to contribute to local social capital by participating in political and civic institutions (Putnam [2000]). Including these amenities, public goods, and controls for social capital does not seem to explain away the role of education on city growth. In fact, the amenity variables are mostly insignificant in this specification, although in line with previous research there is a very strong negative impact of crime on growth.

19. Glaeser and Gyourko (2001).

Table 4. Reverse Causation: Human Capital and Growth

| | Δshare bachelor's degree | | | | | |
| | Cities | | | Metropolitan statistical area | | |
	(1)	(2)	(3)	(4)	(5)	(6)
Spline growth for declining areas	0.058 (0.014)***	0.055 (0.016)***	-0.311 (0.203)	0.121 (0.024)***	0.087 (0.020)***	1.249 (1.996)
Spline growth for growing areas	0.011 (0.005)**	-0.005 (0.006)	0.057 (0.065)	0.010 (0.007)	0.022 (0.007)***	-0.155 (0.103)
Log of population at t-10		0.000 (0.001)	-0.001 (0.001)		0.007 (0.001)***	0.006 (0.001)***
Share of workers in manufacturing at t-10		-0.048 (0.013)***	-0.063 (0.017)***		0.023 (0.011)**	-0.079 (0.031)**
Share of workers in professional services at t-10		0.074 (0.021)***	0.069 (0.023)***		0.138 (0.016)***	0.060 (0.051)
Share of workers in trade at t-10		-0.081 (0.037)**	-0.086 (0.045)*		0.033 (0.034)	-0.038 (0.054)
Year fixed effects	Yes	Yes	Yes	Yes	Yes	Yes
IV for growth (weather instruments)	No	No	Yes	No	No	Yes
Observations	2709	2169	2160	954	954	918
R squared	0.11	0.15		0.22	0.42	

Note: Robust standard errors in parentheses.

*Significant at 10 percent level.   **Significant at 5 percent level.   ***Significant at 1 percent level.

these variables powerfully predict growth, and we use them as instruments in regressions 3 and 6. Clearly, interpreting the coefficients from the instrumental variables (IV) specification would become problematic if we believed that climate has a direct impact on the skill composition of an area. In regressions 3 and 6 the results are inconclusive, because the standard errors become quite large (especially for the coefficients on decline), but we see little evidence for population growth accompanying skill upgrading among growing cities.

Our interpretation of table 4 is that there is significant potential for reverse causality among those cities that are in decline but little potential for reverse causality among growing cities. We see this as more problematic for the city-level regressions because decline is more common at the city level. To ensure that a tendency for declining metropolitan areas to shed skilled workers is not driving our results in tables 2 and 3, we have run regressions in which we treat all declining cities as having zero population growth. This change has little impact on our estimated coefficient on schooling. We also omitted those areas that are predicted (on the basis of weather) to have population declines. This causes our coefficients to fall but generally remain statistically significant.

Productivity and Amenities: A Theoretical Framework

Tables 2, 3, and 4 suggest that the correlation between human capital and subsequent urban growth is a real phenomenon and not a spurious correlation driven by some obvious omitted variable or reverse causality. We now try to understand this correlation. Following Shapiro, we start with a simple model that helps us to distinguish between consumption and production-led urban growth.[20]

We assume that utility in city j equals $C_j \times U$(Traded Goods, Housing), where C_j represents a city-specific amenity level and housing is a nontraded good. We further assume that output in the city equals: $A_j \times F$(Labor, Capital), where A_j represents a city-specific productivity level, labor is itself a function of skilled and unskilled workers, and capital includes traded and nontraded capital inputs.

Although the details are worked out in appendix B, our key assumptions are that utility ($U(\cdot)$) is Cobb-Douglas in traded goods and housing

20. Shapiro (2003).

and that production ($F(\cdot)$) is Cobb-Douglas in effective labor units, traded capital, and nontraded capital. Effective labor units are themselves produced with a constant elasticity of substitution function of skilled and unskilled labor. In equilibrium, workers are paid the marginal product of labor, and utility levels (within skill categories) are equalized across space.

Our primary focus is on changes in the city-specific productivity level, A_j, and the city-specific consumer amenity level, C_j. These are the only city-specific parameters that we allow to change. We assume that $\log(A_{j,t+1}/A_{j,t})$ = Other Factors + $\delta_A S_{j,t}$ and $\log(C_{j,t+1}/C_{j,t})$ = Other Factors + $\delta_C S_{j,t}$, where S_t is the share of the population that is skilled. These equations can be interpreted as meaning that schooling increases productive innovation or investment in consumer amenities. In these cases, we should think of the previously estimated coefficients as suggesting that schooling has a growth effect. Alternatively, we can think of characteristics as having level effects that change over time. As we show in a companion working paper growth effects and level effects that change over time are empirically indistinguishable in this context.[21]

With these assumptions, in appendix B we show that we can write:

$$(2) \quad \log\left(\frac{\text{Population}_{t+1}}{\text{Population}_t}\right) = \left(\beta_A + \beta_C\right) \times S_t + \text{Other Controls} + \text{Error}$$

where β_A equals δ_A times a positive constant and β_C equals δ_C times a positive constant. Our interest is in the ratio $\beta_A/(\beta_A + \beta_C)$, which reflects the share of the growth-skills connection that can be attributed to productivity growth. The appendix also shows that wage and housing growth regressions can be written:

$$(3) \quad \log\left(\frac{\text{Average Wage}_{t+1}}{\text{Average Wage}_t}\right) = \left(\kappa_A \beta_A - (1 - \kappa_C)\beta_C\right) \times S_t$$
$$+ \text{Other Controls} + \text{Error}$$

and

$$(4) \quad \log\left(\frac{\text{Housing Price}_{t+1}}{\text{Housing Price}_t}\right) = \left((1 + \kappa_A)\beta_A + \kappa_C \beta_C\right) \times S_t$$
$$+ \text{Other Controls} + \text{Error}$$

21. Glaeser and Saiz (2003).

where κ_A is a positive constant equal to ratio of spending on housing (nontraded consumer goods) to spending on traded goods, and κ_C is a positive constant equal to the share of producer spending on labor divided by total producer spending on labor plus producer spending on nontraded capital. Comparing equations 2–4 tells us that the coefficients on schooling in the wage and population regressions should add to equal the coefficient on schooling in the housing price regression.

Using calculations in appendix B and the notation $\hat{B}_{Pop}$, $\hat{B}_{Price}$, and $\hat{B}_{Wage}$ to denote the coefficients on schooling in population growth, housing price growth, and wage growth regressions respectively, it follows that:

$$
(5) \quad \frac{\beta_A}{\beta_A + \beta_C} = \frac{\left(\dfrac{\hat{B}_{Price}}{\hat{B}_{Pop}} - \kappa_C \right)}{1 + \kappa_A - \kappa_C} = \frac{\left(\dfrac{\hat{B}_{Wage}}{\hat{B}_{Pop}} + 1 - \kappa_C \right)}{1 + \kappa_A - \kappa_C}
$$

$$
= \frac{\left(\dfrac{\hat{B}_{Wage}}{\hat{B}_{Price} - \hat{B}_{Wage}} + 1 - \kappa_C \right)}{1 + \kappa_A - \kappa_C}
$$

Equation 5 serves as the basis for our subsequent discussion.

Distinguishing between Productivity and Amenity Effects

We now use the equations in the previous section to measure the extent to which the connection between skill and growth stems from productivity or amenity effects. We know from Rauch's work that, holding one's own skill level constant, wages in a city rise with the skill level of that community.[22] We also know that prices are higher in both cities and metropolitan areas with more skilled workers. Moretti extends Rauch and identifies human capital externalities by using instrumental variables related to human capital but plausibly exogenous to wages.[23] He finds that, after controlling for the private returns to education, a 1 percentage

---

22. Rauch (1993).
23. Moretti (forthcoming); Rauch (1993). Moretti uses the demographic structure of the city and the presence of "land grant" colleges from the Morrill Act (1862).

Figure 3. MSA IPUMS Adjusted Real Wages and Human Capital, 1990

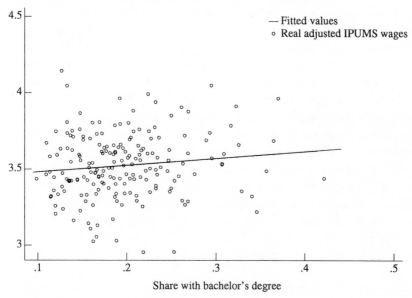

Real wage 1990 = 3.436 + 0.447 × share with bachelor's degree in 1990.
(0.031) (0.175)
R squared: 0.015, N: 191.

point increase in the share of the college educated in a metropolitan area raises average wages by 0.6 percent to 1.2 percent. Moretti finds more direct evidence of human capital externalities by using plant-level production functions.[24] Of course, since not all individual skills are observed by the researcher, it is arguable if the previous literature succeeds in addressing the problem that selection of more skilled workers into these cities might be driving the correlations.

Figure 3 shows the relationship between wages, adjusted for individual characteristics and local prices, and local human capital across metropolitan areas in 1990. The individual characteristics include age, schooling, and gender, and we use the American Chamber of Commerce Research Analysis data to correct for local price levels. The overall correlation is strong and positive. If we believe these price levels, it seems appropriate to think that in the cross section the primary impact of human capital is to increase productivity, at least at the metropolitan-area level.

24. Moretti (2002).

Our focus is, of course, on changes over time, not on the level effects. So to address these changes we turn first to results from looking at housing price growth at the city and metropolitan-area levels. We are implicitly assuming the relative home quality changes across metropolitan areas are small. The available evidence supports that this assumption is not particularly problematic. Table 5 (panels A and B) reproduces tables 2 and 3 with the change in the logarithm of median housing values as the dependent variable. These are self-reported housing values taken from the census. In these regressions we add the initial housing values as an added control to correct for mean reversion.

Regressions 1 through 6 of panel A in table 5 show the impact that initial human capital has on later housing price appreciation at the metropolitan-area level. The magnitude expands dramatically between regression 1 and regression 2 as the coefficient on percent college educated rises from .18 to 1.17. If we believe the coefficient in regression 1, then a 10 percent increase in the percent college educated at the metropolitan-area level is associated with a 1.8 percent increase in housing prices during the next decade. If we believe the coefficient in regression 2, then a 10 percent increase in the percent college educated increases the expected growth rate of housing prices by almost 12 percent during the next decade.

The difference between the two coefficients is entirely the result of controlling for the initial housing price in each community. There is an extraordinarily large amount of mean reversion in housing prices across metropolitan areas. In general, the high-price areas have also had higher levels of human capital, so controlling for the natural tendency of high-price places to mean revert causes the coefficient on initial share with college degrees to increase.

Regressions 3 through 6 show that at the metropolitan-area level the coefficient on schooling in housing price growth regressions is extraordinarily robust statistically when we control for initial housing price. Even with state or metropolitan-area fixed effects, the t statistic never drops below four. Regression 6 shows that the presence of colleges before 1940 also predicts housing price growth during the past 30 years. Panel A in table 5 certainly seems to make it clear that higher levels of education increase both the population of metropolitan areas and the price that this population is paying for the privilege of living in the area.

In panel B (table 5) we examine housing price growth at the city level, and the results essentially reproduce the findings of panel A. Housing price growth is weakly positively associated with human capital when we fail to control for initial housing prices. When we control for mean reversion, the effect becomes extremely large and extremely robust. The only substantive difference between panel A and B is that in panel B the presence of colleges before 1940 is not a good predictor of housing price growth over the past thirty years. We are certainly struck by the extraordinary power of human capital in predicting housing price growth.

In panels C and D (table 5) we look at the connection between income growth and human capital. Panels C and D essentially reproduce tables 2 and 3 with the log of family income as the dependent variable. These regressions are useful in that they are directly comparable to the previous regressions, but they are flawed by the fact that these results will be biased because of the rise in returns to skill over this time period. Because the compensation for skilled workers has generally risen over the period, we should expect to see incomes rising more quickly in more skilled cities. Average family income, or other aggregate income measures, cannot control for the general change in the skill premium. Nevertheless, for completeness we present these results.

Panels C and D show a systematic positive relationship between initial human capital levels and later growth in family income at the metropolitan-area and city levels. As in panels A and B, there is a big difference in the coefficients between regressions 1 and 2 (in both panels C and D) where the coefficient on schooling is much bigger in regression 2. Just as for housing prices, there is substantial mean reversion in family incomes, and just as for housing prices, skilled cities look much better once we account for this natural tendency of high income places to become relatively poorer over time.

In panels C and D the baseline impact of having an extra 10 percent of an area's adult population with college degrees is an increase in expected income growth of 2 percent. When we control for mean reversion, that impact increases to more than 10 percent. Given that wages for workers with college degrees expanded (relative to noncollege degree workers) by less than 50 percent over the entire thirty-year period, the pure compositional effect of a 10 percentage point increase in the share of adults

Table 5. Education, Home Value, and Income Growth

	(1)	(2)	(3)	(4)	(5)	(6)
Panel A: Δlog(MSA median house value)						
Share with bachelor's degree (age 25+) at t-10	0.185 (0.083)**	1.166 (0.186)***	2.324 (0.237)***	2.258 (0.518)***	0.902 (0.220)***	
Log median house value at t-10		-0.417 (0.036)***	-0.71 (0.041)***	-1.183 (0.060)***	-0.422 (0.035)***	-0.333 (0.036)***
Unemployment rate at t-10					-0.881 (0.344)**	
Share of high school dropouts (age 25+) at t-10					-0.053 (0.109)	
Log colleges per capita in 1940						0.032 (0.012)***
Panel B: Δlog(city median house value)						
Share with bachelor's degree (age 25+) at t-10	0.226 (0.045)***	1.619 (0.116)***	2.25 (0.118)***	1.869 (0.222)***	1.097 (0.151)***	
Log median house value at t-10		-0.376 (0.024)***	-0.602 (0.029)***	-1.096 (0.026)***	-0.41 (0.025)***	-0.169 (0.017)***
Unemployment rate at t-10					-1.483 (0.279)***	
Share of high school dropouts (age 25+) at t-10					-0.377 (0.083)***	
Log colleges per capita in 1940						-0.002 (0.008)

Panel C: Δlog(average MSA family income)

	(1)	(2)	(3)	(4)	(5)
Share with bachelor's degree (age 25+) at t-10	0.191 (0.029)***	0.761 (0.082)***	0.849 (0.090)***	1.769 (0.171)***	0.59 (0.090)***
Log average family income at t-10		-0.291 (0.029)***	-0.359 (0.036)***	-1.155 (0.043)***	-0.336 (0.030)***
Unemployment rate at t-10					-0.307 (0.161)*
Share of high school dropouts (age 25+) at t-10					-0.186 (0.054)***
Log colleges per capita in 1940				0.019 (0.004)***	-0.143 (0.025)***

Panel D: Δlog(average city family income)

	(1)	(2)	(3)	(4)	(5)
Share with bachelor's degree (age 25+) at t-10	0.275 (0.020)***	0.632 (0.052)***	0.671 (0.056)***	1.624 (0.094)***	0.434 (0.057)***
Log average family income at t-10		-0.135 (0.016)***	-0.167 (0.020)***	-1.091 (0.031)***	-0.231 (0.020)***
Unemployment rate at t-10					-0.709 (0.118)***
Share of high school dropouts (age 25+) at t-10					-0.313 (0.041)***
Log colleges per capita in 1940				0.015 (0.003)***	0.042 (0.009)***

	(1)	(2)	(3)	(4)	(5)
Year fixed effects	Yes	Yes	Yes	Yes	Yes
Region fixed effects	No	Yes	No	No	Yes
State fixed effects	No	No	Yes	No	No
MSA fixed effects	No	No	No	Yes	No
Other variables in table 2	Yes	Yes	Yes	Yes	Yes

Note: Robust standard errors in parentheses.
*Significant at 10 percent level. **Significant at 5 percent level. ***Significant at 1 percent level.

Table 6. Human Capital and Wage/Value Growth: IPUMS

	Log IPUMS wage	Log IPUMS house value
	(1)	*(2)*
Share with bachelor's degree	0.527	0.389
at t-10*1980 dummy	(0.459)	(1.550)
Share with bachelor's degree	0.738	2.205
at t-10*1990 dummy	(0.347)**	(1.087)**
Share with bachelor's degree	0.785	1.698
at t-10*2000 dummy	(0.271)***	(0.855)**
MSA fixed effects	Yes	Yes
Year fixed effects	Yes	Yes
Observations	1026867	1222890
R squared	0.33	0.64
Average growth in education effect		
per decade	0.26	0.57

Note: Robust standard errors clustered by MSA-year in parentheses.
*Significant at 10 percent level.   **Significant at 5 percent level.   ***Significant at 1 percent level.
Wage regressions include year and MSA fixed effects, controls for age, age squared, education dummies interacted with year, race, Hispanic ethnicity, marital status, and veteran status. Observations include males over 21 years old with complete observations.
Value regressions include year and MSA fixed effects, controls for number of rooms and bedrooms, quality of plumbing and kitchen facilities, and age of the building. The results use a 50 percent random sample of the IPUMS data for all single units with the relevant information.

with a college degree should be less than 2 percent per decade.[25] Using a back of the envelope estimate, if workers of category X have had their wages increase by Y percent over a time period, then an upper bound for the purely compositional effect of having an extra 10 percent of a place's labor force in category X is $.1*Y$.[26] Thus the large magnitudes of the effects seem incompatible with the view that the only effect is that skilled workers are getting higher wages: workers in skilled cities are getting paid more relative to skilled workers elsewhere.[27]

To show this, in table 6, column 1, we use the Census Individual Public Use Microsample (IPUMS) from 1970 to 2000 to control for individual characteristics in a wage regression that includes MSA education lev-

25. Katz and Murphy (1992).
26. The initial share of the highly educated may also be positively correlated with changes in that share. The microdata regressions will dispel any concerns in that direction.
27. The results cannot be accounted for by the fact that higher-educated people have a higher propensity to be married, and thus (median) higher family incomes: using income per capita at the MSA level we found very similar results.

els as explanatory variables. We look at the wages of males over 21, and we control for schooling, age, and race, and metropolitan-area fixed effects. In these regressions the coefficients on schooling and age were allowed to differ by time period. We also include a control for the schooling in the area. We decided to use the lagged share of the percent of the area with college degrees as our measure of education. The decision to use lagged value is an attempt to make these results more comparable with the growth regressions and an attempt to reduce the causality problems inherent with regressing wages on the population composition of an area. Although this would certainly not eliminate causal issues, our results are essentially unchanged if we use schooling in 1970 as our measure of MSA schooling throughout the time period.

Since we are controlling for metropolitan-area fixed effects, we can only estimate the coefficient on area-level schooling in three decades, and we chose 1970 as the excluded decade. As such, differences in our estimated coefficients on the interaction of schooling and decade should be interpreted as the extent to which the coefficient on average schooling in the area has increased over time. Our results suggest that the coefficient on schooling increased by .58 between 1970 and 1980, and then by .21 between 1980 and 1990. Between 1990 and 2000 the coefficient increased by .047.

On average during the three decades, the coefficient on the share with college degrees increased by .25 per decade, which is comparable to a coefficient in a growth regression of .25. This is comparable to the coefficient in the first regressions of table 5 (panels C and D), not the subsequent regressions, because table 6 does not allow high-wage cities to mean revert and become lower wage over time.

In the second column of table 6 we include housing value regressions that are similar in character to the wage regressions. In this case, we are able to control for housing characteristics and thus to control for any changes in the hedonic value of housing characteristics over time. Just as in the wage regression, we are able to control for metropolitan-area fixed effects, and we identify a tendency of the houses in high-schooling metropolitan areas to increase over time. On average, the coefficient on schooling rises by more than .5 each decade over the thirty years, but all of this increase occurs between 1970 and 1990. Between 1990 and 2000, the coefficient on schooling actually falls.

Interpreting the Coefficients with the Model

We first focus on metropolitan areas and then turn to cities and begin with our estimates of $\hat{B}_{Pop}$, $\hat{B}_{Price}$, and $\hat{B}_{Wage}$. At the metropolitan-area level, the coefficient of schooling in the population growth regressions in table 2 ranges from .42 to .58. This is a fairly narrow band, and not much is gained by focusing on the extremes; as such we will use .5 as value of $\hat{B}_{Pop}$.

The estimates of $\hat{B}_{Price}$ in table 5 range from .2 to 2.4, but the bulk of them are clustered around 1. In table 6 our estimate of $\hat{B}_{Price}$ is .55. We will use .5 and .75 as two estimates of $\hat{B}_{Price}$. Table 5 gives a range of estimates for $\hat{B}_{Wage}$ between .2 and 1.8. In the case of $\hat{B}_{Wage}$, we are inclined to put more weight on table 6's estimate of .25, since this is the only estimate that controls properly for individual characteristics.

To produce a reasonable set of estimates, we rely on the fact that the model implies that $\hat{B}_{Pop} + \hat{B}_{Wage} = \hat{B}_{Price}$, the sum of the coefficients on wages and population, should equal the coefficient on prices. It is not true that this holds perfectly empirically—for table 6's estimates and for the estimates in table 5, the value of $\hat{B}_{Price} - \hat{B}_{Wage}$ ranges from .3 to .5. The two cases where the difference is outside of this range are the case for which there are no controls and the case for which we have state fixed effects. So we calibrate the model with a range of .1 to .5 for $\hat{B}_{Wage}$ and an associated range of .6 to 1 for $\hat{B}_{Price}$, which implies that $\hat{B}_{Price}/\hat{B}_{Pop}$ ranges from 1.2 to 2 or $\hat{B}_{Wage}/\hat{B}_{Pop}$ ranges from .2 to 1.

We must also have an estimate of κ_A—the share of spending on nontraded goods divided by one minus the same share. We can calculate this parameter by using the 2001 Consumer Expenditure Survey to estimate the share of shelter in overall expenditure, which is .19. Shelter is pretty clearly a nontraded good, but as there are other elements of consumption that are nontraded, this estimate qualifies as something of a lower bound.

The second way of estimating κ_A is to use a city-level price index (from the American Chamber of Commerce) and regress the log of this price index on the log of housing prices. If the Cobb-Douglas assumption is correct, and if we assume that the consumption amenity is constant, then the derivative of the logarithm expenditure function (that is, household budget requirements as a function of local prices and constant utility) with respect to the logarithm of local prices equals the share of spending on nontraded goods. Since price indexes are supposed to measure the amount of money needed to provide a fixed level of utility, they are ideally the expenditure function. Therefore we obtain an estimate of κ_A as the extent that local price levels rise with increases in housing prices.

Using the 2000 cross section, we estimate:

(6)   log(Price Level) = − 2.2 + .29 * log(Median Housing Price)
                    (18) (.015)

The R squared is .63, and there are 220 observations. We can also estimate this relationship from a panel with MSA and year dummies:

(6′)   log(Price Level) = MSA and Year Dummies + .21
                                              (.028)
                    * Log(Median Housing Value)

In this case, the R squared is .986, and there are 505 observations. Together, these two methods confirm that a reasonable estimate of the share of spending on nontraded goods lies between .21 and .29, and we use $.33[0.25/(1 − 0.25)]$ as our estimate of κ_A.

The value of κ_C equals the ratio of producer spending on labor divided by producer spending on labor plus producer spending on nontraded capital goods. Although we lack any compelling figures for this ratio, we do not believe that spending on nontraded capital goods can be more than one-third of the wage bill. Thus this parameter is bounded between .75 and 1.

Using the parameter estimates $\kappa_A = .33$, we know that $\beta_A/(\beta_A + \beta_C)$ cannot fall below 1 as long as a $\hat{B}_{Wage}/\hat{B}_{Pop} \geq .33$ regardless of the value of κ_C. This result comes from the fact that if $\hat{B}_{Wage}/\hat{B}_{Pop} \geq \kappa_A$ then real wages are increasing with initial schooling, which can only mean that amenity levels are falling. Even if $\hat{B}_{Wage}/\hat{B}_{Pop} = .2$, then the lowest possible estimate of $\beta_A/(\beta_A + \beta_C)$ is .6. To believe that the majority of the skills effect on growth comes from an amenity effect it must be that $\hat{B}_{Wage}/\hat{B}_{Pop} < .1$ or equivalently $\hat{B}_{Price}/\hat{B}_{Pop} < 1.1$. We do not believe that either of those conditions holds, and as such we are led to the view that the bulk of the skills-growth connection at the metropolitan-area level comes from the fact that skills predict productivity growth.

As final check on this, in table 7 we look at the growth of real wages and the relationship to initial human capital. As argued before, if human capital increases amenities at the metropolitan-area level, then real wages should be falling. We again use the American Chamber of Commerce data for local price levels. We use three different measures of MSA-level wages. First, we use the average wage in the area according to the Bureau of Economic Analysis. Second, we use the average manufacturing wage in the area from the Bureau of Labor Statistics. Third, we use a wage variable that we construct using data from the Individual Public Use Micro-Sample, which corresponds to the MSA fixed effect of a regression of wages on individual characteristics. This can be interpreted as the average wage in the metropolitan area net of the impact of individual characteristics. We present results with and without other controls. In all cases, we find a positive or a zero coefficient on human capital. There is no regression where human capital is associated with declining real wages at the city level. This evidence again pushes us to the conclusion that rising wages at the city level have everything to do with rising productivity and nothing to do with rising amenities.

Results at the City Level

We can distinguish between the impact of human capital on the growth of metropolitan areas and the impact of human capital on the growth of cities (holding metropolitan-area growth constant). The overall growth of cities is driven by factors similar to the ones driving growth in metropolitan areas that surround them. The growth of cities, *holding metropolitan-area growth constant,* enables us to really focus on city-specific factors. There has been little work on this issue, but in many respects it is a natural area for research on amenities. Cities within a metropolitan area have radically different levels of amenities but supposedly are part of the same labor market. After all, metropolitan areas are defined to capture a local labor market. Moreover, many people work outside of their city (within their metropolitan area), but their city still determines their quality of life, thousing prices, and public goods.

If wages are the same across cities within a metropolitan area, then changes in the price of the nontraded good (housing) can only reflect changes in the consumption amenity. The previously discussed framework then implies that:

Table 7. Human Capital and Real Wages: Direct Approach

	Δlog(average wage/ Accra prices)		Δlog(average manufacturing wage/Accra prices)		Δlog(IPUMS adjusted wage/ Accra prices)	
	(1)	(2)	(3)	(4)	(5)	(6)
Share with bachelor's degree (age 25+) at t-10	0.78 (0.217)***	1.78 (0.239)***	-0.003 (0.178)	0.213 (0.297)	0.045 (0.088)	0.057 (0.144)
Log of population at t-10		-0.03 (0.011)***		-0.018 (0.010)*		-0.018 (0.005)***
Log average heating degree days (1961–90)		-0.033 (0.024)		0.028 (0.024)		0.011 (0.007)
Log average annual precipitation (1961–90)		-0.03 (0.029)		0.024 (0.040)		0.031 (0.014)**
Share of workers in manufacturing at t-10		-0.029 (0.212)		0.188 (0.182)		-0.069 (0.080)
Share of workers in professional services at t-10		-1.362 (0.318)***		0.203 (0.389)		-0.08 (0.177)
Share of workers in trade at t-10		2.063 (0.505)***		0.505 (0.476)		0.262 (0.371)
Decade fixed effects	Yes	Yes	Yes	Yes	Yes	Yes
Region fixed effects	No	No	No	No	No	No
Observations	238	234	135	135	130	129
R squared	0.11	0.37	0.06	0.22	0.58	0.64

Note: Robust standard errors in parentheses. We use Boston in 1990 as baseline, the evolution of Urban CPI and of relative prices from Accra to calculate prices by MSA and year.
*Significant at 10 percent level. **Significant at 5 percent level. ***Significant at 1 percent level.

(4') $\log\left(\dfrac{\text{Housing Price}_{t+1}}{\text{Housing Price}_t}\right) = \dfrac{\kappa_A \tilde{\delta}_C}{1 + \kappa_A} \times S_t + \text{MSA Fixed Effect}$

$+ \text{ Other Controls } + \text{ Error}$

where $\tilde{\delta}_C$ represents the impact of characteristic k on consumption amenity growth at the local level, which may be slightly different than the impact of the growth of this variable at the MSA level. As shown in Glaeser and Saiz, if the skill level of the city is constant over time, then it also follows that:

(2') $\log\left(\dfrac{\text{Population}_{t+1}}{\text{Population}_t}\right) = \dfrac{\kappa_A \tilde{\delta}_C}{1 + \kappa_A} \times S_t + \text{MSA Fixed Effect}$

$+ \text{ Other Controls } + \text{ Error}$

Somewhat surprisingly, the Cobb-Douglas utility function implies that the effect of consumption amenity growth on prices and people should be the same.[28] Equations 2' and 4' inspire us to run regressions within metropolitan areas controlling for MSA, decade fixed effects. These are shown in table 8, and the regressions should be interpreted as capturing the impact of city-specific human capital controlling for the average growth rate of the metropolitan area over the decade. The first thing that the regressions show is that the impact of human capital on prices and population is not the same, despite the implications of the model. Human capital has a much stronger effect (at least when we control for initial price levels) on price growth than on population growth.

The second implication of the regressions is that human capital powerfully predicts housing price and population growth. Interestingly, the impact of the highly educated capital residents (college graduates shown in regressions 1 and 3) is stronger in the housing price growth regressions. High human capital workers seem to be highly correlated with rising prices. The impact of less educated residents (high school dropouts shown in regressions 2 and 4) is stronger in the population growth regressions. All four regressions can be interpreted to mean that human capital is associated with rising consumer amenity levels at the local level, but the regressions do not tell us a simple story.

28. Glaeser and Saiz (2003).

Table 8. Within MSA Regressions: Minor Civil Divisions within MSA

| | $\Delta log(population)$ | | $\Delta log(median\ value)$ | |
	(1)	(2)	(3)	(4)
Share with bachelor's degree (age 25+) at t-10	0.179 (0.031)***		0.49 (0.035)***	
Share of high school dropouts (age 25+) at t-10		-0.274 (0.028)***		-0.079 (0.025)***
Log of population at t-10	-0.03 (0.002)***	-0.029 (0.002)***	-0.019 (0.001)***	-0.019 (0.001)***
Share of workers in manufacturing at t-10	-0.12 (0.045)***	-0.068 -0.045	-0.099 (0.026)***	-0.105 (0.027)***
Share of workers in professional services at t-10	-0.512 (0.059)***	-0.518 (0.053)***	-0.264 (0.041)***	0.033 -0.034
Share of workers in trade at t-10	-0.245 (0.080)***	-0.363 (0.082)***	-0.143 (0.049)***	-0.249 (0.051)***
Log median value at t-10			-0.111 (0.012)***	-0.019 (0.011)*
Decade fixed effects	Yes	Yes	Yes	Yes
MSA-year fixed effects	Yes	Yes	Yes	Yes
Observations	13752	13752	13645	13645
Minor civil divisions	4584	4584	4584	4584
R squared	0.24	0.25	0.59	0.59

Note: Robust standard errors in parentheses.
*Significant at 10 percent level. **Significant at 5 percent level. ***Significant at 1 percent level.

One possible way to reconcile these regressions is to drop our simple assumptions about housing supply being essentially perfectly elastic (subject to the constraint of the fixed amount of nontraded commodity). Indeed, the impact of housing supply is the most important missing element in understanding city growth. If we assume that there are limits to new construction, such as zoning or land use regulation, and we assume that these were more binding in high-skill, rather than low-skill, cities, then we might expect this pattern. In high-skill cities, supply is relatively inelastic so increasing demand operates mainly by increasing prices. In low-skill cities, supply is more elastic, so increasing demand operates mainly by increasing quantities. This is a possible reconciliation of the four regressions in table 8, but it properly belongs as a subject for future research.

If we accept the assumption that a metropolitan area is a common labor market, with common wages, then table 8 seems to imply that there is a significant impact of skills on consumption amenity growth at the local level. Of course, that assumption may not hold perfectly. Some sub-areas of a metropolitan region may be much more productive than others, and productivity heterogeneity could explain the results. These findings are best thought of as suggestive evidence supporting the link between skills and amenity growth at the local level.

Understanding the Productivity Effect

The evidence suggests that the skills-growth connection at the metropolitan area is fueled primarily by productivity effects. As suggested earlier, the basic data on wage, price, and population growth cannot distinguish among different stories about the connection between human capital and productivity. However, we use other available evidence to check the validity of two of these stories.

First, we address the hypothesis that an environment dense with the highly educated leads to faster technological innovation and that this explains the connection between metropolitan-area growth and human capital. To test this idea, we turn to the patents data. We are able measure patents by MSA for the period 1990–99, so we focus on growth during the 1990s. We first regress patents per capita on the human capital level, and then see how much of the skills-growth connection is explained by greater patenting activity.

Table 9. Human Capital and Technological Growth

	Log patents per worker (1)	Δlog(population) (2)	(3)
Share with bachelor's degree (age 25+) at t-10	9.135 (0.903)***		0.781 (0.119)***
Log patents per worker at t-10		0.02 (0.006)***	0.003 (0.006)
Log of population at t-10	0.156 (0.040)***	0.001 (0.005)	−0.011 (0.005)**
Log average heating degree days (1961–90)	−0.208 (0.080)***	−0.026 (0.010)**	−0.037 (0.010)***
Log average annual precipitation (1961–90)	−0.014 (0.107)	−0.038 (0.017)**	−0.05 (0.018)***
Share of workers in manufacturing at t-10	5.894 (0.740)***	−0.226 (0.109)**	−0.047 (0.122)
Share of workers in professional services at t-10	−0.485 (1.341)	−0.213 (0.157)	−0.756 (0.162)***
Share of workers in trade at t-10	1.832 (2.367)	−0.229 (0.287)	0.232 (0.297)
Region fixed effects	Yes	Yes	Yes
Observations	304	304	304
R squared	0.56	0.38	0.46

Note: Robust standard errors in parentheses.
*Significant at 10 percent level.   **Significant at 5 percent level.   ***Significant at 1 percent level.

In table 9, regression 1, we find (like Carlino, Chatterjee, and Hunt) that the share with a bachelor's degree is an important predictor of technological growth.[29] We find that a 10 percent increase in the share of college graduates increases the number of patents by .09 log points (approximately 9 percent). This certainly supports the idea that the better educated are more technologically innovative.

Moreover, in regression 2 we show that there is a connection between patents and growth in regressions where we do not control for human capital. Of course, no causality is posited by these regressions. Patents are as much a sign of a healthy urban environment as a cause. However, the important fact is shown in regression 3. Once we control for human capital, there is no meaningful relationship between patents and urban growth. As such, human capital may matter because it makes people more creative, but the important elements of this creativity must be in areas beyond the formal patenting sector.

29. Carlino, Chatterjee, and Hunt (2001).

Figure 4. MSA Growth, 1980–2000, and Human Capital, Warm MSAs, 1980[a]

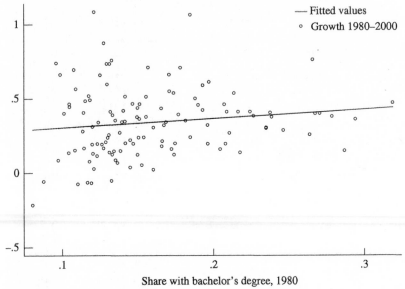

Share with bachelor's degree, 1980

Log(pop2000) − log(pop1980) = 0.615 + 0.242 × share with bachelor's degree in 1980.
                              (0.429) (0.072)
R squared: 0.0171, N: 120.
a. January temperature over 40 degrees.

The Reinvention Hypothesis

We finally turn to the puzzle created by figures 4 and 5: human capital predicts growth much more sharply for cold places than for hot places. Figure 4 shows the relatively mild (0.13) correlation between skills and growth among those metropolitan areas with January temperatures above 40 degrees on average. Figure 5 shows the 47 percent correlation between the initial share of the population with college degrees and the growth of the logarithm of population between 1980 and 2000 for those metropolitan areas with average January temperatures below 40 degrees. The regression (reported in the figure) suggests that as the share of college educated increases by 1 percent, the growth rate of the period increases by 1.3 percent. Previous literature has pointed to warm weather as an exogenous amenity that has fostered growth in the late twentieth-century United States.[30] Sun, coupled with the availability of air condi-

30. Glaeser, Kolko, and Saiz (2001); Glaeser and Shapiro (2003).

Figure 5. MSA Growth, 1980–2000, and Human Capital, Cold MSAs, 1980[a]

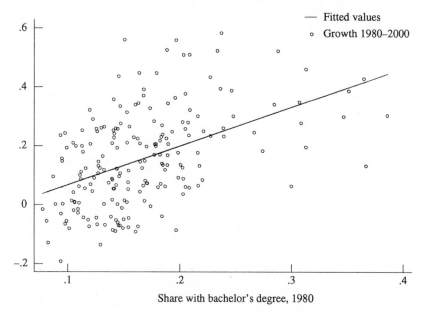

Log(pop2000) – log(pop1980) = –0.064 + 1.317 × share with bachelor's degree in 1980.
(0.031) (0.175)
R squared: 0.222, N: 198.
a. January temperature under 40 degrees.

tioning systems, may have given some areas in the South and West a competitive advantage, but skill appears to be a good substitute.[31]

This fact may be explained by Jacobs's view that cities need to constantly reinvent themselves. Specialization in one area may yield brief success, but eventually the area fades, or the city's comparative advantage in the area decays, and reinvention is necessary. Glaeser details at least four periods in Boston's history when the city reinvented itself.[32] Conversely, in areas with positive exogenous growth shocks, human capital may have less of a role, since reinvention is not necessary.

In table 10 we look at this hypothesis more thoroughly. In regressions 1 through 3 we repeat our benchmark specifications for population, wage

31. Alternatively, the weather variable may be capturing the impact of other variables, though the effect of weather on population growth holds after controlling for state fixed effects. What matters for our argument is not so much the causal impact of weather but the strong predictive power of the part of the signal in this variable that is orthogonal to education.

32. Jacobs (1969); Glaeser (2003).

Table 10. The "Reinvention" Hypothesis

	Panel A: All MSA					
	Δlog (population) (1)	Δlog(wage) (2)	Δlog(house value) (3)	Δlog (population) (4)	Δlog(wage) (5)	Δlog(house value) (6)
Share with bachelor's degree (age 25+) at t-10	0.945 (0.138)***	2.541 (0.230)***	1.264 (0.209)***	0.999 (0.135)***	2.203 (0.226)***	1.046 (0.204)***
Temperature * share with bachelor's degree at t-10	-0.396 (0.112)***	-0.284 (0.137)**	-0.121 (0.133)			
Log of population at t-10	-0.013 (0.004)***	0.424 (0.051)***	0.04 (0.007)***	-0.013 (0.004)***	0.442 (0.052)***	0.038 (0.007)***
Log average heating degree days (1961–90)	-0.143 (0.022)***	-0.075 (0.026)***	-0.06 (0.023)***	-0.093 (0.011)***	-0.052 (0.014)***	-0.021 (0.014)
Log average annual precipitation (1961–90)	-0.027 (0.015)*	-0.015 (0.018)	0.063 (0.017)***	-0.026 (0.016)*	-0.031 (0.019)*	0.078 (0.020)***
Share of workers in manufacturing at t-10	-0.128 (0.087)	-0.151 (0.115)	0.138 (0.114)	-0.145 (0.082)*	-0.185 (0.109)*	0.074 (0.112)
Share of workers in professional services at t-10	-0.295 (0.145)**	-1.266 (0.207)***	-0.139 (0.178)	-0.456 (0.143)***	-1.267 (0.210)***	-0.198 (0.180)
Share of workers in trade at t-10	-0.004 (0.257)	0.088 (0.336)	0.119 (0.307)	-0.05 (0.252)	0.078 (0.333)	0.103 (0.304)
Log average wage receipts per worker at t-10		-0.403 (0.047)***			-0.417 (0.048)***	
Log median house value at t-10			-0.414 (0.036)***			-0.466 (0.042)***
Share immigrant at t-10 * share with bachelor's degree t-10				-5.751 (1.201)***	2.376 (1.897)	3.433 (2.142)
Share immigrant at t-10				0.704 (0.268)***	-0.901 (0.352)**	-0.031 (0.409)
Year fixed effects	Yes	Yes	Yes	Yes	Yes	Yes
Region fixed effects	Yes	Yes	Yes	Yes	Yes	Yes
Observations	918	918	918	918	918	918
R squared	0.52	0.72	0.75	0.54	0.72	0.76

Panel B: 1940–2000

	Share manufacturing (1940–2000)		Δlog(population) (1940–2000)
Share with bachelor's degree in 1940	−0.011 (0.006)*	Share with bachelor's degree in 1940	0.094 (0.017)***
Share in manufacturing in 1940	−0.547 (0.084)***	Log(population) in 1940	−0.139 (0.028)***
January mean temperature	−0.002 (0.0008)**	January mean temperature	0.032 (0.002)***
Share manufacturing 1940 * share with bachelor's degree in 1940	−0.048 (0.018)**	Log average annual precipitation	−0.309 (0.058)***
January mean temperature * share with bachelor's degree in 1940	0.0003 (0.0001)*	Share in manufacturing in 1940	0.046 (0.29)
Log employment in 1940	−0.004 (0.003)	Constant	2.227 (0.371)***
Constant	0.222 (0.050)***		
Observations	293	Observations	293
R squared	0.78	R squared	0.58

Note: Standard errors in parentheses. Panel A: Temperature = 9.27 − log(heating degree days); 9.27 corresponds to the city with max(log heating degree days).
*Significant at 10 percent level. **Significant at 5 percent level. ***Significant at 1 percent level.

growth, and housing price, and we focus on the interaction between initial human capital and warmth. In all three cases, there is a statistically significant negative interaction between warmth and initial skills. The cross effect is strongest in the population regressions, where the regressions imply that a doubling of the number of heating degree days causes the impact of skills to fall by about one-half. The effect on wages is also statistically significant, but smaller in magnitude, at least relative to the benchmark coefficient. The effect on housing prices is the weakest. Although the cross effect is still negative, it is not statistically significant.

One important omitted factor is land use regulations, which seem tighter almost everywhere that there is a high degree of human capital. This would explain why in warm places, skills still matter for housing price growth (because skills are correlated with less elastic housing supply) but not much for population growth. Indeed, if there is a correlation between skills and inelastic housing supply, this would tend to create a perverse negative effect where more skilled places grow less, despite increasing demand for these areas.

In regressions 4 through 6 we look at the share of the population (in the initial time period) that is composed of immigrants. Over this period, immigration was a large source of urban growth, and immigrants tend to settle where other immigrants live.[33] If the reinvention hypothesis is correct, then we should expect to see that human capital does not matter in places with large supplies of immigrants, but it should be important in areas where immigrants are not coming. Indeed, this is exactly what we find in regression 4. Human capital matters much more in predicting population growth in areas without immigrants than areas with immigrants.

One possible explanation for the strikingly different correlation between skills and growth in growing and declining places is that skills allow reinvention. The view that human capital is most valuable because it enables flexibility and the ability to respond to new circumstances was emphasized by Welch.[34] If this view is correct, then we should not be surprised if a high-skill New England city manages to reinvent itself while a low-skill rust belt town does not.

One implication of this hypothesis is that places with high human capital should be better at switching out of declining industries. To test this

33. Altonji and Card (1991); Saiz (2003).
34. Welch (1970).

hypothesis, we gathered data on education and industrial composition in 1940 by metropolitan area (contemporaneously defined). We then tested whether the impact of skills on contributing to the shift away of manufacturing over the next sixty years has been more important in industrial, colder areas of the country (table 10, panel B). The regressions support the view that the skilled rust belt towns were better at reorienting themselves: the importance of education to explain the shift away of manufacturing (the change in the manufacturing share in the lefthand side) in the second half of the twentieth century was stronger in colder areas (interaction between human capital and temperature) and in areas with an initial bigger share of manufacturing (interaction between education and share manufacturing).

Conclusion

Human capital predicts population and productivity growth at the city and metropolitan-area level as surely as it predicts income growth at the country level. High-skill areas have been getting more populous, better paid, and more expensive. Indeed, aside from climate, skill composition may be the most powerful predictor of urban growth. This is a boon to the skilled cities that have done spectacularly during the past two decades and a curse to the cities with less-skilled workers that have suffered an almost unstoppable urban decline.

Why do skilled cities grow more quickly? At the metropolitan area, the available evidence seems to show clearly that skills predict productivity growth and not an increase in amenity levels. The high-skill metropolitan areas are not seeing falling real wages. To the contrary, prices seem not to be rising quickly enough to offset the increases in wages. Standard economic reasoning tells us that this means that high skill levels are associated with decreasing quality of life, perhaps because of increasing population.

Within metropolitan areas, at the very local level, there is some evidence that the prices of skilled places have risen sharply. If the standard assumption that a metropolitan area is a single labor market holds, then the skills-housing price growth connection is best understood as suggesting that skills increase amenities at the very local level, if not at the metropolitan-area level. Thus our results suggest that skills are important because they increase productivity at the metropolitan level and amenities at the local level. On net, the productivity effects appear to be much stronger.

Why are skills so strongly associated with productivity growth at the metropolitan level? Certainly skilled cities are more innovative, but controlling for the rate of innovation does not affect the importance of skills. One clue may be the fact that skills are much more significant in otherwise disadvantaged regions than in exogenously growing regions. This fact might reflect the idea that cities are constantly reinventing themselves—moving from one field of specialization to another. Skills may well be a crucial part of this reinvention as skilled workers react more speedily to painful economic shocks and educated workers find it easier to switch techniques.[35] Although at this point the reinvention hypothesis is only a guess, the fact that skills are so important in the Northeast and almost irrelevant in the West suggests that there is something very significant about the connection between skills and the process of urban decline.

The results in the chapter suggest that city growth can be increased with strategies that increase the level of local human capital. At the regional or metropolitan level, attracting high human capital workers may require provision of basic services, amenities, and quality public schools that will lure the skilled. Conversely, redistributive policies *at the local level* have to be carefully designed to avoid the undesired side effect of repelling the skilled and deterring growth. Generating new technologies *locally* does not seem as important as having the capacity to adapt them. Providing basic quality education (maximizing success rates in high school graduation) may both produce and attract the educated. Since local tax bases are heterogeneous, state and federal funds can help ailing cities to avoid the "low-education" trap.

35. Welch (1970).

Appendix A: Data Appendix

Table A-1. Variables and Sources

Variable	Source	Details
Share of persons 25 or older with a bachelor's degree	HUD State of the Cities Data System (Census)	
Population	HUD State of the Cities Data System (Census)	
Average heating degree days (1961–90)	County and City Data Books, 1994	We match MSAs to the corresponding major city
Average precipitation (1961–90)	County and City Data Books, 1994	We match MSAs to the corresponding major city
Share of workers in manufacturing	HUD State of the Cities Data System (Census)	Employment in manufacturing over total employment
Share of workers in professional services	HUD State of the Cities Data System (Census)	Employment in professional services over total employment
Share of workers in trade	HUD State of the Cities Data System (Census)	Employment in trade over total employment
Unemployment rate	HUD State of the Cities Data System (Census)	Unemployment over labor force
Share of persons 25 or older with less than high school degree	HUD State of the Cities Data System (Census)	
Colleges per capita in 1940	*Peterson's College Guide* (and Census)	*Peterson's* provides foundation dates for all colleges in the United States. We use the foundation date to ascertain if a college was founded before 1940. We match the college zip code with the pertinent county, and then assign counties to MSA using 1999 MSA/NECMA definitions. We have used the Department of Education IPEDS dataset for 1969–99 and confirmed that attrition bias is not an issue: colleges do not seem to disappear from the IPEDS sample at a faster rate in stagnating metro areas.

continued on next page

Table A-1. Variables and Sources (continued)

Variable	Source	Details
Family income	HUD State of the Cities Data System (Census)	
Median house value	HUD State of the Cities Data System (Census)	
Wages	Bureau of Economic Analysis	Average wage and salary disbursements per worker
Manufacturing wages	Bureau of Labor Statistics	Average hourly earnings in the manufacturing industry
IPUMS wages	IPUMS (Census)	
IPUMS house values	IPUMS (Census)	
Adjusted IPUMS wages	IPUMS (Census)	Obtained as the MSA fixed effects of independent cross-sectional regressions where we control for age, age squared, education dummies, sex, race, Hispanic ethnicity, marital status, and veteran status
ACCRA Price index	American Chamber of Commerce Research Analysis Data	A cross section of relative prices for 1970, 1980 (about 36 observations) and 1990 and 2000 (about 210 observations)
CPI-U	Bureau of Labor Statistics	Consumer Price Index - Urban
College enrollment in 1970	IPED/HEGIS database (NCES)	HEGIS/IPEDS offers enrollment for each institution of higher education. We match zip code to counties and add up enrollments for all institutions in a metro area.
Murders per 1,000 population	National Archive of Criminal Justice Data	Originally from FBI. By county, we generate data by MSA.
Teacher/pupil ratio	NCES Common Core of Data	The data are for 1990. We locate the county of each school and aggregate the number of pupils and teachers by county. Then we aggregate the county data to MSA.
Museums	County Business Patterns (1980, 1990)	

continued on next page

Table A-1. Variables and Sources (continued)

Variable	Source	Details
Eating and drinking establishments per capita	County Business Patterns (1980, 1990)	
Motion picture establishments per capita	County Business Patterns (1980, 1990)	
Health establishments per capita	County Business Patterns (1980, 1990)	
Amusement and recreational service establishments	County Business Patterns (1980, 1990)	
Membership organizations	County Business Patterns (1980, 1990)	
Patents per worker	U.S. Patent and Trademark Office	Data on patents by county were generously provided by Robert Hunt. We aggregated at MSA level.

Note: MSA data are for metropolitan areas as defined by the Office of Management and Budget in 1999. We use the county MSA/NECMA definition. In most cases we need to aggregate data by county to obtain the appropriate MSA data. City data are from the Department of Housing and Urban Development State of the Cities Data System. We select those cities with population greater than 30,000 in 1970, the initial year for which the data are available.

Table A-2. Descriptive Statistics for the Main Variables

	1970		1980		1990		2000	
	Mean	Std. dev.	Mean	Std. dev.	Mean	Std. dev.	Mean	Std. dev.
Metropolitan statistical area (N = 318)								
Log population – log population at t-10	n.a	n.a	0.17	0.15	0.10	0.13	0.12	0.10
Share with bachelor's degree (age 25+)	0.11	0.04	0.16	0.05	0.20	0.06	0.24	0.07
Population	504,782	970,639	560,354	981,159	626,707	1,073,780	712,948	1,197,389
Average heating degree days (1961–90)	4,453.08	2,192.30	4,453.08	2,192.30	4,453.08	2,192.30	4,453.08	2,192.30
Average annual precipitation (1961–90)	36.67	13.89	36.67	13.89	36.67	13.89	36.67	13.89
Share of workers in manufacturing	0.23	0.11	0.21	0.09	0.17	0.07	0.14	0.07
Share of workers in professional services	0.19	0.06	0.21	0.05	0.24	0.05	n.a	n.a
Share of workers in trade	0.21	0.03	0.21	0.02	0.22	0.02	0.16	0.02
Unemployment rate	0.04	0.01	0.06	0.02	0.06	0.02	0.06	0.02
Share of high school dropouts (age 25+)	0.46	0.09	0.32	0.08	0.24	0.07	0.18	0.06
Colleges per 1,000 people in 1940	0.02	0.01	0.02	0.01	0.02	0.01	0.02	0.01
Home value	16,022	4,189	47,255	15,616	79,504	45,484	115,785	53,119
Median family income	9,170	1,480	19,585	2,807	34,153	6,101	48,929	8,360
Cities (N = 723)								
Log population – log population at t-10	n.a	n.a	0.03	0.19	0.05	0.14	0.06	0.13
Share with bachelor's degree (age 25+)	0.13	0.08	0.18	0.10	0.22	0.12	0.26	0.14
Population	118,794	363,363	119,624	334,524	127,120	348,124	138,225	378,873
Average heating degree days (1961–90)	4,460.59	2,123.92	4,460.59	2,123.92	4,460.59	2,123.92	4,460.59	2,123.92
Average annual precipitation (1961–90)	35.00	12.80	35.00	12.80	35.00	12.80	35.00	12.80
Share of workers in manufacturing	0.26	0.12	0.23	0.10	0.17	0.08	0.14	0.07
Share of workers in professional services	0.19	0.07	0.22	0.07	0.25	0.07	n.a	n.a
Share of workers in trade	0.21	0.04	0.21	0.03	0.22	0.03	0.15	0.02
Unemployment rate	0.04	0.02	0.06	0.03	0.07	0.03	0.07	0.03
Share of high school dropouts (age 25+)	0.43	0.13	0.31	0.12	0.24	0.10	0.20	0.10
Colleges per 1,000 people in 1940	0.01	0.01	0.01	0.01	0.01	0.01	0.01	0.01
Home value	19,569	7,008	54,847	26,139	113,982	81,750	146,108	103,341
Median family income	10,529	2,299	20,964	4,954	37,382	11,299	50,909	16,288

n.a. Not available.

Table A-3. Further Robustness Tests

	Δlog(population)		
	(1)	*(2)*	*(3)*
Share with bachelor's degree (age 25+) at t-10		0.686 (0.134)***	0.505 (0.166)***
Log of population at t-10	−0.003 −0.004	−0.019 (0.004)***	−0.014 (0.008)*
Log average heating degree days (1961–90)	−0.078 (0.011)***	−0.09 (0.011)***	−0.123 (0.013)***
Log average annual precipitation (1961–90)	−0.02 −0.015	−0.033 (0.015)**	−0.056 (0.016)***
Share of workers in manufacturing at t-10	−0.31 (0.086)***	−0.11 −0.09	−0.349 (0.103)***
Share of workers in professional services at t-10	−0.433 (0.196)**	−0.442 (0.144)***	−0.299 (0.185)
Share of workers in trade at t-10	−0.187 −0.237	−0.005 −0.257	−0.428 (0.302)
College enrollment/population in 1970	0.477 (0.126)***		
Museums			0.000 (0.001)
Eating and drinking establishments per capita			−1.316 (18.143)
Motion picture establishments per capita			64.137 (187.538)
Health establishments per capita			−9.404 (16.920)
Membership organizations			0.000 (0.000)
Amusement and recreational service establishments			0.000 (0.000)
Teacher/pupil ratio			−0.504 (0.298)*
Murders per 100 inhabitants			−3.822 (1.064)***
Year fixed effects	Yes	Yes	Yes
Lagged age distribution	No	Yes	No
Observations	909	915	550
R squared	0.51	0.6	0.57

Note: Robust standard errors in parentheses.
*Significant at 10 percent level. **Significant at 5 percent level. ***Significant at 1 percent level.

Appendix B: The Framework

We assume that there are a large number of cities, and we consider the equilibrium of a single city, denoted "j." There are two types of workers, high skill and low skill, who receive different wages in the city denoted W_j^H and W_j^L. Utility is Cobb-Douglas over a traded good, a nontraded good, and over a place-specific commodity, and as such consumers choose the consumption of the non-traded good (denoted Q) to maximize $C_j(W_j^i - P_j^Q Q)^{1-\gamma} Q^\gamma$, where P_j^Q is the price of that good in city j, and C_j is a city-specific consumer amenity level. Optimization yields $P_j^Q Q = \gamma W_j$. We assume a fixed supply of the nontraded good in city "j," which is denoted $\bar{Q}_j$. If we let N_j denote total city population and $\hat{W}_j$ denote the average wage, then total utility for each person equals $(1 - \gamma)^{1-\gamma} C_j W_j^i (\bar{Q}_j / N_j \hat{W}_j)^\gamma$, which must equal $\underline{U}_i$, the reservation utility for each group H and L. This implies that the ratio of wages in every city equals the ratio of reservation utilities, or $W_j^H / W_j^L = \underline{U}_H / \underline{U}_L$.

We assume a Cobb-Douglas production function that uses capital (denoted K), effective labor units (denoted L and defined later), and a city-specific production input (which is meant to represent commercial land or access to waterways and is denoted F). Total output is $A_j K^\alpha L^\beta F^{1-\alpha-\beta}$, where A_j is a city-specific productivity factor. Capital is available at a national price of r, but there is only a fixed amount, F_j, of the city-specific input. To allow for multiple skill categories, we assume that a unit of effective labor is produced through a constant elasticity of substitution technology that uses both high- and low-skilled workers, i.e. $L = (\theta_j^{1-\sigma} L_H^\sigma + L_L^\sigma)^{1/\sigma}$, where θ_j is a city-specific parameter increasing the relative returns to skilled workers, and L_H, L_L reflect the number of high- and low-skilled workers respectively. Cost minimization implies

$$\frac{L_H}{L_L} = \theta_j \left(\frac{W_j^L}{W_j^H} \right)^{\frac{1}{1-\sigma}} = \theta_j \phi^{\frac{-1}{1-\sigma}},$$

where $\phi = \underline{U}_H / \underline{U}_L$ so the skill composition of the city is determined by the parameter θ_j. Manipulation of the first-order conditions and using the notation $\eta = 1 - \alpha - \beta + \gamma\beta$ implies:

(A1) $$N_j = A_j^{\frac{1-\gamma}{\eta}} F_j^{\frac{(\eta-\gamma\beta)(1-\gamma)}{\eta}} C_j^{\frac{1-\alpha}{\eta}} \bar{Q}_j^{\frac{\gamma(1-\alpha)}{\eta}} \Theta_j^N \Omega_N ,$$

(A2)
$$\hat{W}_j = A_j^{\frac{\gamma}{\eta}} F_j^{\frac{(\eta-\gamma\beta)\gamma}{\eta}} C_j^{\frac{\alpha+\beta-1}{\eta}} Q_j^{\frac{-\gamma(1-\alpha-\beta)}{\eta}} \Theta_j^W \Omega_W,$$

and

(A3)
$$P_j^Q = A_j^{\frac{1}{\eta}} F_j^{\frac{1-\alpha-\beta}{\eta}} C_j^{\frac{\beta}{\eta}} Q_j^{\frac{-(1-\alpha-\beta)}{\eta}} \Theta_j^Q \Omega_Q,$$

where Θ_j^i for $i = N, W, Q$ refers to city-specific terms that are only a function of θ_j and ϕ, and where Ω_i for $i = N, W, Q$ refers to terms that are common across cities, including the reservation utilities, rent level, and the parameters α, β, γ and σ. The values of Θ_N^i and Ω_N are

$$\Theta_j^N = \left(\phi^{\frac{1}{1-\sigma}} + \theta_j\right)\left(\phi^{\frac{\sigma}{1-\sigma}} + \theta_j\right)^{\frac{-\sigma(1-\alpha)+\beta(1-\gamma)}{\sigma\eta}}$$

and

$$\Omega_N = \left(\underline{U}_H^{\alpha-1}\left((1-\gamma)\beta\right)^{(1-\gamma)(1-\alpha)}\left(\frac{\alpha}{r}\right)^{\alpha(1-\gamma)}\right)^{\frac{1}{\eta}}.$$

To manipulate these equations, we will assume that, within a city, the production and consumption amenities are changing over time, that all other city-specific factors are fixed, and that while reservation utilities are changing, the ratio $\underline{U}_H/\underline{U}_L$ is fixed. If we assume that $\log(A_{j,t+1}/A_{j,t}) = \Sigma_k\delta_A^k X_{j,t}^k + \varepsilon_{j,t}^A$ and $\log(C_{j,t+1}/C_{j,t}) = \Sigma_k\delta_C^k X_{j,t}^k + \varepsilon_{j,t}^C$, where $X_{j,t}^k$ are city-specific characteristics as of time t, which include the skill composition of the city, then it follows that:

(A1')
$$Log\left(\frac{N_{j,t+1}}{N_{j,t}}\right) = I^N + \sum_k \left(\delta_A^k \frac{1-\gamma}{\eta} + \delta_C^k \frac{1-\alpha}{\eta}\right)X_{j,t}^k + \mu_{j,t}^N$$

(A2')
$$Log\left(\frac{\hat{W}_{j,t+1}}{\hat{W}_{j,t}}\right) = I^W + \sum_k \left(\delta_A^k \frac{\gamma}{\eta} - \delta_C^k \frac{1-\alpha-\beta}{\eta}\right)X_{j,t}^k + \mu_{j,t}^W$$

$$(A3') \qquad Log\left(\frac{P^Q_{j,t+1}}{P^Q_{j,t}}\right) = I^Q + \sum_k \left(\delta^k_A \frac{1}{\eta} + \delta^k_C \frac{\beta}{\eta}\right) X^k_{j,t} + \mu^Q_{j,t},$$

where I^i for $i = N, W, Q$ is an intercept term that is constant across cities, and $\mu^i_{j,t}$ again for $i = N, W, Q$ is an error term, which has a zero mean and is orthogonal to the X terms as long as the underlying error terms, $\mu^i_{j,t}$, are mean zero and orthogonal to the X terms.

As such, $\beta_A = \delta^k_A[(1 - \gamma)/\eta]$, $\beta_C = \delta^k_C[(1 - \alpha)/\eta]$, $\kappa_A = [\gamma/(1 - \gamma)]$ and $\kappa_C = [\beta/(1 - \alpha)]$.

Comments

Gary Burtless: Edward Glaeser and Albert Saiz have written a lucid, stimulating, and convincing paper. Readers like me who know little about the correlates of metropolitan-area growth will learn a great deal about this fascinating subject. Clearly, my ignorance of the broader literature places me at a disadvantage in assessing how many of the empirical findings represent new knowledge to specialists in the field. But my guess is that many economists who are not specialists in regional economics will be intrigued and largely persuaded by the results.

In looking at U.S. metropolitan area growth during the past three decades, Glaeser and Saiz find that areas with large initial concentrations of college-educated adults have experienced above-average population growth, outsized increases in home prices, and exceptional growth in family incomes.

When they examine population growth more closely, they find that the beneficial impact of college graduates is not uniform across the country. Instead, it is concentrated in parts of the United States with cold winters. In other words, the benefits of college graduates seem to be focused on regions in relative decline. This follows from the fact that the U.S. population is gravitating toward places with warm winters and limited rainfall. In those parts of the country with comfortable winters and low rainfall, heavy concentrations of college-educated workers provide less of an advantage for population growth.

The authors are persuaded that their finding of a beneficial overall impact of college-degree holders on growth is truly causal. They find that metropolitan areas grew faster in the past thirty years if they had a high

95

concentration of colleges as far back as 1940, a year that long predates the era they are studying. Since a concentration of colleges in the prewar era is a good predictor of a concentration of college-degree-holding adults in the more recent period, it seems likely that college concentrations predict growth rather than vice versa.

Glaeser and Saiz pose a question about their basic findings. Do the beneficial impacts of college-degree holders on growth spring from the fact that such concentrations boost average productivity growth? Or are they because such concentrations improve metropolitan-area amenities and hence make certain areas more attractive destinations for migration? The authors argue that the beneficial impacts are from effects on productivity rather than improved amenities, at least at the metropolitan-area level. In view of their evidence, this conclusion seems reasonable.

Finally, the authors offer a conjecture that areas with heavy concentrations of college graduates are more successful than other areas in responding to economic challenges that can lead to urban decline. Perhaps the local availability of workers with advanced skills allows areas faced with decline to attract or develop new industries or reorient old ones so the area can continue to prosper.

To someone unfamiliar with the subject, one of the biggest surprises in the paper is almost independent of its main message about the importance of human capital. I was struck by the importance of winter temperatures and annual rainfall in accounting for recent trends in urban rise and decline. Although the authors treat these findings as though they are well known to readers, I was not aware climate amenities are so critical to regional population growth, home prices, and average incomes. Like any other casual empiricist I recognize that American cities in the Northeast and Midwest have grown more slowly or shrunk in comparison with cities in the South and Southwest. But many differences besides winter temperatures and rainfall might account for the variation in growth rates.

My impression is that cities in the Northeast and Midwest are located in high-tax, high-regulation jurisdictions. Labor laws in those states are more likely to allow unions to compel workers to pay union dues and contribute to union strike funds. Obviously this strengthens union negotiating power compared with the situation in southeastern and western states, where right-to-work laws mean unions cannot force workers to contribute to union operations.

Labor economists probably do not understand all the determinants of plant location, but many of them have the impression that the tax laws and labor regulation in the northeastern and midwestern states are less attractive to firms than regimes in the South and West, which often impose light tax and regulatory burdens on employers. To be sure, state regulatory and tax regimes have some relationship with winter temperatures and annual rainfall. But it seems doubtful that high summer temperatures cause legislators to vote for low taxes, limited regulation, poor unemployment benefits, paltry worker compensation, and modest minimum wages. The association seems statistical rather than causal.

Here is another surprise. Glaeser and Saiz consistently find that high concentrations of college graduates are beneficial for growth of metropolitan areas, increases in home prices, and growth of family income. But they do not find this same consistent pattern for the effects of warm winter temperatures and low rainfall. Warm winters have a significantly positive impact on population growth and house prices but essentially no impact on income growth. Low rainfall tends to boost population growth, but it depresses house prices and growth of family income.

This seems odd. If warm winters and low rainfall are amenities that attract Americans from places with cold winters, why is it that these two amenities have opposite effects on house prices and very different effects on family income growth? Some readers may wonder whether a model placing such heavy emphasis on the influence of climate amenities on population growth might have some limitations. If low rainfall boosts house prices, it seems logical to predict warm winter temperatures do the same thing. Both amenities attract people to a region, but the findings in this paper imply they do not have the same effect on house prices.

These reflections on the impact of temperature and rainfall on metropolitan-area growth make me wonder whether the authors' findings would be duplicated if we examine growth across larger jurisdictions than metropolitan areas. Can we find the same effect of college-degree holders on state population growth as for metropolitan-area growth? At least during the period from 1990 through 2000 the answer is no. Figure 6 shows the simple correlation between states' 1990-2000 population growth and concentrations of college graduates in 1990. States with high concentrations of college graduates grew no faster than states with low concentrations of graduates.

Figure 6. State Population Growth and Human Capital, 1990–2000

Difference in logs, 2000 and 1990 state populations

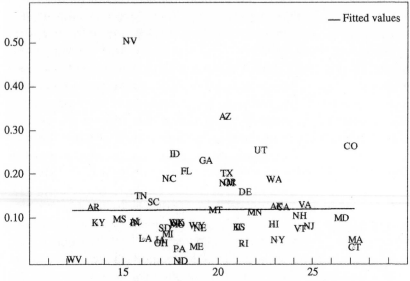

Percent of state's adults with bachelor's degree, 1990

Note: Fitted line from the regression: log(pop2000/pop1990) = 0.12556 + 0.00002 × share with bachelor's degree in 1990. R squared: 0.00000, N: 51.

This pattern is broadly repeated in geographical areas larger than states. The Census Bureau divides the United States into four main geographic regions. In 1990 the Northeast had the highest regional concentration of college graduates, but it also had the slowest regional population growth in the ensuing ten years. This pattern is not new. The Northeast also had the slowest regional population growth in the forty years after 1960. In contrast, during the 1990–2000 decade the South grew three times faster than the college-graduate-rich Northeast, and it grew more than four times faster in the forty years after 1960. This is pretty good performance for the geographical region that has the smallest endowment of highly educated, human-capital-rich workers.

Results in this paper suggest that population growth has been fastest in the areas *within* states and regions that are richest in human capital. These results depend, however, on statistically controlling for the influence of region, mean winter temperature, and annual rainfall when determining the impact of college-degree holders on metropolitan growth. The statistical estimates imply that warm winter temperature and low rainfall are external amenities that are attractive to folks in all educational groups—amenities that irresistibly draw populations toward the South and West.

Another interpretation is that voters in the Northeast and Midwest have devised tax, government transfer, and regulatory policies that increase employer costs and push employers toward places where burdens are lighter. As it happens, those destinations also have warmer winters or less rainfall. But whether it is the government institutions that are pushing firms and workers out of the Northeast and Midwest or warm sunny skies that are drawing folks to the South and West—well, that is a question not settled in this paper.

It may be hard for readers to understand why the beneficial impacts of college graduates at the metropolitan level do not translate into similar benefits at the state and regional level. Why don't concentrations of college graduates in a state or region confer the same benefits that flow to metropolitan areas? One reason may be that concentrations at the urban level matter more than concentrations at the state or regional level. But it is not a straightforward case. The Northeast is the region with the most abundant supply of highly educated workers. It is also the region that has seen the smallest rise in population during the past ten years and forty years.

We are left with the puzzle that the region of the country with the highest concentration of college graduates has grown slowly while a region with an exceptionally small concentration of educated workers has grown much faster. "Holding constant" winter temperatures and rainfall, the puzzle may disappear. But can we really be sure that winter temperature and rainfall are reliable indicators of desirable urban amenities? Or is it possible these variables are proxies for other aspects of the social and legal environment that help create attractive business locations for employers? If the second explanation rather than the first is correct, then we should rethink the ways that endowments of human capital contribute to metropolitan growth. After all, that endowment also influences the social and policy environment in a way that makes some locations attractive and others unattractive to employers.

William C. Strange: The chapter by Edward L. Glaeser and Albert Saiz addresses a fundamental issue in urban economics: the role of human capital in the urban growth process. Several interesting conclusions are reached. First, the chapter shows that there is a large and robust correlation between population growth in metropolitan statistical areas (MSA) and human capital. This result has been obtained elsewhere, so IT is not the chapter's primary contribution.[36] Second, the chapter shows that there is a larger positive effect of skills on wages than on housing prices. This result is new. It is important because it suggests that at the metropolitan level the skills-growth relationship captures productivity effects rather than amenities. Third, the chapter establishes that a somewhat different pattern exists at the city level (rather than MSA), with low-skill workers having the most pronounced effect on growth. This effect is negative, which means that at the microlevel, the absence of local human capital is a disamenity. These results all speak to the way that cities are now about brains rather than brawn and about human capital rather than factories.

The chapter reaches a fourth conclusion, that declining metropolitan areas drive the MSA effects. This result appears first in a spline regression showing that the marginal effect of human capital on growth is larger in MSAs that are losing population than in those that are growing. The result reappears in a model that uses heating degree days to proxy for decline. As is well known, cold cities have declined since World War II, relatively at least, while warm cities have thrived. Glaeser and Saiz find that in cold cities, the effect of human capital is larger at the margin than in warm cities. This result helps us understand why some cold cities have fared better than others during this period. I focus my discussion on this point.

As Glaeser and Saiz observe, the increase in the importance of human capital in declining cities is consistent with Jacobs's analysis of how successful cities reinvent themselves.[37] This is different than the idea that cities are more innovative. Glaeser and Saiz test this "Information City" idea by looking at the determinants of patenting. As might be expected, they find patenting to be correlated with human capital. However, they do not find that controlling for patenting explains the relationship between human capital and growth. Thus the evidence is consistent with

36. Rauch (1993).
37. Jacobs (1969).

reinvention of the sort that Glaeser finds in looking at the history of Boston.[38]

In considering this reinvention, it is best to begin by letting Jacobs speak for herself:

> The process by which one sort of work leads to another must have happened millions of times in the whole history of human development. Every newspaper reports it. From only a few days gleanings in the women's pages, one learns that a cleaner of suede clothing is now starting to bottle and sell her cleaning fluid for people who want to clean their own suede; a chest and wardrobe manufacturer is starting, for a fee, to analyze what is wrong with one's household or office storage arrangements; a playground designer is starting to make and sell equipment for playgrounds and nursery schools; a sculptor is starting a line of costume jewelry; a designer of theater costumes is launching himself as a couturier; a couturier is starting a boutique; an importer of Italian marble is starting to manufacture marble-top tables; a clothing store is starting classes in teen-age grooming and dieting.[39]

This analysis has several key elements. The first is urban reinvention, the idea that successful cities are those where new products and processes are created from established production processes. Jacobs calls this "new work." The second key element is that there are many pieces to the new-work dynamic. These include both endowments and attitudes. Among the most obvious endowments required to create an environment that is friendly to new work is the presence of venture capital. The availability of specialized labor is also implicit in these stories. In regard to attitudes, clearly Jacobs recognizes the importance of an entrepreneurial mindset. The final element in her analysis is one that plays a central role in all of her writings: diversity.

It is interesting to consider how Jacobs's verbal analysis and the systematic econometric work of Glaeser and Saiz might be captured in a simple economic model. One way would be to use a matching model (adapted from Helsley and Strange).[40] Suppose that a city has resources, denoted by addresses $x_i \in [0,1]$, the unit circle. Suppose also that opportunities present themselves, also denoted by addresses $y_j \in [0,1]$, again the unit circle. An opportunity is realized only if it is in some sense "close" to the city's resources: $|x_i - y_j| < d^*$. In this simple model, a city's

38. Glaeser (2003).
39. Jacobs (1969, pp. 53–54).
40. Helsley and Strange (2002).

ability to reinvent itself depends on whether it can realize the opportunities that present themselves.

What are the implications of this simple model for estimating the human capital–urban growth relationship? As just stated, the realization of an opportunity depends on whether there exist resources within some distance on the unit circle (as in Helsley-Strange). This is more likely the more spread out are the resources. This captures the importance of diversity, but diversity is not the only part of the story. This critical "realization distance" $d*$ might also depend on the amount of an MSA's resources of a particular kind, a different sort of effect. The human capital results obtained by Glaeser and Saiz seem to be in this spirit. Smart cities allow opportunities to be realized that would be missed elsewhere. The realization distance might also depend on the entrepreneurial nature of the local business environment or the nature of the local venture capital sector.

This suggests possible extensions of the chapter's intriguing treatment of the human capital–urban growth relationship. The first of these concerns diversity. There is already strong evidence of a diversity-growth relationship.[41] The IPUMs data used in the chapter are amenable to considering the impact on growth of the allocation of skilled workers across sectors. For instance, one might look at the correlation between the Herfindahl-Hirschman index across industries of skilled labor and growth.

The second possible extension concerns entrepreneurship and the local business environment. There are many aspects of the MSA environment that influence the creation of new work. Some of these surely relate to specific kinds of human capital. I discuss one with which I am familiar (and with which I must in honesty admit an interest): management education. There is evidence that this kind of human capital has a different effect than does human capital in general.[42] The U.S.-Canadian productivity gap is large, roughly 25 percent. Among all types of education, the largest difference is in management education, where the U.S. investment is roughly twice as large. Glaeser and Saiz suggest a way that this relationship could be explored further, by looking at relationships between specific kinds of education and growth.

41. Glaeser and others (1992); Rosenthal and Strange (2003a).
42. Institute for Competitiveness and Prosperity (2002).

The third possible extension concerns attitudes. The idea that some cities are more creative than others is present in the work of many authors, including Jacobs. This chapter's finding that cold cities have more reinvention parallels work on European history concerned with why the industrial revolution took place earlier in the colder North. One famous explanation is that the work ethic was different in the North.[43] It is not farfetched to think that there might be differences in attitudes toward work between the warmer and colder parts of the United States. It may be that these attitudes are complementary to human capital, a finding consistent with work on urban labor supply by Rosenthal and Strange.[44]

43. Weber (1958).
44. Rosenthal and Strange (2003b).

References

Altonji, Joseph G., and David Card. 1991. "The Effects of Immigration on the Labor Market Outcomes of Less-Skilled Natives." In *Immigration, Trade, and the Labor Market*, edited by John M. Abowd and Richard B. Freeman, 201–34. University of Chicago Press.

Black, Duncan, and Vernon Henderson. 1999. "A Theory of Urban Growth." *Journal of Political Economy* 107 (2): 252–84.

Berry Cullen, Julie, and Steven Levitt. 1999. "Crime, Urban Flight, and the Consequences for Cities." *Review of Economics and Statistics* 81 (2): 159–69.

Card, David. 1995. "Using Geographic Variation in College Proximity to Estimate the Return to Schooling." In *Aspects of Labour Economics: Essays in Honour of John Vanderkamp*, edited by Louis Christofides, E. Kenneth Grant, and Robert Swindinsky, 202-22. University of Toronto Press.

Carlino, Gerald A., Satyajit Chatterjee, and Robert Hunt. 2001. "Knowledge Spillovers and the New Economy of Cities." Working Paper 01-14. Federal Reserve Bank of Philadelphia.

Eaton, Jonathan, and Zvi Eckstein. 1997. "Cities and Growth: Theory and Evidence from France and Japan." *Regional Science and Urban Economics* 27 (4-5): 443–74.

Glaeser, Edward L. 1994. "Why Does Schooling Generate Economic Growth?" *Economics Letters* 44: 333–37.

———. 2003. "Reinventing Boston: 1640-2003." Discussion Paper 2017. Harvard Institute for Economic Research, Harvard University.

Glaeser, Edward L., and Joseph Gyourko. 2001. "Urban Decline and Durable Housing." Working Paper 8598. Cambridge, Mass.: National Bureau of Economic Research.

Glaeser, Edward L., Heidi D. Kallal, Jose A. Scheinkman, and Andrei Shleifer. 1992. "Growth in Cities." *Journal of Political Economy* 100 (6): 1126–52.

Glaeser, Edward L., Jed Kolko, and Albert Saiz. 2001. "Consumer City." *Journal of Economic Geography* 1 (1): 27–50.

Glaeser, Edward L., and Albert Saiz. 2003. "The Rise of the Skilled City." Working Paper Series. Cambridge, Mass.: National Bureau of Economic Research.

Glaeser, Edward L., Jose Scheinkman, and Andrei Shleifer. 1995. "Economic Growth in a Cross-Section of Cities." *Journal of Monetary Economics* 36 (August): 117–43.

Glaeser E. L. and J. M. Shapiro. 2003. "Urban Growth in the 1990s: Is City Living Back?" *Journal of Regional Science* 43 (1): 139–65.

Helsley, Robert W., and William C. Strange. 2002. "Innovation and Input Sharing." *Journal of Urban Economics* 51 (1): 25–45.

Institute for Competitiveness and Prosperity. 2002. "Closing the Prosperity Gap." *First Annual Report of the Task Force on Competitiveness, Productivity, and Economic Growth.* Toronto.

Jacobs, Jane. 1969. *The Economy of Cities*. Random House.

Katz, L. F. and K. M. Murphy. 1992. "Changes in Relative Wages, 1963-1987: Supply and Demand Factors." *Quarterly Journal of Economics* 107 (1): 35–78.

Lochner, Lane. 1999. "Education, Work, and Crime: Theory and Evidence." Working Paper 465. Rochester Center for Economic Research.

Lochner Lane, and Enrico Moretti. 2001. "The Effect of Education on Crime: Evidence from Prison Inmates, Arrests and Self-Reports." Working Paper 8605. Cambridge, Mass.: National Bureau of Economic Research.

Moretti, Enrico. 2002. "Workers' Education, Spillovers and Productivity: Evidence from Plant-Level Production Functions." UCLA. Mimeographed.

———. Forthcoming. "Estimating the Social Return to Higher Education: Evidence from Longitudinal and Repeated Cross-Sectional Data." *Journal of Econometrics*.

Nardinelli, Clark, and Curtis J. Simon. 1996. "The Talk of the Town: Human Capital, Information, and the Growth of English Cities, 1861 to 1961." *Explorations in Economic History* 33 (3): 384–413.

Putnam, Robert D. 2000. *Bowling Alone: The Collapse and Revival of American Community*. Simon and Schuster.

Rauch James E. 1993. "Productivity Gains from Geographic Concentration of Human Capital: Evidence from the Cities." *Journal of Urban Economics* 34 (November): 380–400.

Rosenthal, Stuart S. and William C. Strange. 2003a. "Geography, Industrial Organization, and Agglomeration." *Review of Economics and Statistics* 85 (2): 377–93.

———. 2003b. "Agglomeration, Labor Supply, and the Urban Rat Race." Working Paper. University of Toronto.

Saiz, Albert. 2003. "Immigration and Housing Rents in American Cities." Working Paper 03-12. Federal Reserve Bank of Philadelphia.

Schultz, Theodore W. 1964. *Transforming Traditional Agriculture*. Yale University Press.

Shapiro, Jesse. 2003. "Smart Cities: Explaining the Relationship between City Growth and Human Capital." Harvard University. Mimeographed.

Simon, Curtis J. 1998. "Human Capital and Metropolitan Employment Growth." *Journal of Urban Economics* 43 (March): 223–24.

Simon Curtis J., and Clark Nardinelli. 2002. "Human Capital and the Rise of American Cities, 1900-1990." *Regional Science and Urban Economics* 32 (January): 59–96.

Weber, Max. 1958. *The Protestant Ethic and the Spirit of Capitalism*. Scribner's Press.

Welch, F. 1970. "Education in Production." *Journal of Political Economy* 78 (January–February): 35–59.

CHRISTIAN A. L. HILBER
London School of Economics

CHRISTOPHER J. MAYER
Columbia Business School and National Bureau of Economic Research

School Funding Equalization and Residential Location for the Young and the Elderly

The share of elderly households is expected to grow strongly in the United States during the next decades. Conventional wisdom, supported by recent research, suggests that spending on local public schools may decline in real terms as a growing percentage of elderly voters becomes more influential.[1]

However, recent research has found that elderly voters are willing to support education spending at the local level but are often opposed to additional state spending on schools.[2] Hilber and Mayer show that house prices may serve as a mechanism to encourage the elderly to support local spending.[3] They show that the percentage of elderly residents is positively associated with additional school spending in certain places where higher school spending raises local house prices. However, the elderly are negatively associated with school spending in places where land is freely available and changes in school spending are likely to have little effect on house prices. These findings imply that the elderly may have a negative effect on public school expenditure levels in locations where state policies (as opposed to local choices) are crucial in determin-

We would like to thank Julie Berry Cullen, Caroline Hoxby, and the participants of the 2003 Brookings-Wharton Conference on Urban Affairs for helpful comments and suggestions. We also thank Dimo Pramatarov for excellent research assistance. Any errors are our own.

1. Poterba (1997).
2. Harris and others (2001).
3. Hilber and Mayer (2002).

ing local spending on schools or in places where school spending is not strongly tied to house prices.

A second mechanism through which an increasing elderly population might not lead to drastic cuts in school spending is Tiebout sorting. For example, well-to-do households with children might choose to live in states that encourage local control over school spending. With local control, elderly households can live in communities that spend little on public schools, while households with children can live in places that have higher levels of school spending. In states with little local control of school spending, such sorting might be less effective in allowing households with children to choose communities with high levels of school spending. Thus states with less local control may be less attractive for middle- and high-income households with children. Alternatively, low-income households might choose to live in states with state funding of schools if such funding leads to additional redistribution. Similarly, elderly households would likely prefer to live in places that spend little on public schools.

Of course, much of the recent evidence on Tiebout sorting suggests that Tiebout sorting may not be as powerful a force with the strong rise in two-career couples and the dispersion of employment in rings at the periphery of metro areas. In this context, it is crucial to develop a better understanding of what factors affect the location decisions of households with children and the elderly.

We use recently enhanced U.S. Census microdata on states and census-designated places from the four censuses between 1970 and 2000 to examine changes in the concentration of households with children and the elderly. In the aggregate, the concentration of both groups of households across states has been little changed over the 1970 to 2000 time period. However, these aggregate statistics mask the fact that low-income households have become increasingly concentrated in a small number of states. A very different pattern emerges when one looks at household concentrations within each state. After weighting by the number of households, the data show a strong deconcentration of most household groups across places within each state. The extent of deconcentration is strongest for the elderly and nonwhite populations but is also strong for households with children and poor households with children (that is, households with children that have an income below 100 percent of the poverty level). Such facts are consistent with the diminished importance of Tiebout sorting at the local level.

Next, we consider how "reforms" in state educational spending policies have affected household location choices. State educational spending policies determine the constraints that local governments face in providing local school services. Although some U.S. states have removed school spending authority from local residents, others encourage local control, potentially leading to Tiebout sorting and maintaining the incentive of residents to support their local schools in order to raise their own house prices. Our results indicate that states with local control and limited redistribution are attractive for middle- and high-income households but not for low-income households. However, in states with significant redistribution mechanisms, nonpoor households with children and elderly have fewer incentives to avoid low-income places and public schools in those places, leading to less concentration of poor households and to less separation of young and elderly. These results indicate that the incidence and overall funding of school services matter for residential location choices in a manner consistent with Tiebout sorting.

Background and Theoretical Predictions

Our analysis is founded on a broad literature that describes the issues that relate household sorting and school finance reforms and also assesses the impact of changes in school funding on performance. This research provides the rationale for our theoretical predictions, which propose that school finances should affect household location choices.

Tiebout Sorting and Household Location Decisions

The seminal work of Tiebout serves as a beginning for most papers that examine issues relating to household location.[4] Tiebout points out that individuals should sort themselves across local jurisdictions according to their local public good preferences. Tiebout's controversial hypothesis is that under certain conditions (for example, free mobility

---

4. Tiebout (1956).

and a large number of local jurisdictions), voting-with-the-feet leads to an efficient provision of local public goods. While the Tiebout hypothesis has been criticized on theoretical grounds based on the strong assumptions needed to derive his results, common wisdom holds that community selection is driven by the same factors that Tiebout noted in his original paper, including the local package of public services (for example, the quality of local public school services) and taxes.[5]

Most empirical research has found evidence of at least some Tiebout sorting, but most papers also conclude that Tiebout sorting is not the only factor that explains where households live. Eberts and Gronberg show that as the number of school districts in metropolitan areas increases, the districts become more homogenous in income, an important prediction of the Tiebout model. Gramlich and Rubinfeld find that the variance in the willingness to pay for local public services is smaller within individual jurisdictions than for state-level populations, another implication from Tiebout. Hoyt and Rosenthal argue that if households sort efficiently across locations, then at a given location households receive the same marginal benefit from locational amenities. In testing the latter proposition, the authors find empirical evidence that is consistent with Tiebout sorting but also that households do not perfectly efficiently sort across locations on the basis of their preferences for local amenities alone. Finally, Rhode and Strumpf examine whether local policies are the dominant motive for residential location choices.[6] They argue that if Tiebout sorting is the dominant motive for residential choice, then the secular decline in mobility costs should lead to greater stratification. Their results, based on across-community heterogeneity between 1850 and 1990, suggest that Tiebout sorting has been historically overwhelmed by forces reducing across-community heterogeneity.

These results imply that factors other than local public services and taxes appear to affect residential location choices. For example, Topel and Ward show that households select communities based on employment opportunities. Costa and Kahn provide evidence that college-educated couples increasingly locate in large metropolitan areas (MSAs).[7]

---

5. See, for example, Bewley (1981); Epple and Zelenitz (1981); Henderson (1985), for theoretical criticism. See also, for example, Epple and Romer (1991); Fernandez and Rogerson (1998); Hoxby (1999, 2000); Nechyba (1999 and 2000).

6. Rhode and Strumpf (2003); Eberts and Gronberg (1981); Gramlich and Rubinfeld (1982); Hoyt and Rosenthal (1997).

7. Topel and Ward (1992); Costa and Kahn (2000).

They argue that this increase in dual-career households in large MSAs can be explained primarily by collocation problems. More generally, changes in the dispersion of employment affect the extent of sorting.

Evidence also shows that households tend to cluster in social groups with similar ethnicity or education. For example, Mincer demonstrates that the proximity to members of the same ethnic group and to family and friends has a strong impact on residential location decisions. Massey and Espana show that this factor is particularly strong for recent immigrants, who tend to locate in ethnic enclaves within metropolitan areas, possibly because of extensive links that are introduced through family ties and ethnic networks. Thus changes in the inflow of recent immigrants are likely to affect sorting outcomes (that is, measures of concentration or segregation respectively). Van Hook and Balistreri provide evidence for California that changes in the student composition have disproportionately occurred in schools attended by Spanish-speaking limited English-proficient students as a result of district-level patterns of segregation by income, race and ethnicity, and language.[8]

Other papers investigate the effects of Tiebout sorting on redistribution.[9] Utilizing a model that assumes free household mobility, Epple and Romer demonstrate that local redistribution induces household sorting, with the poorest households located in the communities that provide the most redistribution. Although the threat of outmigration affects the potential for redistribution, their results imply that local redistribution is nonetheless feasible. On the empirical side, Kremer examines the claims that Americans are increasingly sorting into internally homogenous neighborhoods and schools, and that this sorting has led to increasing inequality. He finds that neighborhood sorting has been stable or decreasing historically and that sorting has limited effect on inequality. This contrasts to propositions of a couple of theoretical studies, which suggest that America may be caught in a vicious cycle of increasing sorting and inequality.[10]

Finally, a growing literature explores the relationship between household sorting, efficiency, and inequality in the context of the American school finance equalization (SFE) reform. According to Hoxby, SFE has

---

8. Mincer (1978); Massey and Espana (1987); Van Hook and Balistreri (2002).

9. For an early discussion see Oates (1972).

10. Epple and Romer (1991); Kremer (1997). For theroretical studies on sorting and inequality see Bénabou (1993, 1996); Fernandez and Rogerson (2001).

affected American schools more than any other reform during the past thirty years.[11] Not only does SFE affect the efficiency of the provision of public school services, it also determines how school spending and taxes are distributed across students.[12] Importantly, the redistribution characteristic of the SFE may also affect migration patterns and the extent of segregation of low- and high-income households or the segregation of young and elderly. While the impact of SFE on school choice, per pupil spending, property prices, efficiency, school productivity, and inequality has recently been studied more widely, to our knowledge there is no empirical study of the effects of SFE on actual sorting outcomes, in particular, on sorting of different income and age groups.[13]

School Spending and Outcomes

Our analysis implicitly assumes that school expenditures are related to learning outcomes of pupils or provide other benefits that matter to parents and homeowners. If this assumption holds, school financing rules that influence local public school expenditures should therefore have an effect on the quality of local public school services. School financing rules would also matter for residential location choices, in particular, for location choices of parents of preschool and school-aged children. Whether school resources are indeed related to perceived learning outcomes is a disputed research question.[14] The disagreement arises in large part because researchers focus on different measures of school performance.

Studies that focus on achievements of children *while they are in school* generally find no powerful evidence that school spending is closely linked to student progress.[15] This puzzling finding may be due to wasteful spending. However, measurement issues provide a plausible alternative explanation. Test scores—the key measure of student achievement—are indeed a quite imperfect measure of effective student out-

11. Hoxby (2001).

12. Hoxby (2001) notes that SFE "differs from conventional redistribution because it is based on property values, which are endogenous to the school's productivity, taste for education, and the school finance system itself."

13. Downes and Schoenman (1998); Fernandez and Rogerson (1998); Hoxby (2000, 2001).

14. For an excellent review of this research question see Burtless (1996).

15. See the metaanalysis by Hanushek (1986).

comes. This is partly because of the "teaching to the test problematic" and partly because test scores do not capture many factors that are most relevant to parents. Examples are the overall happiness of children, their "preparedness for life," the long-term success of the youngsters in the professional world, the provision of arts and music classes, the range of sporting events and quality of sport facilities, or the availability of school dining halls during lunch time. These factors may be more closely linked to school expenditures than are test scores, which may be influenced by parental education and social factors.

Problems with test scores as a measure of school value-added are illustrated by more recent studies that look at the impact of school inputs and education expenditures on students' earnings *after their formal schooling has ended.*[16] While wages of graduates are also imperfect measures of student outcomes (for example, they do not capture the happiness of children while they are in school), they at least measure the market value of the accumulated human capital investment. This is arguably a more inclusive measure than test scores, which merely measure the ability to perform well in a standardized test at a given time during school life. The above mentioned studies that look at graduates' earnings generally find a much stronger link between school resources and schooling outcomes.

Another way to discern how school spending might influence the location decisions of potential residents is to look at whether school spending affects house values using evidence from state-level reforms that affect local spending on schools. Barrow and Rouse show that, on average, additional state aid is valued by potential residents. Similarly, Bradbury, Mayer, and Case use evidence from a property tax limit in Massachusetts, Proposition 2½, to demonstrate that increases in school spending lead to gains in property values, suggesting that additional school spending is valued by marginal homebuyers.[17]

Overall, we view the empirical evidence as supporting the implicit assumption that school resources have a positive impact on the utility of households with children, by improving the quality of local school services or providing other services that parents value. Thus school finance rules may potentially also be important for household location choices.

16. For example, Card and Krueger (1992a ,1992b,1996a ,1996b).
17. Barrow and Rouse (2004); Bradbury, Mayer, and Case (2001).

Theoretical Predictions

Our *first hypothesis* is that states with local control and limited redistribution are attractive for middle- and high-income households but not for low-income households. The *second hypothesis* is that in states with significant redistribution mechanisms, nonpoor households with children and elderly have fewer incentives to avoid low-income places, leading to less concentration of poor households and to less separation of young and elderly. The justification for this hypothesis is that redistribution is borne by all residents of the state and not only by the residents of the local jurisdictions that have an overproportional share of households with children in poverty. The *third hypothesis* is that in states with significant redistribution, nonpoor households with children have fewer incentives to avoid public schools. While these three hypotheses are suggested by some theoretical work, we should note that theory does not necessarily generate unambiguous predictions.

The theoretical analysis of parental school choices is complex because several decision processes are involved and because of interdependencies between individual choices and the overall economic and institutional setting. Nechyba identifies four factors that complicate the analysis. First, parental choices involve judgments about school production functions. Second, choices of residential location often determine the access to primary and secondary schools.[18] Third, private schools offer an alternative to public schools that are linked to the housing markets. And fourth, households may face credit constraints that may not permit them to borrow against human capital investment.

Recently, computer simulation analysis has emerged to help deal with the complexity of general equilibrium models of school finance.[19] Although simulation models are helpful in clarifying important theoretical and quantitative issues, they depend critically on the appropriate assumptions, and different simulations therefore often have diverging outcomes.

One result is especially relevant to our work. Nechyba analyzes the impact of public school financing rules on private school attendance.[20]

18. Nechyba (2003a).
19. See Nechyba (2003a) for a detailed discussion of this research area.
20. Nechyba (2003b).

The theoretical framework points to two distinct effects when pure local and pure state financing are compared. First, state funding has a "direct" (or partial equilibrium) effect on private school attendance; it leads to lower private school attendance in poorer districts where school resources increase (hypothesis 3) and to higher private school attendance in wealthier districts where school resources decrease. Second, an "indirect" (general equilibrium) effect emerges as state financing leads to an increase in the opportunity cost of private school attendees choosing to locate in poor communities in order to take advantage of low-cost housing and low property taxes. Nechyba differentiates between pure state financing and block grants.[21] On balance, the simulations suggest that private school enrollments fall more steeply under block grants (which allow local discretion to spend beyond the grant) than under pure state financing. However, that result is sensitive to particular assumptions. If centralization involves matching grants, then a price subsidy effect emerges, which leads to a further decline in private school attendance.

Overall, Nechyba's simulations suggest that centralization leads to a decrease in private school attendance as stated in hypothesis 3. However, these simulations do not take into account that school finance equalization leads to a decrease in Tiebout choice and therefore may lead to a decrease in the responsiveness to local concerns (that is, a decrease in the efficiency of resource use), which may in turn increase private school attendance.[22] This example illustrates the inherent difficulty of formulating theoretically unambiguous predictions. With this caveat in mind, we describe our empirical findings, which are consistent with the three hypotheses just stated.

Empirical Analysis

Our data are derived from three major sources. The first source is a package of CD-ROMs, compiled by GeoLytics, with long-form data from the 1970, 1980, 1990, and 2000 Decennial Censuses of Housing

21. Nechyba (2003b).
22. Nechyba (2003b). In fact, a decline in responsiveness to local concerns owing to state equalization may explain the empirically documented increase in private school attendance in California after its school finance reform. Downes and Greenstein (1996) and Downes and Schoenman (1998) provide empirical evidence that California's school finance equalization reform was followed by an increase in private school attendance.

and Population. The second source is the Tax Foundation's publication *Facts and Figures on Government Finances*.[23] Finally, we use school finance reform data as reported in table 1 from Hoxby.[24]

The U.S. Census data are compiled on two geographic levels—U.S. states and places. The GeoLytics CD-ROMs have data for all places for the census years 1980, 1990, and 2000. For the census year 1970, the CD-ROMs only include 6,963 (out of 20,768) places. However, these 6,963 places account for more than 95 percent of the U.S. population. To achieve comparability across the years, we limit the sample to the 5,939 places that have data from each of the four censuses. One can assess how representative this sample is by considering that in 2000 there are 161 million people living in those places, 206 million people in all the places, and 281 million people in the entire United States. In earlier years, these places represent a much higher percentage of the U.S. population. As a robustness check, we have performed the regressions reported with the full (unbalanced) sample of all places in each census year but find our conclusions are unchanged.

We examine two different types of household sorting: net flows of various types of households across states and the concentration of households within states. As noted, educational funding reforms may cause households to move to different states or to concentrate in a few places within a state. To measure the state-level concentration of households, we compute Herfindahl indexes from the places dataset. For example, the concentration of elderly in a state is derived by summing across all places in each state the squared market share of elderly households in each place. The market share of elderly households is the percentage of the state's total elderly households living in each place. The Herfindahl index has the advantage of being invariant to changes in the actual number of elderly households in a state over time. So if the number of elderly households in a state doubles, but each place gets its proportional share of the new elderly households, then the Herfindahl index will remain unchanged.

The Tax Foundation publication is used to obtain data on public elementary and secondary school revenues and expenditure for each state.

23. The Tax Foundation publishes this unique one-volume resource on government taxing and spending regularly since 1941. We use several editions to derive data on public elementary and secondary school revenues and expenditure for each state and for the school years that come closest to the 1970, 1980, and 1990 census years.

24. Hoxby (2001). See "Limitations to the Analysis" for a discussion of the appropriateness of using these measures.

The revenue data consist of series for federal, state, and local funding sources, and those are for the 1971–72, 1980–81, and 1991–92 school years. The expenditure data include current spending, capital outlay, and interest payments for the 1969–70, 1980–81, and 1990–91 school years. We use current spending to compute per pupil spending, recognizing the lumpiness of capital spending over time and across places. Unfortunately, the revenues and the expenditure series are discontinued in the latest edition of *Facts and Figures on Government Finances*. However, we are able to extend the series to the 2000–01 school year by including data available on the Census Bureau website. The Census Bureau is the original source of information for the Tax Foundation's publication, and we have verified consistency by comparing data in both sources from the early 1990s.

We also use various school funding equalization (SFE) measures from table 1 in Hoxby including the minimum and maximum inverted tax price and median foundation tax rate.[25] The inverted tax price is defined as the amount that actual school spending increases for the marginal dollar of revenue raised. For example, a value less than one implies that if a school district raises one dollar, it gets to spend less than a dollar because the state government taxes some of the revenue raised, while a value greater than one suggests that the state subsidizes local expenditures by providing a partial matching of revenues raised. The minimum value is the lowest value of the inverted tax price among all districts in the state, while the maximum is the largest value. Note that the actual values reflect endogenous responses by districts that face sometimes complicated formulas that determine state funding or taxation of local budgets. Nonetheless, there is substantial variation in these inverted tax prices; some states such as California, Hawaii, and New Mexico enact reforms that essentially tax all revenues raised by districts that exceed the state-mandated floor. Other states provide large matching subsidies for the poorer districts.

The median foundation tax rate is a state-mandated floor to the property tax rate that all districts must follow. A higher value of the foundation tax rate implies that all districts must provide relatively large amounts of funds for local schools and limits the gains from Tiebout sorting. That is, even if the elderly concentrate in a few districts, they cannot

---

25. Hoxby (2001).

cut school spending as a percentage of property values below the foundation tax rate.[26]

Nominal values for all variables are converted into constant 1992 dollars by using the implicit price deflator for state and local government purchases, as reported in the 1996 and 2003 *Economic Report of the President.*

Finally, we use the percentage of a state's residents that are foreign born from the U.S. Census. This measure proxies for immigrants who may be more likely to be concentrated in places with other immigrants and may also have more children and be poorer relative to the overall U.S. population. Other measures of social similarity were not available for all four census years (partly because of definition changes) or turned out to be statistically completely irrelevant (for example, the percentage of nonwhites).

The final dataset includes 200 observations, one observation for each of the 50 U.S. states and one for each of the four census years 1970, 1980, 1990, and 2000. Summary statistics are presented in table 1. Overall, the average district spends about $4,200 (constant 1992 dollars). While approximately equal amounts of that spending are funded from state and local sources, there is appreciable variation, so some districts receive virtually all of their revenue from state sources, while other districts receive almost all funding from local taxes and fees. Much of that variation across districts is because of differences in state policies on school funding. The concentration measures show that poor households with children (that is, households with income below 100 percent of the poverty line that have at least one child under 18 years) are relatively more concentrated within states than all households with children or elderly households (that is, households with at least one householder older than 64 years). Nearly 40 percent of all households have at least one child under 18 years old, and about one in eight households with children is below the poverty line. Nearly 12 percent of all children attend private schools. About 20 percent of all households have an elderly householder.

Table 2 examines aggregate trends over time in basic demographics, school spending, and private school enrollments. Notice that the percent-

26. For the two states excluded from table 1 in Hoxby (2001), Alaska and Colorado, the minimum/maximum inverted tax price is set to one and the median foundation tax rate to zero.

Table 1. Variable List and Means, All 50 U.S. States, 1970–2000
$N = 200$

Variable	Mean	Standard deviation	Minimum	Maximum
Share of school funding from state sources	0.443	0.173	0.053	0.887
Share of school funding from local sources	0.472	0.199	0.001	0.939
Concentration of households with children	0.096	0.086	0.014	0.520
Concentration of poor households with children (household income <100% of poverty level)	0.138	0.119	0.025	0.552
Concentration of households with an elderly householder	0.106	0.097	0.011	0.491
Concentration of nonwhite population	0.216	0.160	0.021	0.738
Concentration of foreign-born population	0.151	0.121	0.025	0.657
Minimum inverted tax price	0.921	0.240	0	1
Maximum inverted tax price	1.028	0.328	0	1.96
Median foundation tax rate, in 1/1000ths	11.99	10.85	0	48
Per pupil school spending	4,199	1,628	1,708	9,392
Share of private school enrollment (among school-aged children)	0.117	0.043	0.031	0.208
Share of foreign-born population (among all households)	0.049	0.045	0.005	0.262
Share of households with children (among all households)	0.389	0.058	0.281	0.574
Share of poor households with children (among all households)	0.053	0.021	0.023	0.158
Share of households with an elderly householder (among all households)	0.205	0.035	0.052	0.289

Source: For all tables in this chapter see text and notes 23 and 24.
Notes: Monetary values are reported in 1992 dollars by using the National Income and Product Accounts deflator for government purchases of goods and services. The sample consists of all the states for the years 1970, 1980, 1990, and 2000.

Table 2. Aggregate Trends

	Averages across states			Weighted averages across states		
Census year	Share of households with children	Share of poor households with children	Share of households with elderly householder	Per pupil school spending (dollars)	Share of private school enrollment	Share of school funding from local sources
1970	0.446	0.055	0.195	2,781	0.123	0.507
1980	0.401	0.052	0.201	3,492	0.133	0.422
1990	0.341	0.054	0.218	5,250	0.128	0.323
2000	0.334	0.049	0.211	6,022	0.137	0.530

Note: Averages and weighted averages across states. The weight used is the number of children (0–17 years old).

ages of households with children and an elderly householder are calculated based on (unweighted) averages across states to capture the effect
of demographics in the average state. Changing demographics owing to
the baby boom or bust and the aging population are clear in the data. The
percentage of households with children has fallen appreciably since 1970
from 45 percent to 33 percent of all households in 2000. Yet the percentage of poor households with children has fallen only slightly. However,
the data show only modest growth in the percentage of households with
an elderly householder. The next three columns are weighted by the number of children to represent aggregate U.S. trends in schooling. Despite
the fact that real per pupil spending has more than doubled, the percentage of private school enrollment is rising over time, suggesting some dis-
satisfaction with public schools for some parents. Of additional interest is
the strong time-series variation in the sources of local school funding.
Although the percentage of funds coming from local sources fell from
1970 to 1990, it grew appreciably between 1990 and 2000, possibly
caused by the strong across-the-board increase in house prices during the
most recent decade, leading to a rise in property tax collections in many
local communities.

To get a sense of how the number of elderly households and the
shrinking number of households with children are distributed around the
country, tables 3 and 4 examine time trends in sorting within and across
states. Of particular interest, table 3 shows that the concentration of all
household types within states has fallen appreciably between 1970 and
2000, suggesting that Tiebout sorting has become much less important
for both elderly households and households with children. This observation is consistent with long-run trends in Tiebout sorting as documented
by Rhode and Strumpf.[27] However, the data show that the within-state
concentrations have fallen fastest for elderly households, suggesting that
employment-based explanations like increasing dispersion of jobs across
the MSA and the growth of dual-career couples are not the only factors
that are driving reduced Tiebout sorting.

While sorting within states has been falling, sorting across states has
remained relatively unchanged for households with children and elderly
households over the same period. (See table 4, which computes the
Herfindahl measure based on state market shares of various household

27. Rhode and Strumpf (2003).

Table 3. Concentration of Household Types within States

Census year	Households with children	Poor households with children	Households with elderly householder	Nonwhite population	Foreign-born population
1970	0.090	0.162	0.116	0.305	0.179
1980	0.080	0.153	0.091	0.237	0.152
1990	0.075	0.133	0.077	0.203	0.150
2000	0.074	0.127	0.069	0.166	0.140

Note: Concentration measure is weighted Herfindahl index averages across states. The weight used is the number of households.

Table 4. Concentration of Household Types across States

Census year	Households with children	Poor households with children	Households with elderly householder	Nonwhite population	Foreign-born population
1970	0.042	0.039	0.042	0.045	0.159
1980	0.040	0.042	0.041	0.056	0.143
1990	0.042	0.045	0.041	0.068	0.149
2000	0.043	0.051	0.041	0.069	0.154

Note: Concentration measure is Herfindahl index.

groups using the national total of each group by year.) Note that these numbers mask significant variation in overall population growth rates, which vary widely across states. The data indicate that growing states appear to have proportional increases (or decreases) in households with children and elderly households relative to national percentages of each of these groups. However, the aggregate stability in sorting across states does not hold for poor households with children and nonwhite households. These subgroups have become much more concentrated in some states relative to others.

Limitations to the Analysis

A limitation to our analysis is based on the fact that we rely on aggregate data. In this context, we want to clarify that our state equalization variables are quite imperfect measures of the impact of school finance equalization on location choices. As noted by Hoxby, the maximum and minimum inverted tax price and the median foundation tax rate do not fully describe SFE schemes.[28] That is, these variables do not adequately

---

28. Hoxby (2001).

describe the variation in how tax prices and foundation tax rates are distributed within each state. The utilized SFE measures also do not reveal information about flat grants and school-related income and sales taxes. Furthermore, the utilized SFE measures incorporate the endogenous responses of school districts, an issue that also potentially affects most other analyses using state-level policies such as SFEs.

An analysis using more disaggregated data (including school finance variables measured at the school district level rather than at the state level) might be more revealing and would likely generate more robust results. This is partly because of more precise measurement of SFE schemes and partly because it would provide greater degrees of freedom to carry out more specific empirical tests. For example, a much larger sample size might provide enough degrees of freedom to address the policy endogeneity issue by comparing court-ordered versus legislative SFE reforms or by applying an instrumental variable strategy.[29]

However, it is important to note that—as our empirical analysis reveals—even these rough measures of state-level SFE schemes have an economically and statistically significant effect on residential location outcomes within and between states. Data limitations may mitigate the estimated effects of SFE on residential location choices, but they do not eliminate them.

Results

In examining whether trends in school finance equalizations can help explain the patterns described earlier we begin by considering whether states that enact SFEs that allow for more local control over school spending have a greater degree of within-state sorting compared with states that give local school districts relatively little control over school spending. As noted, the benefits of sorting may be stronger in states where local communities can appreciably vary the public services tax and expenditure bundle to address the desires of local residents. Table A-1 in the appendix to this chapter presents regressions that examine the determinants of concentration (Herfindahl indexes) for three types of households: households with children, poor households with children,

29. We intend to address the outlined data limitations and endogeneity issues in future research.

and elderly households.[30] All regressions are at the state level and include state and year fixed effects. We include three measures of local control, along with the percentage of a state's residents who are foreign born. The latter variable serves as a proxy for the location decisions of immigrants, who may be more likely to concentrate in places with other immigrants.

Our results are consistent with the view that less local control leads to a smaller degree of Tiebout sorting. The first column presents results for the concentration of households with children. States that enacted SFEs with high foundation tax rates, which set a floor on the amount of money districts must spend on schools, have much lower concentrations of households with children. The magnitudes of the effects are fairly large. A state that increased its foundation tax rate from 0 to the sample average of 12 would have seen a decrease in concentration of about 0.0065, or more than 40 percent of the decline in within-state concentration of households with children that was observed in the United States between 1970 and 2000. For states that enacted the highest foundation tax rates (Arizona, 47 percent, and New Mexico, 48 percent), these results suggest very high deconcentrations of households with children. These results are intuitively appealing. Suppose a household with children was considering where to live within a metro area. In many cases, households face a trade-off between being closer to work or living in a school district that provides strong support for schools. A high foundation tax rate will equalize spending across districts, so it is easier for households with children to locate in communities based on nonschool reasons, including proximity to employment or locational amenities such as lakes, theaters, museums, or good restaurants.

For poor households with children, redistribution appears more important than a floor on the overall property tax rate. In states with a higher maximum inverted tax price, which is an indicator of redistribution inherent in the SFE, poorer households are less concentrated. To understand this behavior, one might think about the location decisions of middle- or upper-income households. These well-to-do households are more likely to avoid living in communities where there are poor households if the local taxes of the wealthier households effectively subsidize the school services

30. Data on high-income households are not available for all four census years. Thus, unfortunately, we cannot examine the determinants of concentration for this particular household type.

utilized by the children of poor households. However, if the state government provides subsidies to schools based on the number or percentage of poor households, wealthier households—that for some reason have chosen to live in a state with equalization mechanisms in the first place—may not have the same strong economic incentives to avoid locations where poor households locate, at least not because of any fiscal externality.

Finally, for elderly households, concentration is negatively related to both the maximum inverted tax price and the minimum foundation tax rate. As with other households, the benefits from Tiebout sorting are reduced if the state requires all school districts to substantially fund public schools and provides state funds to subsidize school districts with many poor households. One might easily interpret this finding to suggest that elderly households have greater incentive to sort when communities have more flexibility to reduce school spending or when redistribution is greater so that local residents face less of a burden to fund schools for poor households with children.

Next we examine a second margin that might be affected by SFEs: the percentage of a state's school-aged children that attend private schools. Private schools are, after all, an alternative to Tiebout sorting. We regress the percentage of private school enrollment on our three SFE variables and year and state fixed effects. The results, shown in table A-2, are consistent with our previous findings and the predictions in Nechyba's work. Private school attendance is negatively related to the maximum inverted tax price and the minimum foundation tax rate in regressions that include state and year fixed effects. These results suggest that SFEs that ensure adequate local school funding and have an element of redistribution can result in a lower concentration of households with children, especially poor households, and also result in an increased attendance in public schools relative to private schools. These findings get even stronger when we control for the level of real per pupil spending, an attempt to control for the possibility that private school attendance might also be related to the overall school spending in a state, and the percentage of foreign-born individuals in column 2. The quantitative effects are significant. Based on more conservative estimates in column 1, an increase in the maximum inverted tax price of one standard deviation (0.33) reduces private school enrollment by about 0.5 percentage point (0.53 percentage point based on estimates in column 1) or by about 4.4 percent (4.7 percent). The same one-standard deviation increase in the median foundation tax rate (11/1000ths) reduces private school enrollment by 0.58 percentage point (0.73 percentage point) or about 5.2 percent (6.6 percent).

Our findings so far have examined the extent to which SFEs have an impact on the concentration of various types of households within states. We also consider whether SFEs result in net flows on households between states. To do this, we regress the percentage change in the number of households with children on the change in variables related to SFEs, the lagged amount of per pupil spending, and the percentage change in all households. The latter variable controls for non-school-related factors that can influence mobility decisions. For example, we know that strong employment growth, climate, concentrations of immigrants, and land availability lead southern and western states to have strong growth in population. Effectively, we want to examine how SFEs impact the location decisions of households with children, holding the movements of all households constant. In all of our regressions, the coefficient on percentage change in all households is very close to one (we cannot reject that the coefficient is different from one), as one might expect if the baseline impact of mobility is the same for households with children as for all households. This coefficient is not surprising given that aggregate concentrations of households with children across states are virtually unchanged over the 1970–2000 time period.

The results in table A-3 show that households with children tend to locate in states where local revenues fund a greater percentage of total school spending (relative to federal and state sources of revenue). At first these results might be surprising in that one might have expected that households with children would have preferred states that provided much of the funding at the state level, effectively reducing the incidence of school spending on local communities. However, these findings are consistent with previous research showing that places that rely on local funding may provide greater funding than locations that rely on funding that comes from higher levels of government.[31] We include the lagged real per pupil spending as an indicator of overall support for education so that we do not confuse the ability of communities to vary the local level of spending with the amount of aggregate spending.[32] Unfortunately, the

31. See Fischel (2001) and Hilber and Mayer (2002), for example.
32. Of course, we would prefer to directly control for the current amount of per pupil spending, but current per pupil spending is likely endogenous, and our data do not provide any effective instrument.

overall level of school spending in a state is likely to be endogenously determined with the relative numbers of households with children that move into the state, so we cannot include the current level of spending. The results show that a one-standard-deviation increase in the percentage of school funding that comes from local sources (20 percent) would result in an increase in net migration of households with children relative to all households of about 0.6 percent, which is equivalent to the estimated effect of an additional $909 of lagged per pupil school spending, a relatively large number. SFE indicators such as maximum inverted tax price and minimum foundation tax rate seem to have little impact on the relative locations of households with children across states.

Next we examine whether the impact of SFE variables is stronger when overall school spending is higher. In column 2, we interact the SFE and percentage of local funding variables with the lagged level of per pupil spending. The results suggest that the estimated impact of greater local control is much larger in states where per pupil spending is high (that is, the interaction between change in percentage of school funding from local sources and lagged per pupil spending is positive). Other interactions with SFE variables are not close to being significantly different from zero.

In column 3, we conduct a robustness check by including state fixed effects in place of the variable for percentage change in all households out of concern for possible endogeneity in the flow of all households. The results are reassuring. While this regression has a much worse fit (lower R^2) than the equivalent regression in column 1, the coefficient on percentage change in local funding is nearly unchanged. However, the standard errors of the individual point estimates rise so that the coefficient is no longer statistically different from zero.

Our final examination in table A-4 conducts the same regressions as in table A-3, except that we replace the dependent variable with the percentage change in poor households with children. Our hope is to see if SFEs or sources of school funding help explain the sharp rise in the state-level concentration of poor households with children (table 4). These regressions give some additional insights into the factors that affect the net flows of poor households with children and suggest that SFEs have had a modest impact on the relative household location decisions of poor households with children. As with all households with children, poor households with children tend to migrate to states with higher levels of lagged real school spending, although the coefficient is lower for poor households with children than for all households with children. In addition, households with children appear to favor states with a relatively high minimum foundation tax rate. The estimated impact of a one-standard-deviation increase in the minimum foundation tax rate is about the same as a $1,000 increase in lagged real per pupil spending. Given that a high minimum foundation tax rate leads to a lower concentration of poor households with children within a state, we should not be surprised that poor households with children find states with a high minimum foundation tax rate relatively attractive when they are choosing where to live.

The additional regressions in the next two columns provide few new insights. The interactions of SFE variables with lagged real per pupil spending do not provide additional insights for poor households with children in column 2. In column 3, the coefficients on other variables again are smaller but relatively stable when we use state fixed effects instead of the percentage change in all households to control for other factors affecting migration across states.

Conclusion

Our empirical evidence shows that state-imposed redistribution through school funding equalization affects the location choices of households, consistent with the Tiebout model. States with policies that place a high floor on the spending of local schools—a high foundation tax rate—have less sorting of households with children. States that provide redistribution in the form of tax-subsidized inducements to districts with poorer students—a high maximum inverted tax price for expenditures—have less sorting of poor households with children. Both redistribution and a floor on spending reduce the sorting of the elderly. We also show that the same factors that reduce sorting are also associated with decreased private school enrollments.

Next we examine mobility across states and demonstrate that school funding policies have an impact on the net migration of households with children relative to all households. Not surprisingly, households with children are attracted to states with higher spending levels and also to states where more of the funding comes from local (rather than state or federal) sources. Poor households with children also move to states with high per pupil expenditures and to states that have a high foundation tax rate. The latter may well be attractive to poor households with children because it is associated with reduced sorting of poor households at the local level.

Similar to Rhode and Strumpf, we show that Tiebout sorting by many household characteristics has been decreasing over time.[33] However, our results differ in emphasis from those in Rhode and Strumpf in that we find that local public schools are an important factor in determining the residential location choice.[34] The fact that public school funding plays a role in household location decisions may help explain the reduced Tiebout sorting that has taken place during the past three decades. After all, many states have passed school finance equalization packages, which, according to our results, lead to reduced concentration of elderly households, households with children, and poor households with children.

The finding that local public school services—and more specifically school funding equalization—matter for the residential location choice has broader policy implications when we consider the impact of a growing elderly population. Tiebout sorting provides a mechanism through which households with children can choose to live in communities that specialize in providing the services that they prefer, such as good quality and well-funded local schools. However, school funding decisions are often made by state governments. Harris and others and Hilber and Mayer show that while elderly voters are often opposed to state expenditures on schools, they are willing to support local expenditures in some circumstances.[35]

Consider some of the policy options for maintaining or increasing financial support (and redistribution) for public schools. While, according to Hoxby, some of the SFE reforms undertaken in the past thirty years have been successful in increasing spending, many of these reforms were passed by legislatures and thus could be repealed by voters.[36] Economists often propose school vouchers as a solution to the inequality prob-

---

33. Rhode and Strumpf (2003).
34. While Rhode and Strumpf (2003) document this trend for a very long time period, from 1850 to 1990, we look at a much shorter period (1970 to 2000) and find that the trend has continued during the past decade. The authors are careful to point out that their results do not imply that public goods have no impact on location, only that other factors are more important.
35. Harris and others (2001); Hilber and Mayer (2002).
36. Hoxby (2001).

lem. However, vouchers also suffer from the drawback that the funding for vouchers typically comes from state government. Fischel describes another potential drawback of school vouchers, arguing that the public benefit of local schools accrues to the parents and not the children.[37] Having children in local public schools enables adults to get to know other adults better, reducing the transaction costs of citizen provision of true local public goods. In other words, vouchers disperse students from their communities and thereby reduce the communal social capital of adults. Our results provide partial support for Fischel's view in that many SFEs also produce a deconcentration of certain groups of households, leaving communities with fewer common bonds.

A final factor to consider is the extent to which mobility and competition across states might affect household locations and state policies. While the concentration of households with children across states has changed little in the past thirty years, we show that such households do consider school funding issues in their choices of where to live. While the estimated coefficients suggest that school funding plays a relatively small role right now, the influence of state policies might become more important if states further differentiated themselves according to their educational policies. Evidence from the location of poor households with children and welfare recipients suggests that state policies can have an important impact on location decisions.

37. Fischel (2002).

Appendix

Table A-1. Do States with Greater Local Choice Have More Within-State Sorting?[a]

	Weighted regressions with year and state fixed effects		
	1	*2*	*3*
Explanatory variable	*Concentration of households with children*	*Concentration of poor households with children*	*Concentration of households with elderly householder*
Share of school funding	–0.00037	0.011	0.0055
from local sources	(0.0055)	(0.0099)	(0.0082)
Maximum inverted tax	0.0032	–0.013**	–0.021**
price	(0.0067)	(0.0063)	(0.0087)
Median foundation tax	–0.00054**	–0.000021	–0.00091**
rate	(0.00026)	(0.00048)	(0.00041)
Share of foreign-born	0.053	0.012	–0.099
population	(0.060)	(0.067)	(0.085)
Dummy year, 1980	–0.0068**	–0.00071	–0.020**
	(0.0030)	(0.0049)	(0.0054)
Dummy year, 1990	–0.012**	–0.014**	–0.029**
	(0.0027)	(0.0040)	(0.0050)
Dummy year, 2000	–0.013**	–0.020**	–0.035**
	(0.0032)	(0.0056)	(0.0059)
State fixed effects	Yes	Yes	Yes
Constant	0.086**	0.16**	0.14**
	(0.011)	(0.014)	(0.017)
Adjusted R^2	0.98	0.98	0.96
Number of observations	200	200	200

Note: Numbers in parentheses are standard errors. The weight used is the number of households.
*Significantly different from zero with 90 percent confidence.
**Significantly different from zero with 95 percent confidence.
a. Dependent variables: Herfindahl concentration measures for households with children, poor households with children, and households with elderly householder.

**Table A-2. Do More Children Go to Private Schools in States with
Greater Local Control?[a]**

Explanatory variable	Weighted regressions with year and state fixed effects	
	1 *Percent private* *school enrollment*	*2* *Percent private* *school enrollment*
Share of school funding from local	0.0028	−0.0016
sources	(0.0060)	(0.0060)
Maximum inverted tax price	−0.015**	−0.0159*
	(0.0062)	(0.0084)
Median foundation tax rate	−0.00053**	−0.00066**
	(0.00024)	(0.00024)
Per pupil spending ($\times 10^{-3}$)		−0.0052*
		(0.0026)
Share of foreign-born population		−0.0997
		(0.0768)
Dummy year, 1980	0.013**	0.019**
	(0.0042)	(0.0044)
Dummy year, 1990	0.011**	0.026**
	(0.0035)	(0.0069)
Dummy year, 2000	0.020**	0.044**
	(0.0042)	(0.0093)
State fixed effects	Yes	Yes
Constant	0.1384**	0.162**
	(0.0093)	(0.015)
Adjusted R^2	0.89	0.89
Number of observations	200	200

Note: Numbers in parentheses are standard errors. The weight used is the number of children (0–17 years).
*Significantly different from zero with 90 percent confidence.
**Significantly different from zero with 95 percent confidence.
a. Dependent variable: share of private school enrollment.

Table A-3. Do More Households with Children Move to States with Greater Local Control?[a]

Explanatory variable	Percent change in number of households with children		
	1	*2*	*3*
Change in percent of school funding from local sources	0.030**	−0.077*	0.025
	(0.013)	(0.043)	(0.022)
Interaction of change in percent of school funding from local sources * Lagged per pupil spending ($\times 10^{-3}$)		0.025**	
		(0.0097)	
Change in maximum inverted tax price	−0.021	0.0047	−0.024
	(0.016)	(0.084)	(0.032)
Interaction of change in maximum inverted tax price * Lagged per pupil spending ($\times 10^{-3}$)		−0.0076	
		(0.027)	
Change in median foundation tax rate	0.00064	−0.00012	0.00026
	(0.00053)	(0.0025)	(0.0011)
Interaction of change in median foundation tax rate * Lagged per pupil spending ($\times 10^{-3}$)		0.00025	
		(0.00094)	
Lagged per pupil spending ($\times 10^{-3}$)	0.0066*	0.0033	0.025**
	(0.0036)	(0.0038)	(0.011)
Percent change in number of households	1.01**	1.01**	
	(0.035)	(0.035)	
Dummy year,1990	−0.064**	−0.055**	−0.22**
	(0.010)	(0.010)	(0.017)
Dummy year, 2000	0.041**	0.049**	−0.13**
	(0.012)	(0.013)	(0.031)
State fixed effects	No	No	Yes
Constant	−0.12**	−0.12**	0.11**
	(0.016)	(0.016)	(0.032)
Adjusted R^2	0.91	0.91	0.75
Number of observations	150	150	150

Note: Numbers in parentheses are standard errors.
*Significantly different from zero with 90 percent confidence.
**Significantly different from zero with 95 percent confidence.
a.. Dependent variables: percentage change in number of households with children.

Table A-4. Do More Poor Households with Children Move to States with Greater Local Control?[a]

Explanatory variable	Percent change in number of households with children		
	1	2	3
Change in percent of school funding from local sources	0.015 (0.056)	0.10 (0.19)	0.030 (0.060)
Interaction of change in percent of school funding from local sources * Lagged per pupil spending ($\times 10^{-3}$)		−0.021 (0.043)	
Change in maximum inverted tax price	0.0014 (0.070)	0.087 (0.37)	0.068 (0.090)
Interaction of change in maximum inverted tax price * Lagged per pupil spending ($\times 10^{-3}$)		−0.029 (0.12)	
Change in median foundation tax rate	0.0039* (0.0023)	0.0056 (0.011)	0.0022 (0.0029)
Interaction of change in median foundation tax rate * Lagged per pupil spending ($\times 10^{-3}$)		−0.00064 (0.0042)	
Lagged per pupil spending ($\times 10^{-3}$)	0.043** (0.015)	0.046** (0.017)	0.058* (0.032)
Percent change in number of households	0.45** (0.15)	0.44** (0.16)	
Dummy year, 1990	−0.020 (0.043)	−0.027 (0.046)	−0.10** (0.046)
Dummy year, 2000	−0.22** (0.053)	−0.23** (0.056)	−0.32** (0.085)
State fixed effects	No	No	Yes
Constant	−0.045 (0.068)	−0.049 (0.070)	0.044 (0.087)
Adjusted R^2	0.21	0.19	0.15
Number of observations	150	150	150

Note: Numbers in parentheses are standard errors.
*Significantly different from zero with 90 percent confidence.
**Significantly different from zero with 95 percent confidence.
a. Dependent variable: percentage change in number of poor households with children.

Comments

Caroline Hoxby: Christian A. L. Hilber and Christopher J. Mayer ask an important question: Do school finance laws affect where people live? In other words, if we pass a new school finance law in our state, should we expect a reshuffling of the population so that we will all have new neighbors? Will our state draw in certain people from other states or make certain people depart for other states? The answers to these questions are important because American states regularly revise their school finance laws and sometimes revise them in dramatic ways that might trigger sizable reshuffling. States' school finance formulas allocate $370 billion a year. To see how large an amount this is, compare Medicare at only $245 billion, all federal income support programs combined at only $330 billion, and national defense at a similar $376 billion. The amount of money affected by school finance laws is so large and the laws vary so widely, over time and among states, that school finance could easily be *the* government policy that affects where people live. This is not to say, of course, that other factors do not affect where people live. It is just that most of those other factors are not in policymakers' control.

Lurking in the background of this research is the implicit assertion that where people live *matters*. If neighbors do not have a causal effect on a person's outcomes, then it is unclear why we should care who is the neighbor of whom. Here it is important to distinguish between neighbors' correlations and neighbors' causal effects. We have a lot of evidence that there are correlations among neighbors; the evidence on neighbors' causal effects is limited. Indeed, some of the best research, based on the Moving to Opportunity experiment, suggests that neighbors' causal effects are very small.[38] The question of neighbor effects is beyond the scope of Hilber and Mayer's study or this comment, but it is important to flag the issue. We know that we care about whether someone is richer or poorer. It is not so obvious that we care about how people reshuffle themselves if there are no causal effects of sorting. After all, John Smith or Jane Doe is always *someone's* neighbor.

Hilber and Mayer test three hypotheses. First, do middle- and upper-income families prefer to live in states where school districts are relatively independent fiscally? The logic is that fiscally independent districts' resources tend to reflect the resources and tastes of the people who live in them. Therefore, an affluent, well-educated person living in a district with affluent, well-educated neighbors can probably obtain public schools that suit his desires. Conversely, if his district cannot spend money on its schools without giving the state a commensurate amount for other districts' schools, or if his district is forced by the state to spend the same amount as every other district, an affluent, well-educated person's local public schools may fall short of his desires. Indeed, he may abandon the expensive and frustrating task of trying to obtain public schools that suit him and may use private schools or move to another state instead.

The second hypothesis is that, in states that aggressively redistribute funds among their school districts, middle- and upper-income families and the elderly need not avoid living in districts with poor school-aged children as they might in states with financially independent districts. The logic behind this hypothesis is not so clear. If states that equalized school finance always "leveled up," then districts that served poor children would usually (though not always) look more attractive to middle- and upper-income families than they did before equalization.[39] However, more than half of school finance equalizations "level down" because their formulas contain parameters that implicitly penalize districts for higher spending.[40] After a leveling-down equalization such as the Serrano II equalization in California, well-off families have *more*, not less, reason

38. See Kling and Liebman (2004) and Katz, Liebman, Kling, and Sanbonmatsu (2004) for work based on the Moving to Opportunity experiments, in which poor households were given an incentive to move outside of poor neighborhoods.

39. Even this mild statement does not always hold for reasons described in the next paragraph.

40. See Hoxby (2001).

to avoid districts with poor children. Well-off parents do not think, "Our current school will spend less, but it will spend about the same as the school serving the poor children, so I am indifferent about which school my children attend." Instead, they think, "Our current school will spend less and have fewer resources to counteract deficiencies that children bring from home. Therefore, I am even more keen to have my child in a classroom with other children from affluent, well-educated parents." Essentially, when better-off families cannot get resources into their schools, they substitute good peers (which they still can get) for resources.

The logic behind the second hypothesis does not always work for another reason. In many school finance equalizations, the formula forces property tax rates to rise dramatically in property-poor districts.[41] Rising property tax rates tend to drive away, not attract, the elderly because they do not have schoolchildren who benefit from the higher spending that accompanies the higher tax rates. With rising property tax rates in property-poor districts, even better-off families with children may have more, not less, incentive to avoid property-poor districts. If better-off families would want to live in unusually nice houses in property-poor districts, then rising tax rates in those districts could easily mean that they would pay *more* for living there. We can only assert that better-off families with children will be more willing to live in property-poor districts after school finance equalization if they (the better-off families) were glad to live in houses that are typical of those districts.

Hilber and Mayer's third hypothesis is that, after a school finance equalization, fewer better-off families will want to send their children to private schools. This hypothesis is simply wrong for the vast majority of actual school equalizations, which nearly always raise the "price" that well-off families face for obtaining a resource-rich school. With the exception of a handful of equalizations in which the state depends exclusively on income and sales taxes for revenue, even leveling-up equalizations make richer families pay more for each dollar of public school spending relative to a dollar of private school spending. That is, school finance equalization nearly always lowers the relative price of private schools for the well-off population.

41. For instance, the so-called Robin Hood formula in Texas and New Jersey's most aggressive school finance formula both drove up property tax rates dramatically in property-poor districts. See Hoxby (2001, 2004).

After this review of the three hypotheses, it is easy for me to make the first of my comments about Hilber and Mayer's study. Their predictions are mainly right, which is good, but they are wrong for some outcomes and wrong for some families in some states. The reason that Hilber and Mayer sometimes make the wrong predictions is that they are trying to describe equalizations at the state level, when equalizations actually work at the district level. There is just no substitute for figuring out what incentives an equalization gives to each district. To do this, one needs to think about how the formulas' parameters apply at the district level. Probably the best way to generate predictions is to do as Nechyba does.[42] His basic method is to invent simple school finance formulas; make some assumptions about how people react to school spending, property tax, house prices, and peers; and use computable general equilibrium methods to simulate the effects of the invented formulas under a range of plausible assumptions. The alternative procedure is to be purely empirical: use real school finance formulas (not invented ones) and see how families, house prices, and districts react to them.

This brings me to the second of my comments. The district is the natural level of aggregation for a study of school finance. The outcomes that interest us are mainly at the district level. For instance, "How mixed, in terms of household income, is this school district following the school finance equalization?" The data that we need in order to create variables that describe the school finance formula are all district level data: property value per student, the local property tax rate, and so on. Hilber and Mayer make extra work for themselves by starting with data collected at the Census of Population and Housing place level (hereafter the census). I worry a fair amount about the representativeness of their sample. Since their balanced panel focuses exclusively on places that were populated enough in 1970 to have made it into the census summaries, one worries that their data underrepresent areas that were exurbia in 1970 but that are metropolitan now. What if inner-ring suburbs that have become more heterogeneous in income are overrepresented, while outer-ring suburbs that have been more affluent and homogeneous are underrepresented? The data could present an unbalanced picture of actual trends.

However, concerns about the representativeness of the sample are not my primary objection to place level data. My primary objection is simply that place level data make it hard to answer interesting questions and make it impossible to describe school finance formulas accurately. For instance, if I wanted to know whether affluent families move away from districts that have their spending capped, place data could not give me the answer because spending caps apply at the district level. If I wanted to know how property-rich but income-poor elderly people (who are quite common) react to a school finance formula that raises property tax rates in their district, place data could not give me the answer because property tax rates apply at the district level. Overall, Hilber and Mayer have done a great job with data on places. They describe them accurately and use them well. However, next time it would be easier to start with the four datasets that summarize the census at the school district level.[43]

Hilber and Mayer describe outcomes and predictions in terms of data "cells" at the state-year-affluence-elderliness level. On the whole, this is an excellent way to summarize the effects of school finance on how people locate. They have found a few, concise dimensions on which to measure sorting, and others should follow them in this approach, even if they use district data for its myriad advantages.

Because of problems with the predictions and the data, I am hesitant about some of Hilber and Mayer's results. The result that is probably most sound, because the hypothesis has the strongest logical underpinnings and is simplest to test, is that states that allow districts more fiscal independence have more middle- and upper-income households. The causality is probably in the direction Hilber and Mayer describe (taking away independence drives out better-off families), but the evidence on timing is too weak to rule out reverse causality (states with lots of better-off families make political decisions that keep local districts fiscally independent). If the causality runs from school finance to location decisions, then courts contemplating school finance need to be cautious about driving out the tax base on which the state depends. If the causality runs from location decisions through politics to school finance, then courts' interventions may be very helpful. The direction of causality is another item for Hilber and Mayer's future "to do" list.

School finance *is* complicated. The formulas can be difficult to understand. It is the nature of the formulas to have different effects on different districts. This makes them hard to summarize. One has always to remem-

---

43. See U.S. Department of Education (1994, 2003a, b, c).

ber that the formulas are largely about property values, *not* households' income. Households' incomes are easy because they are mainly exogenous, but property values react significantly when households move or when a state changes its school finance formula. Complicated or not, school finance is important. Economists really cannot let courts play with $370 billion a year and move households around without having any notion of what the consequences are. Ultimately, the data are so good and the variation in formulas is so great that research on school finance will deliver rich rewards. Hilber and Mayer have begun down a research path that will undoubtedly produce important results over the course of several studies.

Julie Berry Cullen: The authors provide an empirical exploration of issues that are at the heart of state and local public finance. They ask how two related but distinct factors—the degree of local control over spending and the extent of redistribution across localities—affect how individuals sort both across and within states. They use the school finance equalization movement as the source of variation in these two factors across places and time. This movement began in the 1970s and was a reaction to the striking disparities in per pupil expenditures and property tax burdens across high- and low-wealth communities under predominantly local finance. School finance became more centralized as states reduced inequities directly by imposing spending ceilings and floors and/or indirectly through tax and subsidy schemes.

The role of the two factors in determining *within-state* sorting derives from the Tiebout model. If individuals choose communities according to their tastes for local public goods, then factors that facilitate such sorting should lead to more complete sorting. Conversely, restrictions on local discretion, such as tax or spending limits, reduce the gains from conglomerating with others who have like tastes. Concentration according to willingness to pay will also fall if the form of implicit redistribution through state aid weakens the link between where one lives and how much one pays in taxes or receives in benefits. From these perspectives, the empirical analysis of changes in within-state concentration of various groups in response to changes in the net benefits of concentrating tests the basic force underlying the Tiebout model.

The companion analysis of *cross-state* migration patterns can be thought of as a test of one of the principles of optimal fiscal federalism.

The premise is that there are limits to the amount of redistribution that can be done at subnational levels of government. The simple reason is that individuals who are transferring resources to others on net can move away. States that implement school finance equalization that involves aggressive redistribution across individuals should experience outmigration among the cross-subsidizers.

Besides contributing to the broader literature on local public finance, this paper fits into a growing literature about general equilibrium responses to alternate school funding mechanisms. Although prior theoretical work has considered the relationship between school finance and household location choice, this is one of the first empirical studies to focus on this relationship. It makes a significant contribution as far as the scope of the question, and the primary weakness is the lack of attention to heterogeneity in the structure and content of the various school finance formulas. This inattention leads to hypotheses that are less refined and empirical constructs that are less meaningful than they could otherwise be.

Theoretical Issues

The main difficulty with the three hypotheses presented is that they are unlikely to generally hold across the wide variety of state school finance contexts. I focus on ambiguities within the two hypotheses regarding within-state mobility.

The first within-state hypothesis states that "in states with significant redistribution mechanisms, nonpoor households with children and elderly have fewer incentives to avoid low-income places." The authors do not provide a framework for readers to allow them to characterize more and less significant redistribution in ways that would be relevant for the mobility of these groups. I could imagine a school finance program that transferred more resources from high- to low-wealth districts than another but that provided greater incentives for individuals to sort according to income. It is not just the quantity of redistribution that matters, but the means by which this redistribution is undertaken (for example, by means of a state sales or income tax or by redirecting locally raised property tax revenues).

Besides the structure of the finance program mattering, the environment within which that program operates could be important. As an example, consider that state school finance policies target resources to communities with low property wealth rather than communities with low family income. The authors presume, as many proponents of school finance equalization (and theorists) have, that low-income individuals are disproportionately located in areas with low assessed property value per pupil. However, a large fraction of property wealth is commercial property, which tends to be located in urban areas. In a comprehensive evaluation of California's history with school finance equalization, Sonstelie and others discover that families from different places in the income distribution were relatively evenly distributed across localities of varying property wealth.[44] The disparities in per pupil spending by district wealth were not matched by disparities according to family income. If income and property wealth are not closely correlated, then interventions that redistribute resources according to property wealth should have little effect on the incentives for families to sort according to income. If income and property wealth are negatively correlated, school finance equalization policies could lead to *increased* sorting by income. Clearly, the initial conditions in a given state would determine the sign of the impact of a redistributive reform.

The second within-state hypothesis is that "in states with significant redistribution, nonpoor households with children have fewer incentives to avoid public schools." If Tiebout sorting and private schooling are substitutes and school finance equalization restricts Tiebout sorting, one would expect the opposite prediction. Yet, as the authors concede, there are several conflicting factors at play.

Those families that choose to send their children to private schools should locate in places where the tax burden is lowest. That means that changes in the level of spending at their neighborhood public school will affect a private school family's choice of sector only indirectly through the implications for the tax payments associated with living there—not directly through changes in the quality of *that* public school. To determine who might be drawn into the public sector, one would have to know how a school finance equalization policy affects the distribution of public school quality at next-best alternatives, wherever they may be, as well as the degree of double taxation associated with attending private school.

44. Sonstelie and others (2000).

Knowledge of the means through which equalization is achieved can provide useful information about likely private school enrollment responses. If equalization occurs primarily by lowering expenditures in previously high-spending districts, then presumably families in those districts could face both lower-quality public schooling alternatives and reduced opportunity costs to attending private school. This is exactly what happened in California, where the gap in per pupil expenditures across localities was virtually eliminated along with an overall decline in resources, and is a more natural explanation of the increase in private school enrollments than the one the authors provide (see note 22). In contrast, Michigan's recent school finance reform infused new resources into previously low-spending districts while leaving spending at other districts largely unaffected. Leveling-up reforms like this are more likely to lead to the reduced private school enrollment rates the authors expect. Although hypotheses about the average impact of heterogeneous redistributive policies are not particularly meaningful, less ambiguous predictions could be generated given a careful classification of equalization policies.

Empirical Issues

The main empirical results are based on regressions relating statewide concentration indexes for three types of households to three state school finance policy measures for the years 1970, 1980, 1990, and 2000. From specifications that include state and year effects, the authors uncover statistically significant relationships between relative changes in concentration and their measures of local control and redistribution. While the empirical results are intriguing, it is difficult to assign the desired interpretation to them.

Starting with the left-hand side of the equation, the dependent variables are not sufficient statistics for the kind of mobility the authors predict should be happening. For one, the Herfindahl indexes are defined based on underlying data for places and not school districts. They, therefore, incorporate deconcentration that takes place *within* the relevant jurisdictions while only deconcentration *across* these jurisdictions is of interest. And school districts can become more deconcentrated even if the underlying flows are completely inconsistent with changes in fiscal incentives. In the absence of disaggregated data, the authors could attempt to characterize the changes in the allocation of individuals across communities according to initial community characteristics to ensure that the flows are in the direction anticipated. For example, if school districts are ranked according to property wealth in the initial period, then Gini indexes derived from the fraction of each type of household in communities of ascending initial wealth could be calculated in subsequent years.[45]

The weakness with the key right-hand side variables is that they are not adequate to summarize the incentives for concentration across the demographic groups. Rather than simply being noisy indicators, these indicators could conceivably be even negatively correlated with the incentives they are meant to capture. To illustrate some of the key omissions, I outline the two main methods of state finance of elementary and secondary schools: foundation programs and guaranteed tax base programs. Foundation programs in their purest form guarantee a fixed amount of revenue per pupil (g) in return for a district levying a required minimum tax rate (t_f), so that per pupil aid is equal to: $a_i = g - t_f v_i$, where v_i is the district's per pupil property wealth. Guaranteed tax base (GTB) programs provide a guaranteed yield for each unit of local tax effort, so that per pupil aid is equal to: $t_i(v_m - v_i)$, where t_i is the local property tax rate and v_m is the guaranteed per pupil tax base. Each of these programs may or may not involve *recapture*, so that districts that would receive negative aid may or may not participate at all, and may or may not allow *local leeway* to set property tax rates without limit.

One of the three measures the authors include is the maximum inverted tax price, which is the maximum subsidy from a GTB program. This basically reflects the ratio of the guaranteed wealth level to the wealth of the poorest district. It is possible that a GTB with recapture could lead to a greater compression in tax burdens across communities than a GTB with a higher guaranteed tax base (and higher associated maximum subsidy) and no recapture. Not only would low-wealth districts be able to both spend more per pupil and reduce their tax rates, but high-wealth districts might also have to raise taxes to maintain spending.

45. Farnham and Sevak (2004) are conducting related work that looks directly at migration flows of the elderly. Using the University of Michigan's Health and Retirement Survey, they find that empty-nest movers who relocate within the same state are less able to reduce their exposure to local school taxes when strong equalization policies are in place.

Although the authors' measure captures how much less onerous living in a low-wealth district is, it misses how much less beneficial it is to live in a high-wealth district.

Ignoring the presence of local leeway leads to similar slippage between the underlying incentives and the measures included. A state with a lower foundation tax rate that also does not permit localities to raise revenue above that rate could be associated with fewer incentives for sorting than one that has a higher foundation rate but permits districts to tax themselves above that rate. The inclusion of the third measure, the fraction of revenues raised locally, helps to make these dissimilar district schemes somewhat more comparable. While these omitted variables and others (such as the existence of property tax circuit breakers for the elderly) are likely to be correlated with the included variables and currently confound the interpretation of the results, these program features could be incorporated in the authors' future work as a source of useful variation across states and demographic groups in the incentives to sort.

A final concern with the empirical analysis is that policy endogeneity makes it hard to tell whether state aid policies are determining residential location patterns or vice versa. As work by Loeb and Fernandez and Rogerson demonstrates, whether a state's median voter would prefer to finance local public schools through local or more centralized finance schemes depends on the distribution of income and property wealth across communities.[46] Thus changes in the concentration of groups across a state could change the identity or the preferred policy of the median voter. That the timing of the analysis is fairly crude, so that ten-year changes in school finance policy may reflect recently enacted or stale policy changes, heightens the possibility that the observed changes in concentration are driving the changes in school finance policy through public choice mechanisms, rather than the policy changes driving mobility as individuals "vote with their feet." Focusing on court-mandated reforms, instead of all movements in state school finance, could help the authors to get around this problem.

46. Loeb (2001); Fernandez and Rogerson (1999).

References

Barrow, Lisa, and Cecilia Elena Rouse. 2004. "Using Market Valuation to Assess the Importance and Efficiency of Public School Spending." *Journal of Public Economics* 88 (August): 1747–69.

Bénabou, Roland. 1993. "Workings of a City: Location, Education, and Production." *Quarterly Journal of Economics* 108 (August): 619–52.

———. 1996. "Heterogeneity, Stratification, and Growth: Macroeconomic Implications of Community Structure and School Finance." *American Economic Review* 86 (June): 584–609.

Bewley, Truman F. 1981. "A Critique of Tiebout's Theory of Local Public Expenditures." *Econometrica* 49 (May): 713–40.

Bradbury, Katharine L., Christopher J. Mayer, and Karl E. Case. 2001. "Property Tax Limits, Local Fiscal Behavior, and Property Values: Evidence from Massachusetts under Proposition 2½ ." *Journal of Public Economics* 80 (May): 287–312.

Burtless, Gary, ed. 1996. *Does Money Matter? The Effect of School Resources on Student Achievement and Adult Success.* Brookings.

Card, David, and Alan B. Krueger. 1992a. "Does School Quality Matter? Returns to Education and the Characteristics of Public Schools in the United States." *Journal of Political Economy* 100 (February): 1–40.

———. 1992b. "School Quality and Black-White Relative Earnings: A Direct Assessment." *Quarterly Journal of Economics* 107 (February): 152–200.

———. 1996a. "Labor Market Effects of School Quality: Theory and Evidence." In *Does Money Matter? The Effect of School Resources on Student Achievement and Adult Success,* edited by Gary Burtless, 97–140. Brookings.

———. 1996b. "School Resources and Student Outcomes: An Overview of the Literature and New Evidence from North and South Carolina." *Journal of Economic Perspectives* 10 (Autumn): 31–50.

Costa, Dora L., and Matthew E. Kahn. 2000. "Power Couples: Changes in The Locational Choice of the College Educated, 1940-1990." *Quarterly Journal of Economics* 115 (May): 1287–1315.

Downes, Thomas A., and Shane Greenstein. 1996. "Understanding the Supply Decision of Nonprofits: Modeling the Location of Private Schools." *RAND Journal of Economics* 27 (Summer): 365–90.

Downes, Thomas A., and Dana Schoenman. 1998. "School Finance Reform and Private School Enrollment: Evidence from California." *Journal of Urban Economics* 43 (May): 418–43.

Eberts, Randall W., and Timothy J. Gronberg. 1981. "Jurisdictional Homogeneity and the Tiebout Hypothesis." *Journal of Urban Economics* 10: 227–39.

Epple, Dennis, and Allan Zelenitz. 1981. "The Implications of Competition among Jurisdictions: Does Tiebout Need Politics?" *Journal of Political Economy* 89 (December): 1197–1217.

Epple, D., and T. Romer. 1991. "Mobility and Redistribution." *Journal of Political Economy* 99 (August): 828–58.

Farnham Martin, and Purvi Sevak. 2004. "State Fiscal Policy and Local Residential Sorting: Are Tiebout Voters Hobbled?" University of Michigan and Hunter College. Mimeo.

Fernandez, Raquel, and Richard Rogerson. 1998. "Public Education and Income Distribution: A Dynamic Quantitative Evaluation of Education-Finance Reform." *American Economic Review* 43 (September): 444–71.

———. 1999. *Equity and Resources: An Analysis of Education Finance Systems.* Working Paper 7111. Cambridge, Mass.: National Bureau of Economic Research.

———. 2001. "Sorting and Long-Run Inequality." *Quarterly Journal of Economics* 116 (August): 1305–41.

Fischel, William A. 2001. "Homevoters, Municipal Corporate Governance, and the Benefit View of the Property Tax." *National Tax Journal* 54 (March): 157–73.

———. 2002. "An Economic Case against Vouchers: Why Local Public Schools Are a Local Public Good." Economics Department Working Paper 02-01. Dartmouth.

Gramlich, Edward E., and Daniel L. Rubinfeld. 1982. "Micro Estimates of Public Spending Demand Functions and Tests of the Tiebout and Median-Voter Hypothesis." *Journal of Political Economy* 90 (June): 536–59.

Hanushek, Eric A. 1986. "The Economics of Schooling: Production and Efficiency in Public Schools." *Journal of Economic Literature* 24 (September): 1141–77.

Harris, Amy R., William N. Evans, and Robert M. Schwab. 2001. "Education Spending in an Aging America." *Journal of Public Economics* 81 (September): 449–72.

Henderson, J. Vernon. 1985. "The Tiebout Model: Bring Back the Entrepreneurs." *Journal of Political Economy* 93 (April): 248–64.

Hilber, Christian A., and Christopher J. Mayer. 2002. "Why Do Households without Children Support Local Public Schools? Linking House Price Capitalization to School Spending." Research Working Paper 02/10. Federal Reserve Bank of Philadelphia.

Hoxby, Caroline M. 1999. "The Productivity of Schools and Other Local Public Goods Producers." *Journal of Public Economics* 74 (January): 1–30.

———. 2000. "Does Competition among Public Schools Benefit Students and Taxpayers?" *American Economic Review* 90 (December): 1209–38.

———. 2001. "All School Finance Equalizations Are Not Created Equal." *Quarterly Journal of Economics* 116 (November): 1189–1231.

———. 2004. "Robin Hood and His Not-So-Merry Plan." Working Paper. Harvard University.

Hoyt, W. H., and S. S. Rosenthal. 1997. "Household Location and Tiebout: Do Families Sort According to Preferences for Locational Amenities?" *Journal of Urban Economics* 42: 159–78.

Katz, Lawrence, Jeffrey Liebman, Jeffrey Kling, and Lisa Sanbonmatsu. 2004. "Moving to Opportunity or Moving to Tranquility? The Effects of Neighborhoods on Low-income Household Heads." Working Paper 481. Princeton University.

Kling, Jeffrey, and Jeffrey Liebman. 2004. "Experimental Analysis of Neighborhood Effects on Youth." Working Paper 483. Princeton University.

Kremer, Michael. 1997. "How Much Does Sorting Increase Inequality?" *Quarterly Journal of Economics* 112 (February): 115–39.

Loeb, Susanna. 2001. "Estimating the Effects of School Finance Reform: A Framework for a Federalist System." *Journal of Public Economics* 80 (2): 225–47.

Massey, Douglas S., and Garcia Espana. 1987. "The Social Process of International Migration." *Science* 237: 733–38.

Mincer, Jacob. 1978. "Family Migration Decisions." *Journal of Political Economy* 86 (October): 749–73.

Nechyba, Thomas. 1999. "School Finance Induced Migration and Stratification Patterns: The Impact of Private School Vouchers." *Journal of Public Economic Theory* 1 (January): 5–50.

———. 2000. "Mobility, Targeting, and Private-School Vouchers." *American Economic Review* 90 (March): 130–46.

———. 2002. "School Finance, Spatial Income Segregation, and the Nature of Communities." Working Paper 02-17. School of Economics. Duke University.

———. 2003a. "What Can Be (and What Has Been) Learned from General Equilibrium Simulation Models of School Finance?" *National Tax Journal* 56 (June): 387–414.

———. 2003b. "Centralization, Fiscal Federalism and Private School Attendance." *International Economic Review* 44 (February): 179–204.

Oates, William. 1972. *Fiscal Federalism.* Harcourt Brace Jovanovich.

Poterba, James. 1997. "Demographic Structure and the Political Economy of Public Education." *Journal of Public Policy and Management* 16 (January): 48–66.

Rhode, Paul W., and Koleman S. Strumpf. 2003. "Assessing the Importance of Tiebout Sorting: Local Heterogeneity from 1850 to 1990." *American Economic Review* 93 (December): 1648–77.

Sonstelie Jon, Eric Brunner, and Ken Ardon. 2000. *For Better or for Worse? School Finance Reform in California.* Public Policy Institute of California Report. San Francisco.

Tiebout, Charles. 1956. "A Pure Theory of Local Expenditures." *Journal of Political Economy* 64 (October): 416–24.

Topel, Robert H., and Michael P. Ward. 1992. "Job Mobility and the Careers of Young Men." *Quarterly Journal of Economics* 107 (May): 439–79.

U.S. Department of Education, National Center for Education Statistics. 1994. *School District Data Book: 1990 Census School District Special Tabulation.* Arlington, Va.: MESA Group.

———. 2003a. *School District Demographics: 2000 Census School District Special Tabulation* (electronic file).

———. 2003b. *1970 Census Fourth Count (Population): School District Data Tape* (electronic file). ICPSR version. Washington, DC: U.S. Department of

Education, National Center for Education Statistics (producer, 1970). Ann Arbor, Mich.: Inter-university Consortium for Political and Social Research (distributor, 2003).

U.S. Office of Education. National Center for Education Statistics. 2003c. *National Institute of Education (NIE) Special Tabulations and 1970 Census Fifth Count Data File* (computer file). ICPSR version. Ann Arbor, Mich.: Inter-university Consortium for Political and Social Research (distributor). Washington: AUI Policy Research (producer, 1981).

Van Hook, Jennifer, and Kelly S. Balistreri. 2002. "Diversity and Change in the Institutional Context of Immigrant Adaptation: California Schools 1985-2000." *Demography* 39 (November): 639–54.

ERICA GREULICH
University of California, Berkeley

JOHN M. QUIGLEY
University of California, Berkeley

STEVEN RAPHAEL
University of California, Berkeley

The Anatomy of Rent Burdens: Immigration, Growth, and Rental Housing

During the past three decades, shelter payments for renter households have become more burdensome, especially for poor households and households residing in large urban areas. Between 1970 and 2000, the median rent burden increased from 20 to 25 percent of income. For the poorest fifth of households, the proportion of income devoted to housing increased from 0.51 to 0.55. Concurrently, the proportion of low-income households devoting greater then 30 percent of their income to housing expenditures increased from 67 percent to 79 percent.[1] There have been no comparable increases in housing expenditures among high-income renters or high-income homeowners.

During this period, the foreign-born population residing in the United States has experienced sustained growth and has contributed disproportionately to overall population growth. In 1970 the foreign born accounted for 4.7 percent of the resident population of the United States. As of 2000, this figure had increased to 10.4 percent. In these three decades, the resident immigrant population increased by 16.2 million persons, accounting for roughly one-quarter of overall net population growth in the United States.[2]

Several factors, in combination, suggest that international migration may affect the housing outcomes of many households headed by the native born. Within the United States, the foreign born are disproportion-

1. Quigley and Raphael (2004).
2. U.S. Census Bureau (2001).

149

ately concentrated in six states (in order of importance, California, New York, Florida, Texas, New Jersey, and Illinois) and a handful of metropolitan areas. The concentration of immigrants in selected metropolitan areas coupled with very low housing supply elasticities implies that a large influx of immigrants may result in substantial increases in housing prices and rents in those areas.

Moreover, recent immigrants to the United States are, on average, considerably less educated than natives, have lower incomes, and are more likely to reside in rental housing.[3] Immigrant households are thus likely to compete for housing with low-income natives—the very group that has experienced increasing rent burdens in recent decades.

The effect of immigration on housing prices depends on two factors: the extent to which the U.S. destination choices of international immigrants are exogenous to the current economic conditions at those destinations; and the speed at which population flows among U.S. cities and housing supplies in those cities adjust to variations in exogenous immigration. There is a wealth of literature suggesting that the destinations chosen by international immigrants are heavily dependent on noneconomic factors—the prior decisions of extended family members and the prior existence of enclaves of immigrants from the same country or region of origin, speaking the same language, with the same cultural tradition. Documentation of these locational proclivities among cities and regions (but also across neighborhoods) exists for nineteenth-century immigration to the United States and for twentieth-century migration.[4] Current U.S. immigration policy, with its explicit preference for family reunification, suggests that the choice of destination for new immigrants is less responsive to economic conditions at the destination than would be expected on the basis of a utility-maximizing calculus explicitly taking housing costs into account.[5]

There is convincing evidence that large-scale international immigration to an exogenously determined destination *does* affect housing prices in the short run. Independent studies by Susin and Saiz analyzed the effects of the Mariel Boatlift, in which 125,000 Cubans migrated to

3. Borjas (1999).
4. For nineteenth-century immigration see, for example, Quigley (1972), and for twentieth-century migration see Duncan and Lieberson (1959).
5. Roback (1982).

Miami over a five-month period in 1980.[6] Both authors found a consequent rise in rental housing prices in Miami, especially for lower-quality housing in minority neighborhoods. These price changes were observed over a relatively short time interval, 1979 to 1983.

Over a longer period, it is less clear that exogenous levels of immigration affect price levels. Indeed, in a model of systems of cities, the effect of an exogenous shock of international migration to housing prices in a given city must be vanishingly small.[7] In the absence of transaction costs, the effects of an exogenous increase in immigration to a single city will be partially offset by outmigration of both the native born and earlier cohorts of immigrants. The effects of immigration will also be partially offset by increases in housing supplies. In equilibrium, the utilities of residents with the same endowments must equalize across all cities. Thus an exogenous, immigration-induced population increase to one city will eventually decrease the utility of each resident (in all cities) by a very small amount.[8]

Research on the determinants of the price of low-quality housing has focused largely on the effects of zoning and land use regulation, increasing income inequality, and the profitability of constructing low-quality housing.[9] With the exception of the work by Susin and Saez, however, there has been little research on immigrant housing consumption patterns and the link between international immigration and the price of urban housing.[10] In this paper, we investigate the effects of the growth in the immigrant population during the past two decades on the housing consumption opportunities of native-born renter households.

We begin with a brief description of the evolution of rent burdens across the largest U. S. metropolitan areas (MSAs) during the past two decades. From the Public Use Microdata Sample (PUMS) of the census, we estimate the distribution of rent burdens for each metropolitan area in

6. Susin (2001); Saiz (2003a).

7. See, for example, Fujita, Krugman, and Mori (1999).

8. If housing supply is not perfectly elastic, or if the increase in aggregate population increases aggregate transport costs more than proportionately, the utilities of residents with the same endowments will decline. But unless immigration is large relative to the number of households in the system, this reduction in individual well-being will be quite small. See Abdel-Rahman and Anas (forthcoming) for an extensive review of these models.

9. Malpezzi and Green (1996); O'Flaherty (1996); Ohls (1975).

10. Susin (2001); Saiz (2003a, 2003b). There is, however, at least one recent analysis of immigrant homeownership propensities. See Borjas (2002).

1980, 1990, and 2000. We investigate the shapes of these distributions and their changes across MSAs and decade, separately for all renter households and for poor renter households. We also present a focused analysis of rent burdens in five metropolitan areas with large immigrant populations.

Next, we describe and analyze the housing consumption patterns of immigrants. Using a synthetic cohort framework, we assess the extent to which the housing conditions of immigrants converge to those of the native born as they spend more time in the United States. We model the empirical relationship between housing characteristics and the nativity status of the household head and use this empirical model to identify and describe those native households that are most and least likely to compete with immigrants in the housing market.

Finally, we test for a relationship between the proportion of an MSA's population that is immigrant and a host of housing outcomes for native households. We present estimates using cross-sectional analysis and an analysis of within-MSA changes. We present separate estimates for native households with high and low probabilities of competing with immigrants for housing.

In the cross section, we find that the monthly housing expenses of natives are higher in metropolitan areas with large immigrant populations. However, these marginal effects are comparable both for native households in direct competition with immigrants and for native households unlikely to compete with immigrants in the housing market, suggesting that housing in immigrant cities is more expensive for reasons that are distinct from the issue of immigration. Moreover, while average rents paid by native households increase with the proportion of immigrants in a given metropolitan area, the same is not true for rent-to-income ratios. In fact, there is no within-MSA relationship between rent burdens and the relative size of the immigration population. Thus, based on housing expenditures, there is little evidence supporting the contention that the level of immigration adversely affects the housing outcomes of the native-born population.

We do, however, find that native households in metropolitan areas with high proportions of immigrants consume less housing and are more likely to reside in crowded conditions compared with native-born households in metropolitan areas with relatively small immigrant populations. This result holds in the analysis of cross-sectional variation as well as the analysis of changes within MSAs. In cross-section regressions, the relationship between the proportion immigrant and these measures of housing consumption is considerably stronger for those native-born households who are more likely to be in competition with immigrants in the housing market. This relative pattern, however, does not hold when we estimate the model using decade-level changes in the dependent and explanatory variables.

Rent Burdens in U.S. Metropolitan Areas

We extracted each household's income and its monthly rent from the Public Use Microdata Samples (PUMS) of the 1980, 1990, and 2000 censuses, thus permitting us to estimate the complete distribution of rent burdens (that is, rent-to-income levels) for the 106 largest metropolitan areas (MSAs) during two decades.[11]

The distribution of the median rents across these MSAs, reported in figure A-1 in the appendix to this paper, has changed substantially during this time period. Median rent-to-income ratios increased between 1980 and 1990. In fact, three-quarters of these MSAs experienced increases in median rent burdens during the 1980s.[12] Although the mode of this distribution increased further during the 1990s, median rent burdens declined in the 1990s in about 60 percent of these MSAs.

The pattern of changes in median rent burdens for poor households during this period is similar. Although the distribution of median rent burdens for the poor is centered on 0.60 as opposed to 0.25 for all renters, this distribution shifted slightly to the right during the 1980s and to the left during the 1990s.

Figure 1 summarizes changes in the median rent burdens in the largest U.S. metropolitan areas during the past two decades. The figure plots the 1980–90 changes in median rent burden versus the 1990–2000 changes for each MSA. Figure 1, part A, reports the changes for all renters, and

11. This analysis is based on the 5 percent PUMS samples from the 1980 and 1990 censuses and the one-percent PUMS sample from the 2000 Census. The 2000 sample necessarily restricts our analysis to 106 MSAs, but these account for 56 percent of the native-born population and 84 percent of the immigrant population in 2000.

12. The distribution of rent burdens for these MSAs in 1990 stochastically dominates the distribution in 1980.

Figure 1. Changes in Median Rent Burdens, 1980–90, versus Changes to Median Rent Burdens, 1990–2000

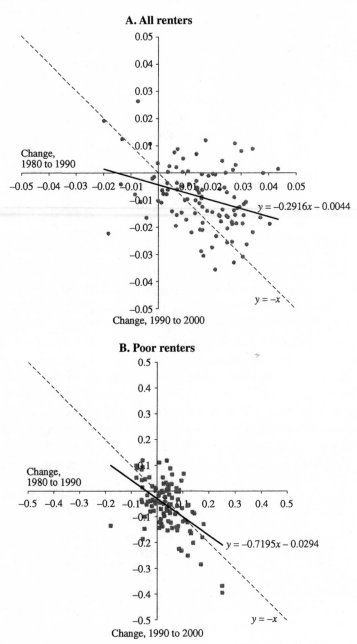

A. All renters

Change, 1980 to 1990

$y = -0.2916x - 0.0044$

$y = -x$

Change, 1990 to 2000

B. Poor renters

Change, 1980 to 1990

$y = -0.7195x - 0.0294$

$y = -x$

Change, 1990 to 2000

Note: 106 largest metropolitan statistical areas (MSAs).

figure 1, part B, reports the changes for renters with incomes below the poverty line. As indicated in figure 1, part A, there are few MSAs where median rent burdens declined during the 1980s. But it is also clear that there were more pronounced declines in rent burdens during the 1990s in those MSAs in which there had been more pronounced increases during the 1980s. This is true for more than three-quarters of the MSAs.

This mean reversion across MSAs is even more pronounced for poor renters (figure 1, part B). Larger increases in MSA median rent burdens for poor households in the 1980s are associated with larger decreases in the 1990s.

Individual Metropolitan Areas with Large Immigrant Populations

The immigrant population in the United States is heavily concentrated in a handful of large metropolitan areas. Thus, to the extent that immigration affects the rent burdens of the native born, one would expect to observe changes in the distributions of rent-to-income ratios in metropolitan areas with large immigrant populations. We explore this question more systematically later; here we simply describe the evolution of rent burdens in five principal urban destinations for immigrants: New York City, Los Angeles, Houston, Miami, and Chicago. These MSAs collectively accounted for roughly 45 percent of the foreign-born population in the United States in 2000.

Figure 2 presents frequency distributions of rent-to-income ratios for all renters in these metropolitan areas. With the exception of the distribution for New York, the distributions of rent burdens were quite stable across decades. In New York City, the variance of the distribution of rent ratios increased in each decade since 1980. However, there is no evidence of a substantial shift. In Los Angeles, the rent burden distribution shifted to the right during the 1980s and receded slightly during the 1990s. A similar pattern is observed for Chicago. For Houston and Miami, there were no apparent changes in the distribution of rent burdens between 1980 and 2000.

These patterns also appear in the median rent-to-income ratios for these cities. The median ratio for New York increased slightly between 1980 and 1990, from 0.24 to 0.25, and then remained constant through 2000. Los Angeles experienced an increase in median rent burdens during the 1980s, from 0.26 to 0.28, and then a decrease of 0.01 during the 1990s, as did Miami (0.28, 0.30, and 0.29 for 1980, 1990, and 2000, respectively). Chicago experienced the largest increase in rent burdens

**Figure 2. Frequency Distribution of Rent Burdens for Metropolitan Areas
with Large Immigrant Populations, 1980, 1990, and 2000**

A. New York

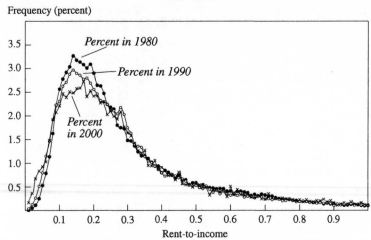

B. Los Angeles

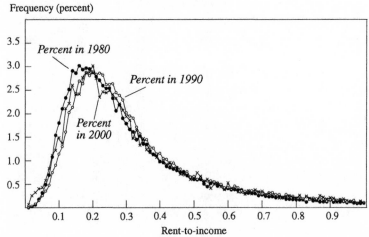

Figure 2. Frequency Distribution of Rent Burdens for Metropolitan Areas with Large Immigrant Populations, 1980, 1990, and 2000 (continued)

C. Houston

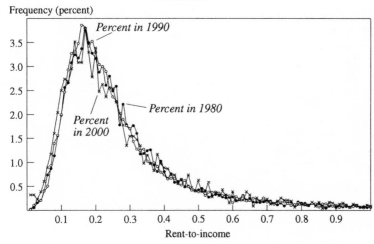

D. Miami

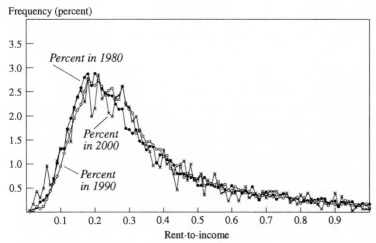

**Figure 2. Frequency Distribution of Rent Burdens for Metropolitan Areas
with Large Immigrant Populations, 1980, 1990, and 2000 (continued)**

E. Chicago

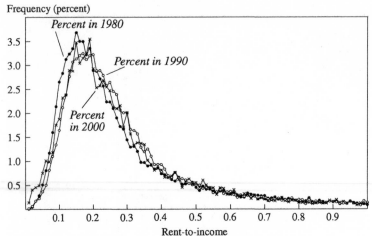

during the 1980s (from 0.22 to 0.25) before a small decline in the 1990s
(to 0.24). The median rent ratio in Houston was stable during the twenty-
year period. Thus, for these heavily immigrant cities, there are no notable
shifts in the rent-to-income distribution during the two-decade period
when their immigrant population grew substantially.

Of course, these patterns may simply be dominated by factors external
to housing markets. For all metropolitan areas, the declines in the median
rent burdens for the poor occurred largely during the 1990s, a period
when the poverty rates declined, and the incomes of the poor increased.
In an analysis of the national distribution of rent-to-income ratios,
Quigley and Raphael show that income growth among the poor lowered
rent burdens, holding the rental distribution constant.[13] Nonetheless, the
patterns in figure 2 suggest that if immigration had any effect on rent burdens in these five cities, the effect was swamped by other factors.

Figures 3 through 6 suggest the importance of several other factors
affecting rent burdens in the 106 largest metropolitan areas. These scatter
plots represent the bivariate relationship between rent burdens and four
factors affecting housing costs: median incomes, new construction,

13. Quigley and Raphael (2004).

Figure 3. Median Rent Burdens versus Index of Regulatory Stringency (Malpezzi Index), 106 MSAs in 1980, 1990, and 2000

Median rent/income

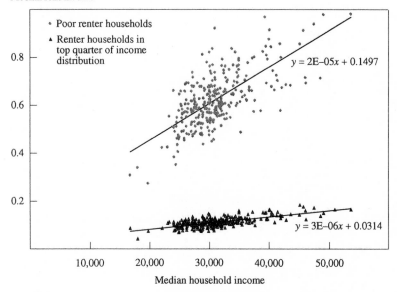

Median household income

recent immigration, and the regulatory stringency of rules governing housing supply.

Figure 3, based on 106 MSAs observed in three censuses, demonstrates that rent-to-income ratios tend to be higher in high-income MSAs. This positive relationship is weak among high-income renters but quite strong for poor renters. Figure 4 assesses whether MSAs where larger proportions of the housing stock are relatively new have lower rent burdens than areas where the housing stock is older. Presumably, new construction in the housing stock reflects greater price sensitivity in housing supply. For high-income renters, there is no relationship between rent burdens and the proportion of the housing stock that is new. For poor households, there is a clearer relationship—a newer housing stock is associated with lower rent burdens for the poor.

Figure 5 plots the bivariate relationship between rent ratios and the fraction of households headed by recent immigrants. Again, there is a weak positive relationship for high-income renters but a much stronger positive relationship for poor renters. Finally, figure 6 relates median rent

**Figure 4. Median Rent Burdens versus Fraction of Newly Built Dwellings,
106 MSAs in 1980, 1990, and 2000[a]**

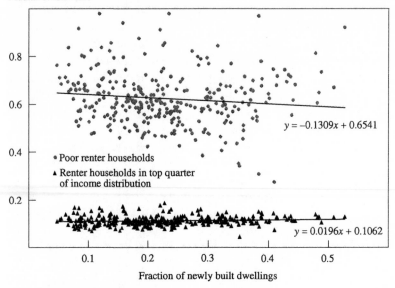

Median rent/income

$y = -0.1309x + 0.6541$

• Poor renter households

▲ Renter households in top quarter
  of income distribution

$y = 0.0196x + 0.1062$

Fraction of newly built dwellings

a. Fraction of dwellings built in past decade.

ratios to the Malpezzi measure of regulatory stringency in building and
residential construction.[14] Metropolitan areas where regulation inhibits
the creation of new housing are those where the rent burdens of the poor
are highest.

The figures suggest that all four factors may have significant impacts
on local rent burdens, especially those of the poor. The relationship
between the proportion of immigrant households and rent burdens is particularly strong for poor renter households. Although figure 2 shows only
small changes in rent burdens in the five largest immigrant-receiving
cities during this period of large-scale immigration, comparisons of
immigrant cities versus nonimmigrant cities reveal a larger differential.
Thus we now turn to a more thorough analysis of immigrant housing
consumption patterns and their impacts on housing outcomes for native-
born households.

14. This measure, see Malpezzi (1996), is only available for the decade of the 1990s.
The scatter diagram in figure 6 thus has only 106 points, rather than 318. A higher index
implies more stringent regulations.

**Figure 5. Median Rent Burdens versus Fraction of New Immigrants,
106 MSAs in 1980, 1990, and 2000[a]**

Median rent/income

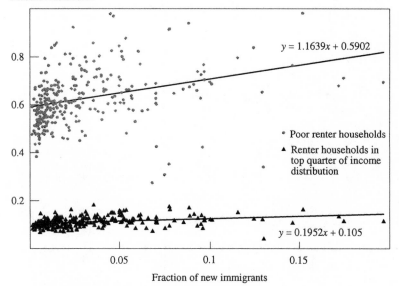

Fraction of new immigrants

a. Fraction of households headed by immigrant arriving in past decade.

Immigrant Housing Patterns and their Convergence
to those of Native Households

A comparison of the conditions under which immigrants and natives
are housed serves two purposes. First, it documents one aspect of the
socioeconomic assimilation experienced by immigrants as their duration
of residency in the United States increases. Several studies document the
degree to which immigrant earnings converge toward those of natives.
There is some evidence documenting the rate at which immigrant homeownership rates converge toward the relatively high homeownership
rates of the native born.[15] We update and extend this research on the
assimilation of the foreign born by documenting the convergence in
housing consumption through 2000 and by considering important dimensions of this convergence beyond tenure choice.

15. For immigrant earnings see Borjas (1985, 1995); Cortes (2004); for homeownership see Myers and Lee (1996, 1998); Borjas (2002).

Figure 6. Median Rent Burdens versus Index of Regulatory Stringency (Malpezzi Index), 106 MSAs in 1980, 1990, and 2000

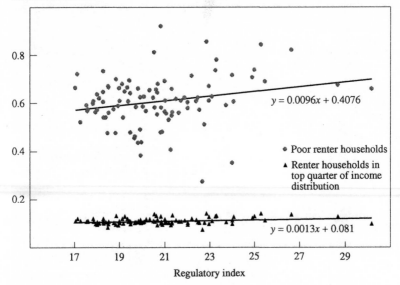

Median rent/income

$y = 0.0096x + 0.4076$

• Poor renter households

▲ Renter households in top quarter of income distribution

$y = 0.0013x + 0.081$

Regulatory index

Second, the comparison of immigrant and native housing consumption patterns reveals the extent to which immigrants compete with natives for different kinds of housing. The degree of intergroup competition will depend on the degree of similarity between housing demands and housing consumption outcomes. The following comparisons assess the extent of overlap. They also facilitate the identification of those native households that are most likely to compete with immigrants for housing.

Table 1 summarizes housing consumption outcomes for immigrant households and native households in 2000.[16] Immigrant households are further stratified by the year of arrival of the household head in the United States. The table reveals several notable differences between the housing patterns of immigrants and natives. First, immigrants are considerably less likely than natives to own their residences. While 69 percent of native households are homeowners, slightly more than half of immigrant households are homeowners. Cohorts of immigrants arriving earlier

16. Households are defined as "immigrant" if the household head is foreign born and as "native" if the household head was born in the United States.

Table 1. Average Housing Consumption Characteristics for Immigrant and Native Households, 2000

	Arrival of immigrant households			*Native households*
	1991 to 2000	*1981 to 1990*	*Before 1981*	
A. Fraction				
Fraction of owner-occupants	0.233	0.439	0.650	0.686
Number of rooms				
One	0.109	0.073	0.038	0.015
Two	0.199	0.154	0.081	0.036
Three	0.211	0.198	0.147	0.083
Four	0.191	0.166	0.146	0.148
Five	0.129	0.155	0.183	0.213
Six	0.072	0.111	0.159	0.198
Seven	0.040	0.062	0.104	0.132
Eight	0.025	0.041	0.071	0.089
Nine or more	0.023	0.039	0.069	0.086
Number of bedrooms				
None	0.133	0.104	0.057	0.020
One	0.324	0.255	0.172	0.115
Two	0.301	0.276	0.259	0.270
Three	0.165	0.231	0.321	0.413
Four	0.062	0.106	0.149	0.149
Five or more	0.015	0.026	0.041	0.032
Number of families in unit				
One	0.806	0.847	0.908	0.903
Two	0.132	0.113	0.076	0.083
Three or more	0.034	0.023	0.011	0.009
Units in structure				
Single-family	0.291	0.464	0.606	0.668
Mobile home	0.037	0.036	0.032	0.073
Two to four	0.165	0.153	0.113	0.081
More than four	0.591	0.413	0.280	0.192
Complete kitchen	0.985	0.986	0.991	0.994
Complete plumbing	0.987	0.983	0.991	0.995
B. Number				
Persons per room				
25th percentile	0.500	0.571	0.333	0.286
50th percentile	1.000	1.000	0.500	0.400
75th percentile	1.333	1.500	1.000	0.600

Source: Figures tabulated from the 2000 One Percent Public Use Microdata Sample (PUMS) from the 2000 Census. Classification of households is based on the immigrant status and year of arrival of the household head.

have higher homeownership rates than cohorts arriving later. These differences may reflect the effect of time in the United States on the likelihood of homeownership (and thus the process of assimilation along this dimension) or systematic differences among cohorts in the economic determinants of home purchases. We return to this question shortly.

Immigrants and natives reside in dwellings of different sizes. Immigrant households generally occupy smaller units than natives, although the differences between the distributions of rooms and bedrooms consumed narrow as immigrants' time in the United States increases. Given that immigrant households are somewhat larger than native households, the smaller unit sizes of immigrants translate directly into a greater likelihood of overcrowding.[17] The median number of persons per room is 1.0 for immigrant households arriving after 1980, 0.5 for immigrants arriving before 1980, and 0.4 for native households.

There are also substantial differences in the likelihood of residing in a single-family detached structure. Only 29 percent of the most recent immigrants reside in single-family detached housing. This figure is larger for immigrants arriving during the 1980s (46 percent) and for immigrants arriving before 1980 (61 percent) but is still lower than the comparable rate for natives (67 percent). Conversely, immigrant households are more likely to reside in large, multiunit structures. While only 19 percent of native households reside in structures with more than four units, 59 percent of immigrants arriving during the 1990s, 41 percent of immigrants arriving during the 1980s, and 28 percent of immigrants arriving before 1980 reside in such structures.

Finally, there are only small differences in the proportion of immigrant- and native-rented units with complete kitchen and plumbing facilities. By the end of the twentieth century, complete kitchen and plumbing facilities are nearly universal.

As noted, differences by arrival cohort may reflect one dimension of a broad assimilation process among immigrants, one in which housing consumption patterns converge toward those of natives over time. Alternatively, the cross-cohort differences in housing outcomes may reflect differences across cohorts in the economic determinants of housing con-

17. The average household size in 2000 was 3.3 for immigrants arriving between 1991 and 2000, 3.9 for immigrants arriving between 1981 and 1990, 3.0 for immigrant households arriving prior to 1980, and 2.5 for native households (authors' calculations with PUMS microdata, 2000).

sumption. Cross-cohort differences in demand may arise from cross-cohort changes in the skill endowments of immigrants and changes in the labor markets in which they compete. Thus cohort effects may create the impression of convergence in housing consumption when little assimilation is actually taking place.[18]

Figures 7, 8, and 9 present synthetic cohort estimates reporting changes in housing outcomes for immigrants with time in the United States.[19] These synthetic cohorts track immigration cohorts across separate censuses. We use data on year of immigration and age to create a longitudinal estimate of the relationship between time in the United States and measures of housing consumption. For example, figure 7 shows homeownership rates for immigrant household heads aged 25 to 34 years at time of arrival, who arrived between 1965 and 1969, at four points in time (1970, 1980, 1990, and 2000). For subsequent censuses, we age the cohort accordingly. Thus the arrival cohort extracts are restricted to those aged 35 to 44 in the 1980 Census, 45 to 54 in the 1990 Census, and 55 to 64 in the 2000 Census. We impose analogous restrictions on the 1975–79, 1985–89, and 1995–99 arrival cohorts.

As shown in panel A, homeownership rates for young immigrants increase sharply during the first decade after arrival and continue to increase in subsequent decades. After a decade in the United States, immigrant homeownership rates for all cohorts triple or quadruple, but the levels remain lower for more recent immigrants than for earlier cohorts. The homeownership rate for the 1965–69 arrival cohort rises from 12.8 per-

18. Borjas (1985, 1995, 1999) documents trends in the absolute and relative educational attainment of immigrant arrival cohorts in the United States. Overall, average educational attainment of subsequent immigrant cohorts arriving since 1965 has increased, with the proportion that are high school dropouts declining and the proportion with a college degree or more increasing. However, the increase in average educational attainment observed for immigrants is considerably smaller than the comparable increases observed among the native population. Consequently, average earnings differentials (measured at either the hourly or annual level) between immigrants and natives have widened over the past three decades. Most of this increase can be explained by the increase in the educational attainment differential between natives and immigrants. Most of the increase in the educational attainment differential is explained by a shift in the national origin composition of the immigrant inflow into the United States from predominantly western European to predominantly Asian and Latin American.

19. The application of synthetic cohorts in this context was first applied by Borjas (1985) in an analysis of convergence in the wages of immigrant and native workers. This technique has now become a standard for analyzing changes in economic outcomes for immigrants with time in the United States.

Figure 7. Measures of Convergence in Home Ownership Rates

A. Immigrant homeownership rates, by census year and arrival cohort, aged 25 to 34 at census year of arrival

Proportion home ownership

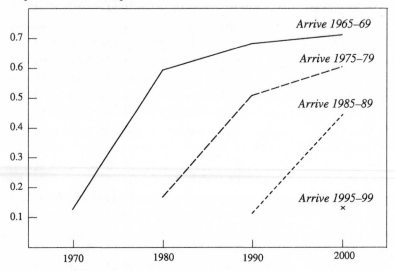

B. Difference in homeownership rate between immigrants and native households of similar ages, by arrival cohort and census year

Native minus immigrant

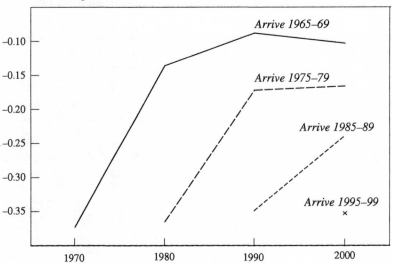

Figure 8. Measures of Convergence in the Proportion Residing in Crowded Conditions

A. Proportion of immigrants residing in crowded conditions, by census year and arrival cohort, aged 25 to 34 at census year of arrival

Proportion in crowded conditions

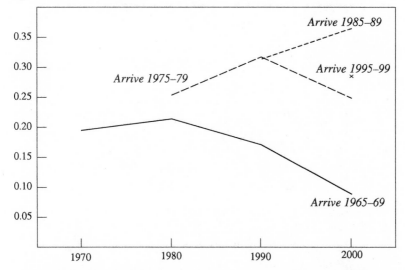

B. Difference in the proportion in crowded conditions between immigrants and native households of similar ages, by arrival cohort and census year

Native minus immigrant

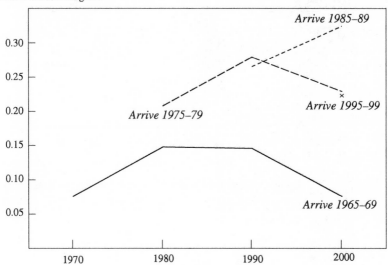

**Figure 9. Measures of Convergence in the Proportion Residing
in Single-Family Structures**

**A. Proportion of immigrants residing in single-family structures, by census year
and arrival cohort, aged 25 to 34 at census year of arrival**

Proportion residing in single-family structures

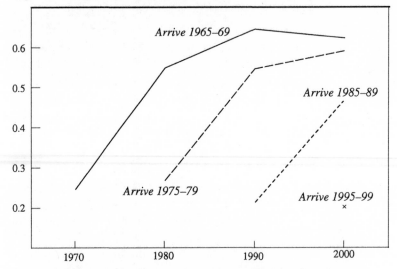

**B. Difference in the proportion residing in single-family structures
between immigrants and native households of similar ages,
by arrival cohort and census year**

Native minus immigrant

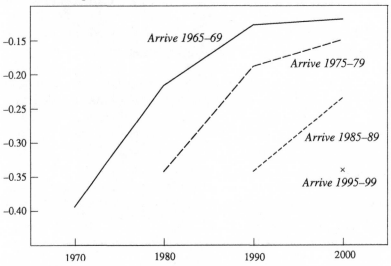

cent to 68.2 percent after two decades and 71.2 percent after three decades. For the 1975–79 cohort, the homeownership rate rises from 16.9 percent to 60.4 percent after two decades in the United States.

Figure 7 also reports the difference in homeownership rates between immigrants and native-born household heads of comparable age as a function of immigrants' time in the United States. [20] Differences in home-ownership rates decline during the first two decades after arrival, though there is a small increase during the third decade for the earliest cohort. This indicates a convergence to the homeownership patterns of native households as immigrants spend more time in the United States.

Adjusting for the household head's educational attainment, age, and household income explains very little of the difference in homeowner-ship rates between immigrants and natives. Borjas shows that the most important factor explaining the immigrant-native homeownership gap is the differential distribution of these two populations across metropolitan areas. [21] Immigrants are highly concentrated in a set of metropolitan areas with below-average homeownership rates for both immigrants and natives. Thus holding the metropolitan area of residence constant explains much of the remaining gap. [22]

Figure 8 reports decennial estimates of the level of overcrowding (that is, more than one person per room) for the same synthetic cohorts. All cohorts experience an increase in overcrowding during the first decade after arrival (and an increased disparity between the overcrowding of immigrants and native-born households of the same age). This increased overcrowding declines with time in the United States for the 1965–69 and 1975–79 arrival cohorts. Given the large increases in homeownership rates experienced over this range of the time-in-U.S. profile, these pat-terns suggest that relatively new immigrant households make an initial trade-off of space for homeownership. Consequently, the immigrant-native difference in the proportion crowded widens initially but then nar-rows in subsequent decades.

20. That is to say, we compare immigrant homeownership rates to a sample of native-born households where the household heads are restricted to the same age range.

21. Borjas (2002) also finds that immigrant homeownership rates increase in the size of the co-national population of the MSA—that is, the bigger the co-ethnic enclave the greater the likelihood that the immigrant households are homeowners.

22. We are unable to adjust for metropolitan area fully due to the fact that the 2000 one percent PUMS separately identifies only 106 of the almost 300 metropolitan areas in the United States.

Figure 9 documents the rates at which immigrant households move out of large multiunit structures and into single-family detached units. The figure shows a pronounced movement of immigrant households into single-family detached housing.[23] There are slight reductions in the rate of convergence for later arrival cohorts. There are also large relative cross-census increases in the population of immigrants residing in single-family homes, compared with native households of the same ages. For example, the 1965–69 cohort differential drops from 39 to 12 percentage points over thirty years in the United States. Comparable changes are observed for the latter cohorts.

As a final comparison of the housing consumption patterns of immigrants and the native born, we characterize the quality of both rental and owner-occupied housing units occupied by immigrants and native households by the position of each unit in its MSA-specific housing price distribution. Specifically, for each housing unit in an identified MSA in the 2000 one percent PUMS, we calculate the unit's percentile position within the MSA's rent distribution (for rental units) or the unit's percentile position within in the MSA's house value distribution (for owner-occupied units). We then calculate the quartile values of these percentile positions for immigrants and natives in rental and owner-occupied housing. If immigrants, on average, consume lower-quality housing, then the quartile values for the immigrant distribution should be below the twenty-fifth, fiftieth, and seventy-fifth percentiles of the housing quality distribution. For example, if the median immigrant in the rental market consumes a unit at the fortieth percentile of the MSA-specific rental distribution, then immigrant households are disproportionately concentrated in lower-quality rental housing.

Table 2 presents these figures for native and immigrant households stratified by arrival cohort. We present separate calculations for those in the rental market and those in the owner-occupied housing market. Consider the rental market: the 1991-2000 cohort of immigrants is not particularly concentrated in low-quality rental dwellings. The immigrant household at the twenty-fifth percentile of the immigrant renter distribution occupies a unit at the twenty-eighth percentile of the quality distribution in its metropolitan area. Similarly, the median immigrant renter

---

23. Note, homeownership and residence in single-family detached housing are not synonymous. Slightly less than one-third of rental units in 2000 were single-family detached dwellings.

Table 2. Position of Immigrant and Native Households in Metropolitan Area Rental and Home Value Distributions, 2000

	Arrival of immigrant households			*Native*
	1991 to 2000	*1981 to 1990*	*Before 1981*	*households*
Position in rent distribution[a]				
25th percentile	28.04	25.61	20.24	26.43
50th percentile	49.40	45.99	43.88	52.44
75th percentile	71.81	68.66	70.80	77.07
Position in housing value distribution[b]				
25th percentile	16.66	16.19	20.32	26.42
50th percentile	39.91	35.82	44.26	51.76
75th percentile	65.45	61.08	68.06	76.11

Note: The sample is restricted to those households residing in one of the 106 metropolitan areas separately identified in the one percent 2000 PUMS. The figures in the table are the quartile break points for immigrant and native renter and homeowner households. Classification of households is based on the immigrant status and year of arrival of the household head, as well as an indicator of whether the household owns or rents the current residence.

a. Percentile position of the reported gross rent in the metropolitan-area-specific rent distribution (as calculated from the PUMS).

b. Percentile position of the reported value of the house in the metropolitan-area-specific rent distribution (as calculated from the PUMS).

household appears to rent the median-quality rental unit. However, immigrants are slightly underrepresented at the higher end of the rental market. For recent arrivals, the renter in the seventy-fifth percentile occupies a unit at the seventy-second percentile of the quality distribution. Interestingly, the quality of units rented by immigrants declines for earlier arrivals (for example, the median immigrant renter for the 1981 to 1990 cohort rents a forty-sixth percentile unit, while the immigrant renter arriving before 1981 rents a unit at the forty-fourth percentile). This decline in rental housing quality for earlier cohorts probably reflects a process by which those who remain in rental housing after lengthy periods of time in the United States are negatively selected in terms of income and assets. The distribution of native households in the rental market is slightly skewed toward higher-quality units.

In the owner-occupied market, the distribution of immigrants in the housing quality hierarchy (as measured by self-reported housing values) is skewed toward lower-quality units for all cohorts. The median immigrant homeowner in the 1991-2000 cohort occupies a unit in the fortieth percentile of the distribution of house values; the analogous values for earlier immigrants are the thirty-sixth percentile for the 1981 to 1990 cohort and the forty-fourth percentile for the cohort arriving prior to

1981. In comparison, the median native homeowner household occupies a unit at the fifty-second percentile of the quality distribution.

The lack of a quality increase in housing consumed across cohorts does not indicate that the quality of immigrant housing is not converging toward the quality of native housing. Movement from the rental into the owner-occupied market is perhaps the clearest indication of an increase in the quality of housing consumed. The large shifts between tenure types, the increase in unit size, and the shift out of multiunit structures into single-family detached housing all support this proposition. Nonetheless, table 2 indicates that immigrants, even when homeowners, are somewhat more concentrated in lower-cost housing.

Identifying Natives Likely to Compete with Immigrants for Housing

The above comparisons indicate that those native households whose housing outcomes are most likely to be affected by competition with immigrants should be relatively low-income renters. Now we use the relationship between housing characteristics and the nativity status of the household head to identify those native households that are the most likely to compete with immigrant households in the housing market.

We begin by modeling the relationship between observed housing characteristics and the nativity of the household head. Specifically, we first estimate the limited dependent variable model

$$(1) \quad \text{Prob}(I_i = 1) = \Phi(\alpha + \beta Owner_i + \delta' Percentile_i + \gamma' Characteristics_i$$
$$+ Owner_i * \varphi' Percentile_i + Owner_i * \kappa' Characteristics_i)$$

where I_i is a dummy variable indicating that household i is an immigrant household, $Owner_i$ is a dummy variable indicating that the unit is owner-occupied, $Percentile_i$ is a vector of two variables, the position of the unit in the MSA-specific rental or home value distribution and the position squared, $Characteristics_i$ is a vector of unit characteristics, α, β, δ, γ, φ, and κ are parameters to be estimated, and Φ is the cumulative normal distribution. This probit model fully interacts all housing unit characteristics with an indicator for owner-occupied units. Table A-1, in the appendix to this chapter, presents the estimation results using household data

Table 3. Average Characteristics of Native Households, by Quartiles of the Likelihood of Competition with Immigrants for Housing

	Quartiles of the distribution of the predicted probability that an immigrant household competes for the unit				Top decile
	Lowest	Q2	Q3	Highest	
Predicted likelihood	0.021	0.046	0.087	0.211	0.299
Renter	0.005	0.068	0.499	0.858	0.948
Age	52.688	51.950	49.099	44.277	43.671
Male head	0.726	0.695	0.560	0.516	0.533
Educational attainment					
<9 years	0.025	0.041	0.068	0.075	0.091
9 to 11 years	0.040	0.064	0.097	0.091	0.090
12 years	0.225	0.276	0.325	0.299	0.280
13 to 15 years	0.285	0.297	0.298	0.298	0.289
16 plus years	0.423	0.321	0.212	0.237	0.250
Black	0.063	0.114	0.201	0.213	0.213
Hispanic	0.037	0.058	0.100	0.156	0.185
Persons per household	2.585	2.783	2.622	2.114	1.858
Persons per room	0.371	0.436	0.505	0.773	1.052
Household income/poverty	4.025	3.656	2.932	2.570	2.384
Housing costs/income (median)	0.145	0.146	0.189	0.245	0.270

Note: Sample of natives is stratified by the predicted probability that an immigrant competes for their housing unit based on the parameters of the probit regression reported in table A-1.

from the 2000 PUMS. The data extract is restricted to those households that are in one of the 106 identified metropolitan areas.[24] We also narrow the definition of immigrant households to those households in which the household head has immigrated during the previous twenty years. The model adjusts for a full set of dummies indicating the number of rooms in the units, the number of bedrooms, and the structure type.

Next, we use the parameters reported in table A-1 to estimate the likelihood that an immigrant competes for the housing unit occupied by each native household in the sample. Natives whose dwellings have higher predicted probability are more likely to be in competition with immigrants.

Table 3 presents average characteristics of native households who fall into four quartiles reflecting the intensity of their competition with immigrants for housing. The first four columns present figures for each quar-

24. We impose this restriction since we cannot calculate a position in the local quality distribution without an MSA identifier.

tile while the fifth column presents average characteristics of the 10 percent of native households most likely to compete with immigrants for housing.

For the native born, the proportion of renters increases uniformly with the predicted probability of competition with immigrants. Approximately 86 percent of households in quartile 4 (those households most likely to compete with immigrants for housing) rent, while less than 1 percent of households in quartile 1 are renters. For the top decile, 95 percent of households are renters. In addition, the proportion of female-headed households rises and the average age of the household head declines with the predicted probability of competition with immigrants. The educational attainment of the household head declines in the predicted likelihood, while the proportion black or Hispanic increases uniformly. Households in the higher quartiles consume less housing per person. For example, the number of persons per room is 0.77 for quartile 4 households compared with 0.37 for households in the first quartile. In addition, higher quartile households have lower incomes relative to the poverty line. Finally, those native households who occupy units that are the most similar to those occupied by immigrant households devote a relatively larger fraction of monthly income to housing expenses.

Thus, based on housing characteristics alone, native households that are poor, minority, and renters are most likely to compete with immigrants for housing. These households tend to reside in more crowded conditions than native households not in competition with immigrants and also tend to devote a larger proportion of household income to housing expenditures. Whether immigration contributes to the higher cost burdens and greater overcrowding is the next question we consider.

The Impact of Recent Immigrants on Native Renter Housing Outcomes

We rely on a series of intermetropolitan area comparisons of native housing outcomes to assess whether native renter households fare worse in metropolitan areas with large immigrant populations. We estimate the cross-sectional relationship between the proportion of recent immigrant households and average native housing outcomes, as well as the relationship between the within-MSA change in the proportion immigrant and the comparable changes in native housing outcomes. Our analysis is limited to the 91 largest MSAs in the nation.[25]

We present alternative sets of regression estimates of the impact of the immigrant population on housing outcomes for natives. First, we assess the impact of immigration on average outcomes for all native renter households. We estimate separate regression models for levels and changes. (Presumably, the regressions in decennial differences provide more stringent empirical tests than the cross-sectional comparisons.) Second, we estimate separate relationships for native renters that are most likely to compete with recent immigrant households for housing and for natives who are least likely. If immigration matters, one would expect its importance to be larger for those native households most likely to compete with immigrant households. We investigate this proposition by testing the interaction between the likelihood of being in competition with immigrants and the proportion immigrant on native housing outcomes.

We estimate the impact of international immigration on four housing outcomes for native renter households: average gross rents (natural log), the median rent-to-income ratio, the average number of persons per room, and the proportion of native households residing in crowded conditions. All outcomes are measured at the MSA level. Gross rents are the simplest and most straightforward measure of housing costs available in the census data.[26] There is some prior evidence that immigration levels are associated with high rents.[27] Rent-to-income ratios provide a measure of housing expenditures that are adjusted for differences in price levels and purchasing power. The analysis of the average number of persons per room provides a consumption-based estimate of the impact of immigrants on native housing outcomes. To the extent that immigrants drive up housing rents, native households should substitute away from housing in their consumption bundles and thus consume less housing per person. Finally, the proportion crowded provides an alternative average measure of consumption that is less sensitive to large households.

25. Of the 106 MSAs separately identified in the 2000 one percent PUMS, only 91 can be matched directly to MSA definitions from 1990 and 1980.

26. Recall that Saiz (2003a) and Susin (2001) found that an exogenous shock of immigration did affect rent levels in Miami.

27. Saiz (2003b) found a positive relationship between growth in the immigrant population and growth in the Department of Housing and Urban Development's (HUD) measures of "Fair Market Rents," that is, estimates of the price of just-standard housing of a given size at either the 40th or 45th percentile of the rental distribution.

*The Effect of Immigrants on Rents and Rent Burdens
of Native Households*

Tables 4 and 5 present regression estimates of the impact of the proportion immigrant in 91 MSAs on two measures of housing outcomes for natives. The regressions control for year effects and for changes in the average observable characteristics of the housing stock. The first two regressions in each table are based on levels. The remaining six regressions are based on within-decade changes. Two models present estimates where the 1980–90 and 1990–2000 changes have been pooled; the final four regressions present separate estimates by decade.[28] For the log rents models in table 4, the regression-adjusted levels model and the regression-adjusted pooled change model yield similar point estimates of the impact of immigration on the average log gross rents paid by native renter households. In both specifications, the coefficient on the proportion immigrant is roughly 0.6. These estimates imply that moving from a metropolitan area where the proportion of recent immigrant households is 0 to one where the proportion is 0.3 (the range of variation observed in the data) would increase average log rents by 0.18, or roughly 20 percent. The separate change estimates by decade indicate larger impacts of immigration during the 1980s and an insignificant impact during the 1990s.

In contrast, table 5 reports little or no evidence that immigrants increase rent-to-income ratios for native households. While the coefficient on proportion immigrant is positive and significant in the simplest specification with no covariates, adjusting for average characteristics of the housing stock eliminates this effect. In the six regressions based on changes, the proportion immigrant is always insignificantly different from zero.

The contrast between the results for gross rents and rent-to-income ratios suggests that while nominal rents are higher in cities with large immigrant populations, real rent burdens are not. That is, a metropolitan area with a large immigrant population generally has higher rents than one with no immigrant population, but a concurrent increase in income in the former city is sufficient to keep rent burdens unchanged.

We next test for the impact of immigration on the housing outcomes of those natives who are most likely to be in competition with immigrants

28. The regression models presented are not weighted. Our conclusions are unaffected by weighting the observations by population.

Table 4. Regression Estimates of the Effect of the Proportion of Immigrant Households on the MSA-Average Log Rents of Native Renter Households

	Levels, all years pooled		Changes					
			All observations		1980–90		1990–2000	
Proportion immigrant	1.783 (0.158)	0.577 (0.280)	0.823 (0.289)	0.655 (0.375)	3.204 (0.804)	1.937 (0.962)	0.437 (0.282)	0.270 (0.400)
Rooms								
Two		6.008 (1.898)		0.165 (1.505)		1.582 (3.476)		0.489 (1.517)
Three		4.142 (1.742)		1.256 (1.507)		4.017 (3.282)		0.958 (1.606)
Four		4.724 (1.658)		−0.089 (1.151)		1.804 (3.371)		0.352 (1.578)
Five		4.995 (1.665)		0.715 (1.496)		3.057 (3.126)		0.406 (1.624)
Six		4.056 (1.752)		0.102 (1.579)		2.156 (3.216)		0.263 (1.727)
Seven		6.013 (2.229)		0.213 (1.738)		5.868 (3.824)		−0.267 (1.866)
Eight		2.652 (2.980)		1.648 (1.964)		0.797 (4.517)		1.808 (2.077)
Nine		2.476 (3.222)		−1.666 (2.292)		1.551 (5.301)		−1.110 (2.540)
Bedrooms								
Two		−4.149 (1.286)		−1.345 (1.441)		−5.711 (3.357)		−0.790 (1.443)
Three		−4.340 (1.233)		−0.845 (1.434)		−4.470 (3.166)		−0.486 (1.495)
Four		−4.741 (1.197)		−1.133 (1.495)		−6.045 (3.253)		0.151 (1.568)
Five		0.377 (1.650)		−1.552 (1.619)		−4.385 (3.497)		−1.265 (1.737)
Six		−4.127 (3.495)		−5.394 (2.894)		−8.738 (6.193)		−3.303 (3.218)
Mobile		−1.394 (0.508)		−1.724 (0.598)		−2.250 (1.139)		−1.711 (0.641)
Single		−0.085 (0.114)		0.209 (0.222)		0.510 (0.340)		−0.677 (0.328)
Less than 4 units		−0.310 (0.129)		0.510 (0.341)		0.288 (0.434)		−0.655 (0.467)
R^2	0.896	0.931	0.767	0.767	0.151	0.307	0.026	0.318
N	273	273	182	182	91	91	91	91

Note: Standard errors are in parentheses. All regressions include a constant term. The level regressions include dummy variables for census year, as do the pooled change regressions. Regressions are based on 91 MSAs observed in 1980, 1990, and 2000.

Table 5. Regression Estimates of the Effect of the Proportion of Immigrant Households on the MSA-Average Rent-to-Income Ratios of Native Renter Households

	Levels, all years pooled		Changes					
			All observations		*1980–90*		*1990–2000*	
Proportion	0.089	−0.034	0.002	−0.023	−0.002	−0.129	0.003	0.058
immigrant	(0.018)	(0.029)	(0.041)	(0.050)	(0.110)	(0.123)	(0.045)	(0.059)
Rooms								
Two		0.070		−0.224		0.642		−0.419
		(0.198)		(0.204)		(0.446)		(0.222)
Three		0.014		−0.004		0.861		−0.158
		(0.182)		(0.204)		(0.421)		(0.235)
Four		−0.169		−0.343		0.823		−0.603
		(0.174)		(0.205)		(0.432)		(0.231)
Five		−0.256		−0.275		0.569		−0.412
		(0.174)		(0.202)		(0.401)		(0.237)
Six		0.008		−0.167		0.723		−0.305
		(0.184)		(0.214)		(0.412)		(0.253)
Seven		0.000		−0.198		0.522		−0.291
		(0.233)		(0.235)		(0.491)		(0.273)
Eight		−0.510		−0.123		0.939		−0.101
		(0.311)		(0.266)		(0.579)		(0.304)
Nine		−0.400		−0.541		0.631		−0.386
		(0.337)		(0.311)		(0.680)		(0.372)
Bedrooms								
Two		−0.112		−0.128		−1.250		0.219
		(0.134)		(0.195)		(0.431)		(0.211)
Three		0.097		0.080		−1.147		0.450
		(0.129)		(0.194)		(0.406)		(0.218)
Four		−0.147		−0.077		−1.068		0.164
		(0.125)		(0.203)		(0.417)		(0.229)
Five		0.249		−0.255		−1.476		0.044
		(0.173)		(0.219)		(0.449)		(0.254)
Six		−0.522		−0.393		−1.595		−0.181
		(0.365)		(0.392)		(0.795)		(0.471)
Mobile		−0.072		−0.131		−0.059		−0.163
		(0.053)		(0.081)		(0.146)		(0.093)
Single		0.062		0.041		0.069		0.007
		(0.011)		(0.030)		(0.044)		(0.048)
Less than 4 units		0.042		−0.008		−0.037		0.045
		(0.013)		(0.040)		(0.056)		(0.068)
R^2	0.132	0.526	0.153	0.340	0.000	0.289	0.000	0.400
N	273	273	182	182	91	91	91	91

Note: Standard errors are in parentheses. All regressions include a constant term. The level regressions include dummy variables for census year, as do the pooled change regressions. Regressions are based on 91 MSAs observed in 1980, 1990, and 2000.

for housing. Using the results presented in table A-1, we estimate the likelihood that each native renter household in each metropolitan area-year combination competes with an immigrant for housing. This probability is used to stratify native households in each metropolitan area and each year into quartiles. We then compute average native housing outcomes by metropolitan area, quartile, and census year. We test whether the effect of immigration on rents and rent burdens is larger for higher quartiles. Specifically, we estimate several variants of the model

$$(2) \quad Outcome_{itq} = \beta_0 + \beta_1 Q_{itq}^2 + \beta_2 Q_{itq}^3 + \beta_3 Q_{itq}^4 + \delta_0 immigrant_{itq}$$
$$+ \delta_1 Q_{itq}^2 * immigrant_{itq} + \delta_2 Q_{itq}^3 * immigrant_{itq}$$
$$+ \delta_3 Q_{itq}^4 * immigrant_{itq} + \varepsilon_{itq},$$

where i indexes metropolitan areas, t indexes census years, and q indexes the four quartiles. $Outcome_{itq}$ is the average housing outcome for native households, $immigrant_{itq}$ is the proportion of households that are recent immigrants, and Q_{itq}^j for $j = (2,3,4)$ are dummy variables indicating the second, third, and fourth quartiles. β_0 through β_3 and δ_0 through δ_3 are parameters, and ε_{itq} is a disturbance term. To the extent that immigrants drive up housing costs for native renter households, one would expect larger impacts for those households in greater competition with immigrants for housing. Thus a fairly stringent test for an effect of immigrants on housing outcomes for natives would be a test of whether the impact increases across quartiles—i.e., $0 < \delta_1 < \delta_2 < \delta_3$.

Table 6 presents estimates of this model for the average log of gross rents and median rent-to-income ratios. For each dependent variable, the table presents four specifications: first, a regression in levels with a complete set of quartile dummies, the proportion immigrant, and interaction terms between the quartile dummies and the proportion immigrant. Second is a regression in levels including the variables in equation 2 as well as all housing characteristics control variables reported in table 5. Third is a regression using decennial changes, including all equation 2 variables. Finally, we present a regression using decennial changes with the variables in equation 2 and the housing characteristics control variables.

The regressions in levels yield little evidence of a progressively larger impact of immigration on the gross rents of native households more likely to be in competition with immigrants. In both regressions, the

Table 6. Regression Estimates of the Effect of the Proportion of Immigrant Households on the Log Rents and Rent-to-Income Ratios of Native Renter Households, by Predicted Competition with Immigrant Households

	Dependent variable: Ln(gross rent)				Dependent variable: Rent/income			
	Levels		Changes		Levels		Changes	
Proportion immigrant	2.628	2.148	0.303	0.673	0.068	0.057	0.041	-0.014
	(0.231)	(0.225)	(0.289)	(0.307)	(0.028)	(0.028)	(0.052)	(0.057)
Proportion immigrant * Q2	0.342	0.005	1.112	0.348	0.039	0.022	-0.126	-0.026
	(0.316)	(0.305)	(0.387)	(0.432)	(0.038)	(0.038)	(0.070)	(0.080)
Proportion immigrant * Q3	-0.116	0.006	0.579	0.011	0.075	0.098	0.050	0.136
	(0.316)	(0.299)	(0.387)	(0.421)	(0.039)	(0.037)	(0.070)	(0.078)
Proportion immigrant * Q4	0.155	0.002	0.596	0.023	0.038	-0.094	-0.176	-0.119
	(0.316)	(0.340)	(0.387)	(0.409)	(0.038)	(0.043)	(0.070)	(0.076)
Q2	-0.264	-0.984	-0.006	0.007	0.006	-0.036	0.009	0.005
	(0.017)	(0.101)	(0.013)	(0.016)	(0.002)	(0.012)	(0.002)	(0.003)
Q3	-0.162	-1.079	0.012	0.019	0.011	-0.052	0.005	0.001
	(0.017)	(0.133)	(0.013)	(0.016)	(0.002)	(0.017)	(0.002)	(0.003)
Q4	-0.353	-1.545	0.043	0.059	0.029	-0.093	0.012	0.008
	(0.017)	(0.208)	(0.013)	(0.017)	(0.002)	(0.026)	(0.002)	(0.003)
Controls	No	Yes	No	Yes	No	Yes	No	Yes
F test[a]	0.792	0.272	2.751	0.332	1.260	6.960	4.540	4.182
(P value)	(0.500)	(0.847)	(0.041)	(0.806)	(0.286)	(0.000)	(0.003)	(0.006)
R^2	0.873	0.893	0.721	0.743	0.291	0.365	0.139	0.171
N	1092	1092	728	728	1092	1092	728	728

Note: Standard errors are in parentheses. All regressions include a constant term and dummy variables for census year. Models with control variables include all variables in table 5. Regressions are based on averages of households in four quartiles of predicted competition with immigrant households, in 91 MSAs observed in 1980, 1990, and 2000.
a. This provides the test statistic from a test of the joint significance of the three interaction terms.

coefficients on the interaction terms between the quartiles and the proportion immigrant are small and insignificant. Moreover, in both specifications a test of the joint significance of the three interaction terms fails to reject the null hypothesis that the coefficients on these terms are zero. The results from regressing the change in gross rents against the change in the proportion immigrant are similar.

The rent-to-income models also yield no evidence of a differential impact of immigrants on the rent burdens of natives. In the simplest levels model without controls, the impact of immigration for quartile 4 is statistically indistinguishable from that for quartile 1. For the specification including controls, the estimated coefficient for quartile 4 is smaller than that estimated for quartile 1. The models of changes confirm that there is no evidence that rent burdens are higher for native households who are more likely to compete with immigrants in the housing market.

Taken together, these results yield little support for the proposition that competition with immigrants increases the housing costs of native renter households, either in gross terms or relative to income. Although there is evidence that gross rents are positively associated with the relative size of the local immigrant population, household income differentials across MSAs are large enough to compensate for higher nominal rents.

The Effect of Immigrants on Persons per Room and Crowding among Native Households

In this section, we test whether immigration affects other dimensions of native housing consumption. Table 7 presents regression estimates of the effect of immigrants on two native housing consumption outcomes, persons per room and overcrowding. The regressions control for year effects, MSA differences in the average size of native households (and changes therein), and differences in household income.[29] Panel A presents regression estimates in which the dependent variable is the average number of persons per room. Panel B presents regression estimates for the proportion of native households residing in crowded conditions. Native households in immigrant cities consume fewer rooms per person relative to comparable native households in areas with smaller immigrant populations. Adjusting for household size reduces the impact of the pro-

29. Here, we do not control for the average characteristics of the housing stock since quantity measures are themselves the dependent variables.

Table 7. Regression Estimates of the Effect of the Proportion of Immigrant Households on the Average Number of Persons per Room and the Proportion in Crowded Conditions among Native Renter Households

	Levels, all years pooled			Changes								
				All observations			1980 to 1990			1990 to 2000		
Panel A: Dependent variable: persons per room												
Proportion immigrant	1.683	1.268	1.343	0.502	0.348	0.282	1.831	0.571	0.517	0.286	0.297	0.230
	(0.099)	(0.058)	(0.073)	(0.123)	(0.064)	(0.075)	(0.374)	(0.183)	(0.201)	(0.096)	(0.065)	(0.081)
Household size		0.256	0.241		0.285	0.281		0.302	0.300		0.227	0.224
		(0.010)	(0.010)		(0.013)	(0.012)		(0.016)	(0.016)		(0.022)	(0.022)
Household income $\times 10^7$			−9.30			8.50			5.10			9.20
			(5.50)			(5.10)			(7.60)			(6.50)
R^2	0.518	0.850	0.852	0.114	0.764	0.768	0.213	0.839	0.839	0.090	0.582	0.591
N	273	273	273	182	182	182	91	91	91	91	91	91
Panel B: Dependent variable: proportion of native households in crowded conditions												
Proportion immigrant	0.744	0.521	0.613	0.155	0.077	0.071	1.010	0.378	0.352	0.017	0.022	0.043
	(0.004)	(0.028)	(0.034)	(0.064)	(0.035)	(0.041)	(0.187)	(0.091)	(0.100)	(0.049)	(0.036)	(0.045)
Household size		0.138	0.132		0.146	0.145		0.152	0.151		0.107	0.108
		(0.005)	(0.005)		(0.007)	(0.007)		(0.008)	(0.008)		(0.013)	(0.013)
Household income $\times 10^7$			−1.10			6.80			2.30			−2.80
			(2.60)			(2.80)			(3.80)			(3.70)
R^2	0.443	0.850	0.860	0.031	0.713	0.713	0.246	0.847	0.848	0.001	0.456	0.459
N	273	273	273	182	182	182	91	91	91	91	91	91

portion immigrant slightly in the levels, pooled changes, and 1980–90 change regressions, yet immigration is still significant in all models. Adjusting for household income does not affect these estimates. The marginal effect of an increase in the proportion immigrant is considerably larger in the levels regressions than in the changes regressions. Again, we find evidence of a considerably larger effect during the 1980s than the 1990s. The results for models of the proportion of native households residing in crowded conditions are analogous.

Table 8 presents tests for an impact of immigration on the housing consumption outcomes of natives, distinguishing (by quartiles) those that are more likely to be in competition with immigrants for housing. In contrast to the housing expenditures results, the regressions in levels for both dependent variables suggest that immigrants have a much larger impact on native households in the higher quartiles relative to the lower quartiles. For all levels regressions, F tests of the joint significance of the three interaction terms clearly reject the hypothesis that the impact of the proportion immigrant is equal across quartiles. However, when the models are estimated using changes, this pattern disappears. For both outcomes, the proportion immigrant has comparable effects on the natives that are the most likely to compete with immigrants (quartile 4) and those that are the least likely (quartile 1). When controls for changes in household size and household income are added, the models indicate that immigrants have the largest effect on the housing consumption of those native households who are least likely to be in competition with immigrants in the housing market.

Conclusion

While rents and rent-to-income ratios for native households are higher in metropolitan areas with large immigrant populations, our findings suggest that this pattern may have little to do with competition from immigrants. First, average gross rents for natives do increase within metropolitan areas when the immigrant proportion of the population increases, but rent burdens do not. Rent increases in cities with a larger fraction of immigrants are matched by income increases in those cities. Thus these findings provide little support for the proposition that immigration increases the real costs of housing.

Second, the housing consumption patterns of recent immigrants are

Table 8. Regression Estimates of the Marginal Effect of the Proportion of Immigrant Households on the Average Number of Persons per Room and the Proportion in Crowded Conditions: Native Renter Households, by Predicted Competition with Immigrant Households

	Dependent variable: persons per room				Dependent variable: proportion crowded			
	Levels		Changes		Levels		Changes	
Proportion immigrant	0.354 (0.109)	0.145 (0.068)	-0.051 (0.148)	0.272 (0.096)	0.148 (0.062)	0.094 (0.044)	-0.002 (0.079)	0.177 (0.061)
Proportion immigrant * Q2	0.362 (0.150)	0.101 (0.079)	0.322 (0.197)	-0.232 (0.121)	0.239 (0.085)	0.089 (0.051)	0.047 (0.107)	-0.214 (0.077)
Proportion immigrant * Q3	0.536 (0.150)	-0.042 (0.081)	0.363 (0.197)	-0.340 (0.123)	0.327 (0.085)	-0.006 (0.052)	0.160 (0.107)	-0.184 (0.077)
Proportion immigrant * Q4	2.346 (0.150)	1.501 (0.082)	0.043 (0.197)	-0.541 (0.122)	1.128 (0.084)	0.639 (0.053)	-0.119 (0.107)	-0.403 (0.077)
Q2	0.086 (0.008)	0.101 (0.004)	-0.007 (0.007)	0.010 (0.004)	0.025 (0.005)	0.031 (0.002)	-0.001 (0.003)	0.006 (0.002)
Q3	0.081 (0.008)	0.207 (0.005)	0.000 (0.007)	0.006 (0.004)	0.021 (0.005)	0.085 (0.003)	-0.000 (0.004)	0.002 (0.003)
Q4	0.292 (0.008)	0.554 (0.007)	0.070 (0.007)	0.054 (0.004)	0.081 (0.005)	0.216 (0.005)	0.037 (0.004)	0.028 (0.003)
Household Size	...	0.271 (0.005)	...	0.271 (0.007)	...	0.143 (0.003)	...	0.129 (0.005)
Household income $\times 10^7$	...	-7.930 (2.60)	...	-3.40 (3.30)	...	-8.30 (1.70)	...	-4.00 (2.10)
F test[a]	98.972	168.123	1.792	6.842	66.512	70.483	2.353	9.192
(P value)	(0.006)	(0.002)	(0.147)	(0.000)	(0.002)	(0.001)	(0.072)	(0.001)
R^2	0.803	0.945	0.293	0.741	0.611	0.862	0.227	0.607
N	1092	1092	728	728	1,092	1,092	728	728

Note: Standard errors are in parentheses. All regressions include a constant term and dummy variables for census year. Regressions are based on averages of households in four quartiles in 91 MSAs observed in 1980, 1990, and 2000.
a. A test of the joint significance of the three interaction terms.

reasonably distinct, and it is thus possible to identify those native households that are most likely to be in competition with recent immigrants in the housing market. In cross-sectional analyses of MSA-level rents and rent burdens, we find no evidence of a disproportionate effect of immigration on the housing outcomes of those native households most likely to compete with immigrants.

We do find some evidence that native households consume fewer rooms and are considerably more likely to reside in crowded conditions in predominantly immigrant cities. However, our statistical results do not provide much evidence of a disproportionate impact on those native households more likely to compete with immigrants for housing. Taken together, these findings indicate that immigration has little effect on the housing outcomes of native renter households.

These results contrast with those of Saiz and Susin, who analyzed the effects of immigration shocks in a single metropolitan area and found large effects upon rents during a four-year interval.[30] Our results, based on decennial changes in immigration and housing conditions, suggest that markets adjust tolerably well over a somewhat longer run. Housing supplies increase, prior residents migrate elsewhere, and others—who would have migrated to cities impacted by recent migrations—are diverted to other destinations. Although the extent of international immigration to U.S. cities is large and increasing, the resulting effects on the housing conditions of natives are quite small—at least when markets have reasonable time periods to adjust.

Our results on the evolution of immigrant housing patterns with time in the United States indicate a fair degree of upward mobility through the housing quality hierarchy. Our findings also indicate a greater degree of convergence to the circumstances of natives along these housing dimensions than is commonly reported in comparable research on labor market convergence. These findings imply that immigrant wealth accumulation increases with time in the United States at a fairly rapid rate. Given the means and asset tests for eligibility in most U.S. public assistance programs, these patterns also suggest declines in immigrant use of public assistance with time in the United States. In addition, the accumulation of housing wealth among first-generation immigrants is likely to foster the intergenerational mobility of future generations.

---

30. Saiz (2003a); Susin (2001).

Appendix

Figure A-1. Distribution of MSA-Level Median Rent-to-Income Ratios, 1980, 1990, and 2000, 106 MSAs

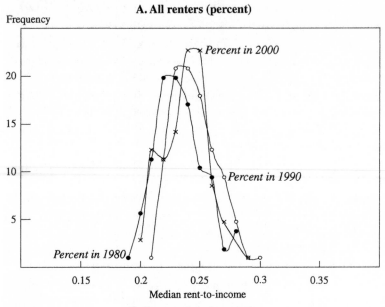

A. All renters (percent)

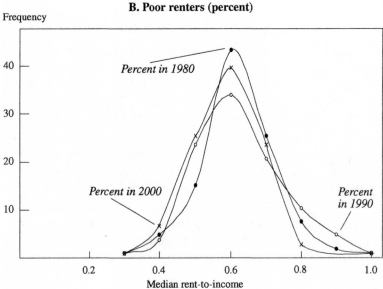

B. Poor renters (percent)

Table A-1. Probability That a Dwelling Is Occupied by a Recent Immigrant, 2000

	Base effect	*Interaction with homeowners dummy*
Owner	−0.076	...
	(0.050)	
Quality percentile	0.013	−0.016
	(0.001)	(0.001)
Quality percentile squared (×10⁴)	−0.0001	0.0001
	(0.005)	(0.008)
Number of bedrooms		
One	−0.037	−0.357
	(0.023)	(0.041)
Two	0.336	−0.466
	(0.027)	(0.045)
Three	0.596	−0.359
	(0.030)	(0.049)
Four	0.869	−0.281
	(0.039)	(0.056)
Five plus	1.135	−0.331
	(0.061)	(0.075)
Number of rooms		
Two	−0.063	0.477
	(0.025)	(0.064)
Three	−0.565	0.733
	(0.027)	(0.064)
Four	−0.956	0.357
	(0.029)	(0.067)
Five	−1.221	0.289
	(0.030)	(0.069)
Six	−1.482	0.342
	(0.034)	(0.070)
Seven	−1.599	0.322
	(0.040)	(0.075)
Eight	−1.713	0.317
	(0.049)	(0.080)
Nine or more	−1.729	0.221
	(0.058)	(0.086)
Units in structure		
Single family	−0.080	0.103
	(0.010)	(0.017)
Mobile home	−0.265	−0.008
	(0.029)	(0.038)
Two to four	0.002	0.344
	(0.009)	(0.023)

Note: Standard errors are in parentheses. The model also includes a constant term not reported in the table. Probit model is estimated using 528,465 observations from 2000 PUMS 1 percent sample with MSA identifier.

Comments

Joseph Tracy: This paper adds to our understanding of the economic impact of immigrants on native residents in U.S. metropolitan areas. There is a growing empirical literature in labor economics that has examined the immigrant impact on wages of native workers. However, to understand the full economic effect of immigration on domestic households it is important to examine the impact in the housing market. And measuring immigrant impacts on wages and rents should provide a more complete test of the prevailing theoretical arguments in the literature.

As discussed in Borjas, Freeman, and Katz, the wage impacts of immigrants on domestic workers tend to be small when measured at the locality and only begin to emerge as significant as the researcher expands the geographic scope of the analysis. An explanation for this finding is that immigrants into a city tend to displace native workers of similar skills.[31] That is, an influx of immigrants into a city does not necessarily lead to an equivalent outward shift in the local labor supply since native workers affected may choose to migrate to another locality.

The displacement hypothesis would also imply little impact on rents by an influx of immigrants into a city. For the same reason that an influx of immigrants into a city need not lead to an outward shift in the local labor supply, it may not lead to an outward shift in local housing demand. A finding of no significant immigrant impact on rents, when combined with the lack of any significant local wage impacts documented in the labor literature, would provide additional support to the displacement

31. Borjas, Freeman, and Katz (1996); Filer (1992); Frey (1995).

188

hypothesis. However, a finding of a significant positive immigrant impact on rents would present a challenge to the displacement hypothesis.

In a recent paper, Saiz finds that on average a 1 percent inflow of immigrants into a city is associated with a 1 percent increase in rents.[32] Greulich, Quigley, and Raphael (hereafter GQR), in contrast, find no significant impact of the share of immigrants in a city on the median rent-to-income ratio (table 5). Both studies look at census data and arrive at different answers.[33] How do we reconcile the two sets of empirical findings?

Although it is beyond the scope of this comment to answer this question, I would like to raise a few issues that may point to a reconciliation of the results. Note first that the immigrant control measures differ between Saiz and GQR. Saiz uses the change in the number of immigrants living in a city over a period of time relative to the city population at the outset of that time interval $(I_{it} - I_{it-1})/P_{it}$, where I_{it} is the number of immigrants in city i in year t, and P_{it} is the population of city i in year t. In contrast, GQR use the immigrant population share in the city or the change in the immigrant population share: I_{it}/P_{it} or $(I_{it}/P_{it}) - (I_{it-1}/P_{it-1})$.

Which immigrant control variable is more appropriate? The answer may depend on the underlying theoretical model that the researcher is trying to test. Saiz is interested in testing whether a presumed outward shift in the demand for housing resulting from an inflow of immigrants affects rents paid by domestic households. He explicitly has a demand and supply of housing framework in mind and presents a formal model along these lines. Seeing the net change in the stock of immigrants into a city as a fraction of the city population would seem to be an appropriate control variable to measure shifts in the immigrant demand for housing.

GQR do not discuss any theoretical framework in their paper. I believe, though, they also have in mind a model of the demand and supply of housing. I would argue, however, that the GQR immigrant control variable—the immigrant share—may be more appropriate for a quality-of-life (QOL) model.[34] Suppose we wanted to think of immigrants in a city as a potential amenity or disamenity that is consumed by residents of the city along with other city attributes. The immigrant population share in the city would be a natural way to measure the magnitude of this particular city attribute. The predicted impact of variations in the immigrant

32. Saiz (2003b).
33. Saiz (2003b) finds that his basic results are robust across several different data sets.
34. See for example Rosen (1979) and Roback (1982) for details.

population share on wages and rents would depend on whether immigrants are a consumption amenity or disamenity and whether they are also a production amenity or disamenity. The two studies may arrive at different answers in part because implicitly their empirical specifications are addressing different questions.

GQR's finding of no overall impact of the immigrant share on rents might mask an underlying positive impact that is localized to those native households most in competition in the housing market with immigrants.[35] To test for this possibility, GQR construct a competition index in the following manner. For their sample of households they estimate a probit model on an indicator that takes a value of one for an immigrant household, using as control variables an own-versus-rent indicator and various attributes of the house. For each native renter household, GQR use the estimated probit model to calculate a probability that an immigrant household would occupy a similar house. They stratify the sample of native renter households into quartiles based on these calculated probabilities and check to see if the immigrant share variable has differential impacts on rent-to-income ratios in each quartile. The fact that GQR find no significant rent-to-income impacts in any of the four quartiles dispels the hypothesis that there is a positive impact of immigrants on rents that is restricted to those households most likely to compete in the housing market with immigrants. However, in a QOL model it is not clear that these fitted probabilities would have any particular bearing on the estimated impact of the immigrant population share.

A final specification difference between Saiz and GQR has to do with how each controls for income effects on the demand for housing. GQR look at median rent-to-income ratios and estimate the specification in levels and not logs. Saiz uses the change in log median rents and frees up the income elasticity by including income as a control variable. For three of the four rent specifications using census data (table 6), Saiz reports an income coefficient that is less than one.

This finding raises the possibility that the GQR-estimated coefficient on the immigrant population share is subject to a form of left-out-variable bias. This is easiest to illustrate assuming that GQR had estimated

35. This is similar to the labor literature that has looked for wage effects specifically on native workers whose skills were close to those of immigrants.

their specification in logs rather than levels. Suppose that the true specification (simplified here) is given as follows.

(1) $$\ln(R_{it}) = \beta_0 + \beta_1 Y_{it} + \beta_2 \left(\frac{I_{it}}{P_{it}} \right) + \varepsilon_{it},$$

where R_{it} is the median rent in city i in year t, and Y_{it} is per capita income in city i in year t. This can be rewritten with the dependent variable normalized by per capita income.

(2) $$\ln \left(\frac{R_{it}}{Y_{it}} \right) = \beta_0 - (1 - \beta_1) Y_{it} + \beta_2 \left(\frac{I_{it}}{P_{it}} \right) + \varepsilon_{it}$$

Assume that the following specification is in fact estimated.

(3) $$\ln \left(\frac{R_{it}}{Y_{it}} \right) = \beta_0 + \beta_2 \left(\frac{I_{it}}{P_{it}} \right) + \varepsilon_{it}$$

Comparing equation 3 with equation 2 illustrates that the estimated specification suffers from a left-out-variable bias problem. If the demand elasticity (β_1) is less than one, then the coefficient on the left-out-variable is negative. GQR establish that the likely correlation between the left-out-variable (per capita income) and the immigrant share is positive. This suggests that normalizing rents by income (in this simple example) will create a downward bias on the estimated coefficient on the immigrant share.

GQR also provide a wealth of descriptive information. Figures 2a–2e show by decade the distribution of rent-to-income ratios for the five SMSAs with the highest immigrant share. The figures show no systematic shifts in these rent burden distributions in the period from 1980 to 2000. GQR comment that this simple descriptive check of the data does not reveal any obvious evidence of a significant immigrant impact on rent burdens. They caution readers, though, that these figures cannot control for the many factors that may be affecting rent burdens in these SMSAs.

Let me add another reason for caution in interpreting these figures. The observed empirical rent burden distribution for any SMSA and year reflects the underlying distribution of rent burdens among all households and the censoring of that distribution by the decisions by households to own versus rent. That is, if a household owns instead of rents in a given year, the researcher does not observe the rent-to-income ratio for that household. If the homeownership rate is roughly unchanged over a period of time, it is likely that changes in the observed distribution of rent burdens reflect changes in the underlying distribution of rent burdens for households. However, in the decade of the 1990s a substantial increase in homeownership rates occurred. This increase makes it difficult to interpret any changes to the observed empirical distribution of rent burdens from 1990 to 2000. Any shifts in the underlying distribution during this period may be masked by changes in the censoring of this information as more households became homeowners.

GQR also explore in figure 4 whether there is a relationship between median SMSA rent burdens and the fraction of the housing stock that is new. They interpret this fraction as a measure of the elasticity of housing supply in the SMSA. For high-income renters there is no relationship, but for low-income renters GQR find that higher proportions of new housing stock are associated with lower rent burdens.

If the primary factors that shift the demand for housing in a local housing market are aggregate in nature, then GQR's interpretation of figure 4 seems reasonable. That is, if most SMSAs experience similar housing demand shocks, then difference in supply responses will reflect underlying differences in housing supply elasticities. However, if there are significant regional patterns to housing demand shocks, then the proportion of new housing across SMSAs could differ even if all SMSAs had similar housing supply elasticities.

The impact of immigration on native households is an important unresolved public policy issue. It is laudable that researchers such as GQR are now looking for immigration impacts in the housing market as well as the labor market. Greulich, Quigley, and Raphael provide a nice contribution to this effort. Empirical work such as this will help point to a unified theoretical framework for understanding the nature of these immigrant impacts.

Guillermina Jasso: Erica Greulich, John M. Quigley, and Steven Raphael address two important questions in the study of migration and in the study of housing: First, what are the patterns of housing behavior among foreign-born persons in the United States and what are the determinants of these patterns? Second, what is the impact of foreign-born housing behavior on the native born? They provide a careful and detailed examination of housing patterns among the foreign born and an equally careful analysis of those patterns and their impact. The data, however, are not equal to the task. As immigration researchers have discussed for almost twenty-five years—and numerous panels in the private and public sectors have concluded—new kinds of data are required in order to provide reliable answers to questions about migration. Understanding the housing behavior of the foreign born, and hence its impact on the native born, requires taking into account the distinctive legal environments faced by different subsets of the foreign born and their differential resources, in a framework attentive to cohort effects and duration effects.

In these comments I discuss conceptual and data challenges and a new longitudinal public-use data resource—the New Immigrant Survey—which will make it possible to answer many questions, especially as time passes and survey rounds accumulate.[36] And I present preliminary evidence on homeownership based on the 1996 and 2003 cohorts of new legal immigrants studied in the New Immigrant Survey.

Conceptual and Data Challenges

There are two major challenges in studying the foreign born. The first is to accurately characterize the environments they face—especially law and policy regimes—so that their behaviors and decisions can be understood and interpreted. The second, arising from the dynamic nature of immigration, is to follow the foreign born over time, so that changes in behavior and characteristics can be mapped and the extent and pace of adjustment to and integration into the United States analyzed.

LEGAL STATUS AND THE ENVIRONMENTS FACED BY THE FOREIGN BORN. Foreign-born persons in the United States are highly heterogeneous. Not only do they come from an extraordinary variety of countries and backgrounds, but, importantly, they face very different U.S. environments, depending on their exact legal status. Housing behavior cannot be understood without understanding the environment faced, and the environment faced cannot be understood without information about legal status. Though anyone, or almost anyone, with sufficient financial resources can

36. www.pop.upenn.edu/nis (May 2004).

purchase a house in the United States, the desire to purchase a house will probably differ across the following types of foreign born: illegal aliens, legal temporary residents (such as foreign students, World Bank staffers, or newspaper correspondents), lawful permanent residents (LPRs), and those among LPRs who have naturalized. A person who does not have assurances of remaining in the United States—a person, say, subject to deportation—will not want to buy a house.[37]

The large databases currently available (such as the census and the Current Population Surveys) do not provide information on legal status (except for information on naturalization). Thus it is difficult to understand and interpret a person's actions based on these data. Net of every other characteristic— income, region of the country, and so on—legal status may play a determining role in the decision to buy or rent.

Accordingly, the practice in Greulich, Quigley, and Raphael of treating "foreign born" and "immigrant" as synonyms and using the two words interchangeably leads to substantial distortion. For example, they state that "recent immigrants to the United States are, on average, considerably less educated than natives."[38] But data on legal immigrants admitted to lawful permanent residence in 1996 indicate otherwise, showing instead that recent legal immigrants have average schooling similar to the native born—and substantially higher than the set of all recently arrived foreign born.[39]

DYNAMIC CHARACTER OF IMMIGRATION. Assimilation occurs over time. The decision to remain in the United States or to leave, the timing of emigration, the accumulation of resources—all occur over time. Thus an important desideratum of data for immigration research is that the data be longitudinal.

The large databases currently available are cross sectional, and thus it has not been possible to follow individual immigrants over time. The synthetic-cohort method is widely used, but it has serious limitations, as we shall see.

INTERACTION OF THE TWO CHALLENGES. The two challenges—of accurately characterizing the environments faced by the foreign born and

37. The acronym LPR will be used for both lawful permanent resident and lawful permanent residence. The context should make clear whether reference is to a person or to a status.

38. The authors cite Borjas (1999).

39. Jasso and others (2000b).

of observing foreign born over time—interact in important ways. For example, it is a universal premise in immigration research, and an empirically documented one, that the returns to experience differ depending on whether the experience is as an illegal alien, or as a legal temporary resident, or as a legal permanent resident (LPR). Moreover, the cohort that is followed over time is most usefully defined in terms of accession to a legal status, in terms, that is, of initiation into a state in which a particular environment is faced uniformly by all members of the cohort. Thus it makes sense to speak of the cohort who became LPRs in 1972 or of the cohort who entered without inspection for the first time in 1992.

There is a still further way in which legal environments play a part. Within the set of LPRs, the specific provision of the law by which LPR was achieved carries with it special features. For example, some immigrants acquire only conditional LPR and must have the conditionality removed two years later. Some require contractually binding affidavits of support. Some have access to public assistance privileges. Only the immigrant class of admission provides this information.

Note also that because requirements differ across visa categories, the immigrant class of admission provides further information about immigrant selection, and thus, potentially, about the resources relevant to housing behavior. For example, a diversity visa requires a high school education (or equivalent). A spouse-of-U.S.-citizen visa, through behavioral mechanisms associated with assortative mating, signals that a U.S. citizen—and Americans are among the most highly educated people in the world—has screened this person for the long term. An employment visa, depending on its particular type, may require a baccalaureate degree.

Finally, note that immigration law and policy are not static. There are many changes, and thus the specific environment and immigrant background signaled by a visa vary with the year in which it is acquired. For example, a spouse-of-U.S.-citizen visa in 2003 provides a different signal than a spouse-of U.S.-citizen visa in 1996, for two reasons: stringent affidavit-of-support provisions are now in effect; and in 1996, persons who had been granted amnesty under the Immigration Reform and Control Act of 1986 (IRCA) were naturalizing and sponsoring their spouses.

INADEQUACY OF THE SYNTHETIC COHORT METHOD. Definition of the cohort—of the formative event that initiates cohort members into a special state—is based on the census question on year of entry. For a long time, immigration researchers have expressed concerns about the question on year of entry, in part because the question is a subjective one, which can be answered in different ways depending on the respondent's legal status, and which can be answered in different ways even by the same person at different points in the life course, and in part because the wording of the question or its associated instruction has changed over time.[40] To illustrate briefly, in 1980 the question asked foreign-born respondents to provide the first year they came to stay. In 1990 the question asked for the latest year they came to stay, and in 2000, for the year they came to live.

Thus one cannot be sure that the people who in 1990 say they came to stay in 1985–90 are the same people who in 2000 said they came to live in 1985–90. Indeed, people who in 1990 say they came to stay in 1985–90 may also have said in 1980 that they came to stay in 1975–80. For example, they may have thought in 1980 that they came to stay for the first time in 1977, but then they left in 1982, returning in 1988.

Moreover, because of emigration selectivity, it is not possible to gauge how much of what appears to be change in behavior—more people buying a house—may instead be change in the composition of the cohort—with renters leaving the country and buyers remaining.

As numerous immigration researchers and panels have concluded, the synthetic cohort method is a poor substitute for longitudinal observation of probability samples drawn from well-defined cohorts.

MIXED-NATIVITY HOUSEHOLDS. Finally, there is one feature of Greulich, Quigley, and Raphael's empirical implementation that ignores immigration realities and potentially exaggerates differences in home-ownership between the native-born and foreign-born populations. The authors classify a household as immigrant or native depending on the nativity of the householder. This means that both the immigrant and native subsets include an unknown proportion of mixed-nativity households. But the mixed-nativity household is very important to study in its own right. Its behavior may differ from that of both pure-native and pure-foreign households. Inclusion in the two sets dilutes the patterns in the two pure sets and may induce differential distortion.

The mixed-nativity household is a critical element in immigration research. Such households are formed by the marriage of a native-born U.S. citizen to a foreign-born person who, typically, is sponsored for

40. Jasso and Rosenzweig (1990); Jasso (2004); Redstone and Massey (forthcoming).

immigration by the U.S. citizen. The spousal route to immigration is a favorite and appealing route. It is the route used by the largest single set of adult immigrants. For example, in the years 1996–2000, the proportion of adult new legal immigrants who obtained a visa as the spouse of a U.S. citizen ranged from 27.2 percent in 1996 to 33.3 percent in 1998.

If there are systematic differences between the U.S. citizen men who marry and sponsor the immigration of wives and the U.S. citizen women who marry and sponsor the immigration of husbands, then inclusion of mixed-nativity households in the foreign-born set and the native-born set introduces differential distortion. For example, if U.S. citizen men and their foreign-born wives have higher schooling than U.S. citizen women and their foreign-born husbands (as suggested by data on the fiscal year 1996 immigrant cohort) and if the census respondents identified as the householder are disproportionately male (for example, 87 percent male in the 2000 Census), then households formed by (the higher-educated) U.S. citizen men and their immigrant wives are included among the native-born households analyzed by Greulich, Quigley, and Raphael, and households formed by (the lower-educated) U.S. citizen women and their immigrant husbands are included among the foreign-born households.[41] Thus the failure to examine separately mixed-nativity households not only misses an opportunity to learn more about the behavior of this important type of household but also exaggerates the differential in homeownership between native-born and foreign-born households.

Homeownership and the New Immigrant Survey

Accurate assessment of the impacts of immigration on native-born housing costs hinges on correct understanding of foreign-born housing patterns. Correct understanding of foreign-born housing patterns in turn requires understanding the decision to buy or rent, taking into account the distinctive legal environments faced by different subsets of the foreign born and their differential resources, in a framework attentive to cohort effects and duration effects. Data recently collected by the New Immigrant Survey (NIS) on the fiscal year 1996 and 2003 cohorts of new legal immigrants provide some initial insights.

OVERVIEW OF THE NEW IMMIGRANT SURVEY. The New Immigrant Survey is a new plan for nationally representative, longitudinal studies of

---

41. For data on the NIS-P1996 immigrant cohort see Jasso and others (2000a).

immigrants and their children that will provide new kinds of data to help answer many important questions about immigration; the data will be publicly available to researchers.[42] In preparation for the full New Immigrant Survey, the New Immigrant Survey Pilot carried out a survey of a representative sample of legal immigrants admitted to permanent residence in July and August of 1996 (148,987 persons). The sample design oversampled employment-based immigrants, in whom there is considerable interest, and undersampled child immigrants, who are numerous. The final sample numbered 1,984 persons, of whom 1,839 were adult immigrants. The first full NIS cohort consists of approximately 11,000 new legal immigrants drawn from among new immigrants in the seven-month period May–November 2003. Of these, approximately 10,000 are adult immigrant and 1,000 are child immigrant principals. The sample design oversampled employment and diversity principals and undersampled the numerous spouse-of-U.S.-citizen category. Interviews were conducted with the adult immigrants, with the parents of the child immigrants, and with the spouses of both sets of adults; as well, up to two children, 8–12 years old, were interviewed, and all children, 3–13 years old, were administered tests of achievement.

HOMEOWNERSHIP IN THE NEW IMMIGRANT SURVEY. The NIS-Pilot (NIS-P) included the question, "Right now, do you own any property in the United States? (By property we mean any commercial or residential property you currently own including your home and any business you own.)" This question was asked at the twelve-month round; the average time since admission to LPR was between twenty-two and twenty-three months. The NIS-2003 baseline-round questionnaire included the question, "Do you [and your spouse, etc.] own this [home or apartment], rent it, or what?" Here we use data from the May, June, and July subsamples. The average time since admission to LPR is 2.75 months. Thus the housing information provided by the NIS-2003 cohort May–July subsample pertains to a much earlier point in the immigrant career than the housing information provided by the NIS-P sample.

Examination of the data yields information about visa effects, duration effects, and cohort effects.

42. A succinct overview of the New Immigrant Survey may be found in Jasso and others (2003).

Figure 10. Homeownership, New Legal Immigrants, 25–64 Years Old, by Visa Class: NIS 2003 Cohort

Percent

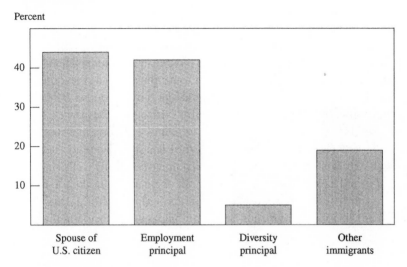

Spouse of U.S. citizen · Employment principal · Diversity principal · Other immigrants

Source: New Immigrant Survey, 2003 immigrant cohort. See text.

Figure 10 shows the proportion of the NIS-2003 immigrants, 25–64 years old at admission to lawful permanent residence, who own their home. Three classes of admission are depicted—spouses of U.S. citizens, employment principals, and diversity principals, as well as a fourth category containing all other immigrants. As shown, 44 percent of the spouses of U.S. citizens and 42 percent of the employment principals own their own home (at less than three months after admission to LPR, on average). The comparable proportions are 20 percent in the other-immigrants category and only 5 percent among diversity principals. Clearly, immigrants screened by an employer or a U.S. citizen spouse have (or acquire) both the resources and the resolve to participate in the "American dream" and to do so almost immediately.

Of course, some immigrants "adjust" their status to LPR after living in the United States with a temporary nonimmigrant visa, such as an F visa for foreign students or an H-1B visa for specialty workers, and so on. If both the requisite resources and the resolve to buy a home increase with time in the United States, adjustee immigrants would have higher rates of homeownership than new-arrival immigrants. Figure 11 reports the pro-

Figure 11. Homeownership, New Legal Immigrants, 25–64 Years Old, by Visa Class and Adjustment of Status: NIS 2003 Cohort

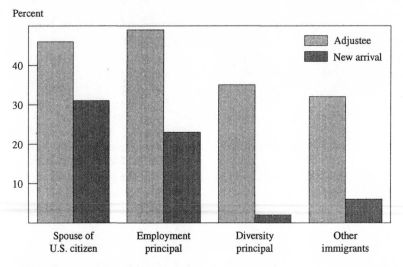

Source: New Immigrant Survey, 2003 immigrant cohort.

portions who own their home, separately for adjustee immigrants and new-arrival immigrants.[43] As shown, there are large duration effects. The proportions who own their home are more than twice as large for adjustee immigrants, compared with new-arrival immigrants, in three of the four admission classes—all except the spouses of U.S. citizens, a visa category in which the sponsor may have already owned a home before marrying and sponsoring the spouse.

It is reasonable to expect nontrivial cohort effects. First, the fiscal year 2003 immigrants are subject to the stringent affidavit-of-support provisions instituted by the Illegal Immigration Reform and Immigrant Responsibility Act of 1996, which went into effect in December of 1997. We thus expect the NIS-2003 immigrants to have more resources than the NIS-P immigrants. Second, the NIS-P immigrants are thought to include an IRCA-aftermath stream consisting of spouses of newly naturalized amnestied aliens. For this reason, the NIS-2003 immigrants may also be thought to have more resources than the NIS-P immigrants.

---

43. The contrast is not exact, as some new-arrival immigrants have in fact been living in the United States but are ineligible to adjust status, for example, because they are currently deportable.

Figure 12: Homeownership, New Legal Immigrants, 25–64 Years Old, by Visa Class: NIS 1996 and 2003 Cohorts

Percent

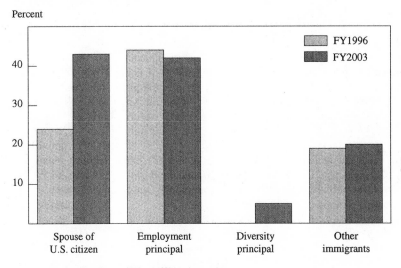

Source: New Immigrant Survey, 1996 and 2003 immigrant cohorts.

Third, the NIS-2003 immigrants include a higher proportion of immigrants who adjusted their status than the NIS-P immigrants (approximately 60 percent in the NIS-2003 compared with 55 percent in the NIS-P). Longer time in the United States is also associated with greater resources. Counterbalancing these three factors, which all favor higher homeownership in the NIS-2003 than in the NIS-P, is that the NIS-2003 immigrants are interviewed twenty to twenty-one months earlier in the immigrant career than the NIS-P immigrants. Which factors dominate is an empirical question.

Figure 12 depicts the proportions reporting ownership of property (1996) or a home (2003). As shown, the proportions who own property or a home are roughly similar in the employment and residual categories, but they are substantially different in the spouse-of-U.S.-citizen category, with higher homeownership rates in the 2003 cohort. Given that the 2003 information was obtained twenty to twenty-one months earlier in the immigrant career than the 1996 information, these results also suggest higher homeownership rates among employment and diversity principals in the more recent cohort. Among the spouses of U.S. citizens, the differential is striking, suggesting a pronounced cohort effect plausibly associ-

Table 9. Logit Estimates of Determinants of Owning Property or Home in the United States, New Legal Immigrants, 25–64 Years Old

	1996 cohort own property	2003 cohort own home
Age	.218	.222
	(2.74)	(4.38)
Age squared	–.00267	–.00252
	(2.70)	(4.23)
Sex (1 = female)	.0670	.127
	(.38)	(1.03)
Total schooling (years)	.0541	.0405
	(2.84)	(3.04)
Adjustee	.731	1.68
	(3.51)	(11.2)
Spouse of U.S. citizen	–.0962	.865
	(.42)	(5.39)
Employment principal	.482	.706
	(2.18)	(4.26)
Diversity principal		–.759
		(2.45)
Constant	–6.53	–7.64
	(4.17)	(7.0)
N	750	1,909

Source: Data are drawn from the New Immigrant Survey, 1996 and 2003 immigrant cohorts. Data for the 2003 cohort are drawn from the subsamples for May, June, and July. Absolute values of asymptotic *t* ratios appear in parentheses next to the corresponding estimates.

ated with the IRCA-aftermath stream consisting of spouses of newly naturalized amnestied persons.

To assess the net effects of cohort, duration, and class of admission, I carry out a binary logit analysis of the probability of owning property (in the 1996 cohort) and a home (in the 2003 cohort). Table 9 reports the estimates. The admission category variables are jointly significant at high levels of significance, indicating the persistence of visa effects in a multivariate context. In 2003, net of duration effects and other variables, visa effects mirror the percentages in figures 10 and 12. Spouses of U.S. citizens have the highest probability of owning a home, followed closely by employment principals. In 1996, however, spouses of U.S. citizens rank lower than the other admission categories in the probability of owning property, a result that departs from that in the raw percentages depicted in figure 12.

The adjustment-of-status variable is statistically significant in both cohorts, underscoring the importance of the duration effects visible in figure 11. The coefficient is larger in the 2003 cohort, suggesting that the more recent set of adjustees was more successful in converting time in the United States into a home. This may be due in part to the fact that, under provisions in effect in 1996, the earlier immigrants could adjust from an illegal status while in the United States. To the extent that illegal migrants have fewer resources than their counterparts who are adjusting from a legal status, the estimated duration effects would reflect the differing composition of the adjustees in ownership-relevant characteristics.

Finally, schooling and age are significant in both cohorts. Schooling exerts, as expected, a positive effect on the probability of ownership. The effects of age are represented by downward parabolas, peaking at forty-one years of age (1996) and forty-four years of age (2003).

SUMMARY. The heterogeneity of the foreign born and the dynamic nature of their attachments to the United States—visible in the visa, duration, and cohort effects documented among new legal immigrants—means that correct understanding of the housing behavior of the foreign born requires attentiveness to these aspects of their personal and social circumstances. And correct understanding of the housing behavior of the foreign born is in turn necessary for correct assessment of its impact on the native born. Change in the composition of the foreign-born population will importantly affect the type and magnitude of its housing impacts.

References

Abdel-Rahman, Hesham M., and Alex Anas. Forthcoming. "Theories of Systems of Cities." In *Handbook of Urban and Regional Economics*, vol. 4, edited by J.V. Henderson and J.F. Thisse. Amsterdam: Elsevier-North Holland Publishing Company.

Borjas, George. 1985. "Assimilation, Changes in Cohort Quality, and the Earnings of Immigrants." *Journal of Labor Economics* 3 (4): 463–89.

———. 1995. "Assimilation and Change in Cohort Quality Revisited: What Happened to Immigrant Earnings during the 1980s?" *Journal of Labor Economics* 13 (2): 201–45.

———. 1999. *Heaven's Door: Immigration Policy and the American Economy.* Princeton University Press.

———. 2002. "Homeownership in the Immigrant Population." *Journal of Urban Economics* 52 (3): 448–76.

Borjas, George J., Richard B. Freeman, and Laurence F. Katz. 1996. "Searching for the Effect of Immigration on the Labor Market." *American Economic Review* 86 (May): 246–51.

Cortes, Kalena. 2004. "Are Refugees Different from Economic Immigrants? Some Empirical Evidence on the Heterogeneity of Immigrant Groups in the United States," *Review of Economics and Statistics* 86 (May): 465–80..

Duncan, Otis Dudley, and Stanley Lieberson. 1959. "Ethnic Segregation and Assimilation." *American Journal of Sociology* 64 (January): 364–74.

Filer, Randall. 1992. "The Effect of Immigrant Arrivals on Migratory Patterns of Native Workers." In *Immigration and the Work Force*, edited by George Borjas and Richard Freeman, 245–69. University of Chicago Press.

Frey, William. 1995. "Immigration and Internal Migration 'Flight' from U.S. Metropolitan Areas: Toward a New Demographic Balkanisation." *Urban Studies* 32 (May): 733–57.

Fujita, Masahisa, Paul Krugman, and T. Mori. 1999. "On the Evaluation of Hierarchical Urban Systems." *European Economic Review* 43 (2): 210–59.

Jasso, Guillermina. 2004. "Have the Occupational Skills of New Legal Immigrants to the United States Changed Over Time? Evidence from the Immigrant Cohorts of 1977, 1982, and 1994." In *International Migration at Century's End: Trends and Issues,* edited by Joaquín Arango, Douglas S. Massey, and J. Edward Taylor. Oxford University Press.

Jasso, Guillermina, Douglas S. Massey, Mark R. Rosenzweig, and James P. Smith. 2000a. "Assortative Mating among Married New Legal Immigrants to the United States: Evidence from the New Immigrant Survey Pilot." *International Migration Review* 34 (Spring): 443–59.

———. 2000b. "The New Immigrant Survey Pilot (NIS-P): Overview and New Findings about U.S. Legal Immigrants at Admission." *Demography* (February) 37: 127–38.

———. 2003. "The New Immigrant Survey in the U.S.: The Experience over Time." Washington: Migration Policy Institute.

Jasso, Guillermina, and Mark R. Rosenzweig. 1990. *The New Chosen People: Immigrants in the United States.* A volume in "The Population of the United States in the 1980s: A Census Monograph Series." New York: Russell Sage Foundation.

Malpezzi, Stephen. 1996. "Housing Prices, Externalities, and Regulation in U.S. Metropolitan Areas." *Journal of Housing Research* 7 (2): 209–41.

Malpezzi, Stephen, and Richard K. Green. 1996. "What Has Happened to the Bottom of the U.S. Housing Market?" *Urban Studies* 33: 1807–20.

———. 2003. *A Primer on U.S. Housing Markets.* Washington: Urban Institute.

Myers, Dowell, and Seong Woo Lee. 1996. "Immigration Cohort and Residential Crowding in Southern California." *Demography* 33 (February): 51–65.

———. 1998. "Immigration Trajectories into Homeownership: A Temporal Analysis of Residential Assimilation." *International Migration Review* 32 (Autumn): 593–625.

O'Flaherty, Brendan. 1995. "An Economic Theory of Homelessness and Housing." *Journal of Housing Economics* 4 (March): 13–49.

———. 1996. *Making Room: The Economics of Homelessness.* Harvard University Press.

Ohls, James. 1975. "Public Policy towards Low Income Housing and Filtering in Housing Markets." *Journal of Urban Economics* 2 (April): 144–71.

Quigley, John M. 1972. "An Economic Model of Swedish Emigration." *Quarterly Journal of Economics* 86 (1): 111–26.

Quigley, John M., and Steven Raphael. 2004. "Is Housing Unaffordable? Why Isn't it More Affordable?" *Journal of Economic Perspectives* 18 (1): 191–214.

Redstone, Ilana, and Douglas S. Massey. Forthcoming. "Coming to Stay: An Analysis of the Census Question on Year of Arrival." *Demography.*

Roback, Jennifer. 1982. "Wages, Rents, and the Quality of Life." *Journal of Political Economy* 90 (6): 1257–78.

Rosen, Sherwin. 1979. "Wage-based Indexes of Urban Quality of Life." In *Current Issues in Urban Economics*, edited by Peter Mieszkowski and Mahlon Straszheim, 74–104. Johns Hopkins University Press.

Saiz, Albert. 2003a. "Room in the Kitchen for the Melting Pot: Immigration and Rental Prices." *Review of Economics and Statistics* 85 (3): 502–22.

———. 2003b. "Immigration and Housing Rents in American Cities." Working Paper 03-12. Federal Reserve Bank of Philadelphia

Susin, Scott. 2001. "The Impact of the Mariel Boatlift on the Miami Housing Market." U.S. Bureau of the Census.

U.S. Bureau of the Census. 2001. *Profile of the Foreign Born Population in the United States: 2000*, P23-206. Government Printing Office.

STEVEN RAPHAEL
University of California, Berkeley

MICHAEL A. STOLL
University of California, Los Angeles

The Effect of Prison Releases on Regional Crime Rates

A DIRECT CONSEQUENCE of the recent increases in the U.S. prison population is the concurrent increase in the number of former inmates and recently released inmates living in noninstitutionalized society. Between 1980 and 2000, the U.S. prison population increased fourfold from 300,000 to more than 1.2 million. During the same period, the number of exoffenders residing in the community increased from 1.8 to 4.3 million.[1] Annually, there are large flows into and out of the state and federal prison systems. For example, in 1999 approximately 550,000 inmates were released from prison, 75 percent being conditionally released into state parole systems. Net of conditional returns to prison, releases in 1999 increased the population of recently released inmates by more than 300,000 people.

The growing numbers of former prison inmates generate a host of problems for receiving communities. Prime among the problems of recent prison releases is the potential effects on local crime rates. By most conventional measures, a large share of exoffenders have postrelease run-ins with the legal system. Approximately 70 percent are rearrested within three years of release, and nearly 50 percent are eventually returned to prison.[2] Moreover, roughly 7 percent of those released to

We would like to thank Steven Levitt for valuable input in the very early stages of this research. This paper has also benefited immensely from the comments of Mark Duggan and Anne Piehl. We also thank the Russell Sage Foundation for generous support of this research project.

1. Bonczar (2003).
2. Langan and Levin (2002).

state parole systems abscond from supervision.[3] Certainly, these figures suggest a level of criminal activity among former inmates that could impose substantial social costs on receiving communities.

The predominantly urban communities that commit and receive a disproportionate share of state and federal prisoners are most likely to be affected by the criminal activity of released prisoners. Within states prisoner releases are increasingly concentrated in the central cities of metropolitan areas. Lynch and Sabol estimate that the percentage of state prison releases to central cities rose from 50 percent in 1984 to 66 percent in 1996.[4] Within central cities, a small number of neighborhoods that are characterized as poor and working class account for a disproportionate share of the concentrations of released prisoners.[5] Thus poor urban communities are likely to bear a disproportionate share of the costs of addressing the problems of prisoner release and reintegration. Moreover, given the current fiscal crises faced by many states and pressure to reduce criminal justice expenditures, the challenges to urban areas posed by prison releases are likely to intensify.

Previous research on the link between prison releases and criminal activity focused largely on the determinants of postrelease parole failure, or recidivism broadly defined. In such research the principal measures of recidivism are being returned to the custody of a state or federal prison, being sanctioned in some other form by the parole system (jail time or forced treatment for substance abuse), or absconding.[6] Although criminal activity is likely to be correlated with these measures of failure, they are at best noisy measures of the crime committed by former inmates. Variation over time and across states in parole failure rates most likely reflects policy variation rather than the underlying criminality of the parole population. Moreover, the fact that many parolees are returned to prison for technical parole violations (and not new crimes) attenuates the link between actual criminal behavior and common measures of recidivism.

In this paper we assess the impact of recent prison releases on regional crime rates. Using state-level data for the time period 1977 to 1999, we test for a direct correlation between net changes in the population of

3. Glaze (2002).
4. Lynch and Sabol (2001).
5. Rose and Clear (1998).
6. Gendreau and others (1996).

recently released prison inmates and changes in violent and property felony crimes. We also present comparable estimates of the effect of new court commitments to prison on state crime rates, interpreting the impact of a new court commitment as that of incarcerating an offender that has never been to prison. We compare the relative impacts of new court commitments and prison releases on crime to gauge the relative propensity of former inmates to engage in crime after release.

We find that a net increase in the population of former inmates positively and significantly affects nearly all felony offenses. For most crimes, a recently released inmate increases crime by less than the absolute value of the crime reduction resulting from the average new court commitment, though the magnitudes are comparable. The magnitude of our estimates suggests that in a typical year during the 1990s, the net increase in the population of exoffenders caused by prison releases during the previous year accounts for approximately 2.0 percent of property crime and 2.5 percent of violent crime.

For the violent crimes of murder and robbery, recent prison releases account for substantially larger proportions. Approximately 14 percent of murder and 7 percent of robbery in 1994 can be explained by the net increase in the population of former inmates over the prior year. In comparison, these new releases amount to roughly one-tenth of a percent of the noninstitutionalized population. The amount of crime attributable to all exoffenders is likely to be larger than our estimates of the amount of crime committed by recent prison releases, given that the population of noninstitutionalized former inmates is many times the population of net prison releases in any year during the 1990s.

However, we find that prisoners released during the 1990s have much smaller effects on crime than prisoners released during earlier time periods. This result, combined with the finding of a diminished marginal effect of new court commitments, suggests that the marginal offender incarcerated in the late 1990s is much less criminally active than the marginal offender incarcerated in decades past. We also find that in states with strong centralized parole boards, prison releases have considerably smaller effects on most crimes, although this pattern is not uniform for all offenses. This result indicates that providing state correction departments with discretion over whom to release and when may result in less postrelease criminal activity. In conjunction, these two results suggest that states could probably reduce their steady-state prison population from current levels in a targeted and deliberate fashion without appreciably affecting crime rates.

The Impact on Crime of Prison Releases and Admits

Inmates released from state and federal prison are released subject to a set of conditions on behavior and postrelease surveillance, or they are unconditionally released. Most conditionally released inmates are remanded to the authority of state parole systems. Parole is technically defined as a period of conditional supervision following release from prison.[7] An inmate can be paroled at the discretion of a state parole board (discretionary parole) or through statutory requirement (mandatory parole).

A sizable minority of inmates leave prison without any form of postrelease supervision or conditions. In states with determinate sentencing policies, inmates who have "maxed out" their sentences in prison are generally released into the community with no form of supervision and no parole conditions. In other instances, early releases that are deemed low risk may avoid parole altogether and be released unconditionally.

Figure 1 shows the distribution of prison releases by type of release for 1999. We compute these tabulations from the National Correctional Reporting Program (NCRP) database.[8] Approximately 68 percent of inmates are released to the authority of the state and federal parole systems, with the majority paroled by mandate (40 percent of all releases). An additional 9 percent are released under some alternative form of conditional release and supervision in the community. The remaining 23 percent of releases are inmates whose sentence expired while serving time.

7. Parole conditions generally vary with the offender. At a minimum, parolees are required to maintain contact with a supervising parole officer, not to abuse drugs, and not to engage in criminal activity of any kind. However, additional conditions may be placed on certain offenders, such as prohibitions against alcohol consumption, requirements that the exoffender stay away from victims, and requirements that the parolee make restitution to the victim. Parole violations can result in a number of alternative sanctions. For example, a parolee that fails a drug test may be fined, required to attend a substance abuse program, or in some instance be returned to prison. In general, length of time on parole does not exceed three years and the average parole term is slightly more than a year.

8. The NCRP provides microdata information on all prison admissions, prison releases, and parole releases occurring during a given calendar year. Currently, 38 state correction departments, the federal correction system, and the California Youth Authority are included. The distribution in figure 1 omits prisoners that are released because of an inter-prison transfer or because of the death of the inmate.

Figure 1. Distribution of Prisoners Released, by Avenue of Release, 1999

Percent of releases

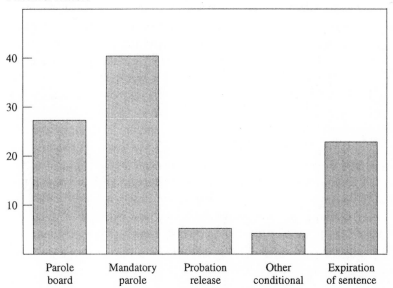

Source: Authors' calculations based on National Corrections Reporting Program database.

The majority of prison inmates will eventually be released, most to some form of conditional supervision. In 1997, 65 percent of surveyed inmates in state and federal prison indicated that they had a definite release date. An additional 32 percent indicated that they anticipated eventually leaving prison. Of the 97 percent of inmates who anticipated being released, nearly 60 percent indicated that their set release date or the soonest possible date of release would occur during the 1997, 1998, or 1999 calendar years.[9]

Research on the impact of changes in the prison incarceration rate on crime decisively demonstrates that incarceration reduces crime rates and that the increase in incarceration during the past two decades has played a key role in reducing crime during the 1990s.[10] Theoretically, an increase in the prison incarceration rate affects crime through two separate effects: it incapacitates convicted offenders by removing them from

9. The figures cited in this paragraph are based on our tabulations of the 1997 Survey of State and Federal Prison Inmates.
10. Levitt (1996, 2003).

society and deters potential offenders through a higher risk of incarceration in the event of detection and conviction. However, deterrent effects are likely to be small. Empirical research on the impact of sentence enhancements on crime generally finds small deterrent effects. Moreover, ethnographic research on criminally active youth tends to indicate a high tolerance for risk, and by extension, a low sensitivity to changes therein.[11] Thus much of the reduction in crime resulting from increased prison incarceration rates is likely to reflect the impact of incapacitating the criminally active.

Put simply, prisoner release may increase crime by reversing the incapacitation effect of incarceration. However, for several reasons, the extent of this reversal may differ from the incapacitation effect of incarcerating a new prisoner. First, the selective releases may result in compositional differences between prison admits and prison releases. And prisoners may undergo personal transformations that increase or decrease their propensity to commit crimes on release. Finally, most prisoners are conditionally released and subject to postrelease supervision, a factor that is likely to suppress criminal activity.

Differences in Characteristics of the Marginal Prisoner Release and Prison Admit

The relative effects on crime of releasing an additional inmate and incarcerating an additional offender will surely depend on the characteristics of the marginal release and the marginal prison admission. To the extent that a select group of prisoners is systematically released from prison, the characteristics of the marginal release and marginal prison admit are likely to be different. As a precursor to our more formal analysis of this question, we present comparisons of the average characteristics and criminal backgrounds of releases and new prison admits.

Table 1 compares the demographic characteristics of released prisoners and prison admits in 1999 using data from the NCRP. For prison releases, the table presents tabulations for all releases, prisoners released to some form of conditional supervision, and releases because of expired sentences. In general, released inmates are quite similar to newly admitted prisoners. The level of educational attainment among prison releases

11. Marvell and Moody (1995); Raphael and Ludwig (2002); Levitt and Venkatesh (2000).

Table 1. Characteristics of Individuals Released and Admitted to State and Federal Prisons, 1999[a]

| | *Prison releases* | | | |
Item	*All releases*	*Conditional releases*	*Expired sentences*	*Prison admissions*
Male	0.903	0.902	0.907	0.900
Race/ethnicity				
White	0.479	0.495	0.430	0.469
Black	0.486	0.468	0.535	0.509
Other	0.035	0.037	0.035	0.022
Hispanic	0.132	0.151	0.060	0.134
Education				
<8th grade	0.116	0.110	0.126	0.129
9th grade	0.117	0.110	0.131	0.116
10th grade	0.158	0.153	0.167	0.155
11th grade	0.165	0.164	0.166	0.158
12th grade/GED	0.363	0.380	0.330	0.363
Some college	0.066	0.066	0.066	0.063
College degree	0.010	0.001	0.010	0.009
Year of admission				
1996 or earlier	0.202	0.201	0.206	0.00
1997	0.131	0.131	0.130	0.00
1998	0.369	0.373	0.357	0.00
1999	0.298	0.295	0.307	1.00
Type of most recent admission				
New commit	0.551	0.498	0.743	0.600
Parole revoked	0.373	0.424	0.197	0.213
Probation revoked	0.040	0.042	0.037	0.047
Prior felony incarceration	0.272	0.232	0.408	0.152
Escapee	0.052	0.065	0.028	0.000
Age at admission				
25th percentile	25.0	25.2	24.3	24.7
50th percentile	31.6	31.8	31.1	31.9
75th percentile	38.4	38.5	38.0	38.9
Age at release				
25th percentile	26.9	27.1	26.1	...
50th percentile	33.4	33.6	32.9	...
75th percentile	40.0	40.0	39.7	...

a. Figures tabulated from the National Corrections Reporting System microdata set for 1999 (parts 1 and 2).

is quite low. Fully 56 percent of releases in 1999 had fewer than twelve years of schooling (compared with 14 percent of the overall adult population in 1999). Releases are half black, 13 percent Hispanic, and 90 percent male. Roughly 80 percent began their current spell in prison within the last three calendar years, with 37 percent having been returned to custody for a parole violation. Almost a third of releases had a felony incarceration before their current prison commitment. Finally, the median released prisoner was 31.6 years of age at admission to prison and left prison at the age of 33.4.

Although there are a few differences between the average characteristics of new prison admits and prisoner releases, the two groups are quite similar. The racial-ethnic distributions, as well as the distribution of prior educational attainment, are nearly identical. The distribution of age at admission is similar for releases and admits, although in 1999 the releases are roughly one to two years older than new admissions. A larger proportion of new prison admits are sent to prison on a new court commitment (0.60), and a smaller proportion is being returned to custody because of revoked parole (0.21). Similarly, a smaller fraction of new admits have a prior felony incarceration (0.152).[12]

Table 2 presents tabulations for the first offense on the commitment sending the inmates into the current spell of prison, and the values of the twenty-fifth, fiftieth, and seventy-fifth percentiles of the maximum sentence, minimum sentence, and time served on the current prison admission distributions (measured in months). There are few differences in offense committed between releases and admissions. Although releases are slightly less likely to have committed murder or a sex offense, releases are slightly more likely to have committed robbery and assault, and in general, a violent crime at a rate comparable to new admits. Similar proportions are in prison for property crime and drug offenses.

---

12. There are a few notable differences between inmates released to conditional supervision and those released because of an expired sentence. Those who max out are somewhat less educated than conditional supervision releases and are considerably more likely to be recently admitted on a new court commitment. Expired-sentence releases are also slightly younger. While we cannot present similar tabulations for the general prison population from the NCRP data, we did calculate some figures in common with those in table 1 from the 1997 Survey of State and Federal Prisoners. The distributions of inmates by race and ethnicity and by educational attainment are nearly identical. The general population of inmates is somewhat older on average than the population of new admits and releases.

Table 2. Offense and Sentencing Characteristics of Individuals Released and Admitted to State and Federal Prisons, 1999[a]

	Prison releases			
Item	All releases	Conditional releases	Expired sentences	Prison admissions
Offense committed				
Murder	0.024	0.025	0.019	0.034
Kidnapping	0.006	0.006	0.006	0.005
Sex offense	0.043	0.040	0.054	0.049
Robbery	0.090	0.096	0.068	0.079
Assault	0.087	0.086	0.093	0.083
Other violent	0.006	0.006	0.006	0.007
Burglary	0.121	0.122	0.116	0.116
Arson	0.004	0.004	0.005	0.004
Auto theft	0.026	0.029	0.013	0.020
Other property	0.156	0.145	0.192	0.152
Drug trafficking	0.163	0.178	0.114	0.146
Drug possession	0.086	0.083	0.097	0.097
Drug unspecified	0.017	0.015	0.023	0.036
Weapons	0.031	0.032	0.027	0.028
Escapees	0.007	0.006	0.011	0.007
DUI	0.033	0.029	0.045	0.038
Maximum sentence, months				
25th percentile	24	24	12	24
50th percentile	36	44	24	36
75th percentile	72	72	60	72
Minimum sentence, months				
25th percentile	5	6	3	3
50th percentile	13	17	9	12
75th percentile	32	36	24	30
Time served on admission, months				
25th percentile	5	5	5	. . .
50th percentile	10	11	10	. . .
75th percentile	24	24	25	. . .

a. Figures tabulated from the National Corrections Reporting System microdata set for 1999 (parts 1 and 2).

Perhaps the best gauges of the relative severity of offending are found in the distribution of the maximum and minimum sentences. The quartile breaks in maximum sentences are identical for releases and admissions (twenty-four, thirty-six, and seventy-two months). The minimum sentences are also similar, with the minimum sentence for new admits generally one to two months lower than those for releases. Prison releases serve considerably less time than the maximum sentence and somewhat less time than the stated minimum sentence on their current prison spell.

The latter fact may be partly because of the high proportion of releases that are in prison owing to a parole violation.[13]

The patterns in tables 1 and 2 suggest that the criminal propensity of new admits and prison releases are similar. Although those released are slightly older than new admits and, thus along this dimension, less criminally prone, released inmates show more evidence of repeat offending (a prior felony incarceration, revoked parole). Both groups commit comparable offenses and have similar sentence length distributions—that is, the severity of offending placing them in prison on the current spell is roughly the same. Thus these tabulations alone suggest that the average incapacitation effect on crime for each new prison admission is likely to be similar in absolute value to the reverse incapacitation effect associated with parole and other avenues of prisoner release.

How Prison May Alter the Criminality of Inmates

One pre-post incarceration change that is likely to increase the criminality of many newly released offenders is that the released inmates have felony criminal records.[14] Employers express an extreme aversion to hiring exoffenders, and an increasing proportion of employers check the criminal history records of job applicants before hiring them. While research investigating the link between employment status and parolee recidivism finds a small effect of employment for recent prison releases overall, being employed tends to have larger effects on those that are the least likely to reoffend.[15] Thus, to the extent that having served time permanently alters one's ability to secure employment, all else equal, those released from prison may be, on average, more criminally active postrelease than before incarceration.

---

13. In other words, a parolee may serve the minimum sentence during a term in prison, be paroled, and then be returned to custody for a parole violation with no new court commitment. Such parolees can only be held in prison for the time remaining on their sentence and are likely to be held in prison for less time. Thus the fact that time served on the current commitment is slightly lower than the minimum sentence does not necessarily mean that releases are serving less than the minimum sentence assigned by the court of commitment.

14. Note that only 27 percent of prison releases in 1999 had a prior felony commitment to prison. Thus, for a majority of released offenders, their criminal history record has been permanently altered.

15. Holzer and others (2001, 2003); Raphael and Weiman (2002).

Figure 2. Participation of State Prison Inmates in Prison Education, Training, Reentry, and Substance Abuse Programs, 1997

Percent of state inmates

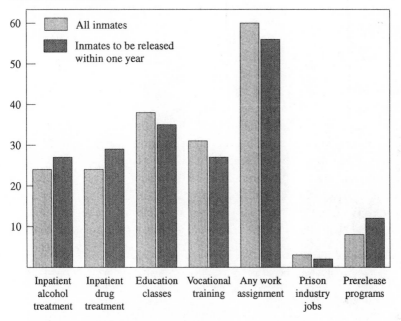

Source: Authors' calculations based on Petersilia (2003).

Similarly, acculturating to the prison environment may adversely affect the criminality of prison releases. In a meta-analysis of 131 recidivism studies, Gendreau and others find that one's companions and the degree to which one exhibits an antisocial personality are among the strongest determinants of recidivism.[16] Serving time clearly exposes inmates to companions strongly predisposed toward committing crimes. Moreover, one may reasonably argue that a spell in prison is likely to engender antisocial feelings and behavior in some individuals.

On the positive side, many inmates do participate in prison programs designed to augment human capital and to address certain needs, and these activities may help militate against potential criminality. Figures 2 and 3 reproduce the tabulations presented by Petersilia on the percentage of state and federal inmates that participate in various prison education

16. Gendreau and others (1996).

Figure 3. Participation of Federal Prison Inmates in Prison Education, Training, Reentry, and Substance Abuse Programs, 1997

Percent of federal inmates

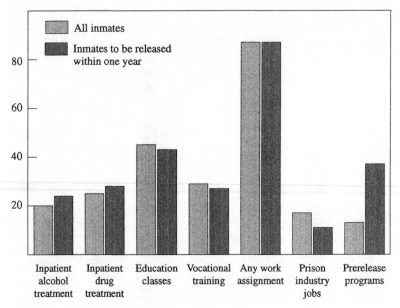

Source: Authors' calculations based on Petersilia (2003).

and substance abuse programs in 1997.[17] Figures are shown for all prisoners and for inmates slated for release within the next twelve months. Roughly 33 percent of state inmates participate in a drug or alcohol abuse program, with 24 percent participating in a drug program and 24 percent participating in an alcohol abuse program. Approximately one-third participates in education programs and vocational training. Only 8 percent of inmates and 12 percent of soon-to-be-released state inmates participate in any prerelease programs. Program participation in federal prison is somewhat higher, especially in prerelease programs intended to smooth the reentry of paroled offenders. Federal prisoners, however, constitute a small fraction of the prison population and of prison releases.

Petersilia argues that the current level of program participation among inmates is distressingly low and notes that in recent years program partic-

17. Petersilia (2003).

ipation rates have declined substantially.[18] Nonetheless, our own tabulations of the survey used to generate the statistics in figures 2 and 3 indicate that while small proportions participate in any given program, a somewhat higher proportion participates in at least one remedial education or job skills program. For example, we calculate that 58 percent of inmates in 1997 participated in a job-training program, an education program, life-skills classes, or a prerelease program. Adding drug and alcohol treatment to the list of possible program increases this figure to 67 percent. To the extent that inmates are self-selecting into prison programs based on self-assessed need, one might conclude that a fair proportion of prisoners do receive some rehabilitative services while incarcerated. Of course, whether these services affect postrelease criminal activity is an open question.

Another factor that is likely to affect postrelease criminal activity is that inmates age while incarcerated. Table 1 shows that released inmates are one to two years older than newly admitted inmates. Moreover, many studies find strong inverse relationships between age and the likelihood of participating in criminal activity. While age is one of the weaker determinants of recidivism among paroled offenders with an effect in cross-tabulations that is often masked by the much stronger effect of prior criminal history, aging should certainly exert some influence on postrelease crime (table 3).[19]

On net, whether offenders leave prison with a higher or lower propensity to commit crime is a theoretically ambiguous question. A felony record and the social and psychological impact of incarceration are likely to increase criminality. Participation in prison programs and the aging of inmates are likely to reduce criminality. In the end, the net effect of serving time on criminal activity is an empirical question.

Postrelease Surveillance and Service Provision

To the extent that parole agents monitor the activities of recently released inmates, the reversal of the prison incapacitation effect is likely

18. For example, inmate self-reports indicate that more than two-third of inmates abuse alcohol or drugs, yet only one-third participate in any form of substance abuse program. In addition, the inmate population is quite undereducated compared with the general population, yet fewer than 40 percent participate in a formal education program.
19. Greenberg (1985); Gendreau and others (1996); Raphael and Weiman (2002).

to be less than complete. Parolees are required to check in with their parole officer within twenty-four hours of being discharged, inform their parole officer if they change address or place of employment, and generally obey the instructions of their assigned officer. Surely, at some level that should help deter parolees from committing further crimes.

However, the number of face-to-face contacts between parolees and parole officers is quite low on average. The required monitoring by a parole agent of a given parolee depends on the assessment by parole authorities of the risk to society posed by the parolee. According to Petersilia, 85 percent of parolees are classified as regular caseload types and meet with a parole officer less than twice a month.[20] The average regular parolee caseload in 2001 was 66 cases per parole officer. Parolees designated for more intensive monitoring may meet with a parole officer four to six times per month and, in certain cases, may be subject to electronic monitoring. Average caseloads for parolees designated as high-risk range from 13 to 32 parolees per officer.[21] And as figure 1 shows, a sizable share of prisoners are released unconditionally and are not subject to parole restrictions.

Postrelease services intended to ease prisoner reentry include halfway houses, work-release programs, and prisoner reentry programs designed to aid the search for employment, housing, and other social services. Only 10 percent of released inmates participate in reentry programs on release, and fewer than 10 percent reside in halfway houses. Hence the impact of postrelease service provision on recidivism is likely to be very small.[22]

Recidivism and Crime Rates

The lion's share of research on postrelease criminal activity focuses largely on recidivism defined as failing to meet the terms of one's parole.

---

20. Petersilia (2003).

21. There is little empirical evidence documenting lower recidivism rates from smaller caseloads per parole officer. Petersilia and Turner (1993) do show that smaller caseloads are associated with higher recidivism rates. With fewer caseloads, parole officers are able to scrutinize parolees' actions. This monitoring is more likely to uncover technical violations of parolees. But parolee crime rates could be higher with higher caseloads as parole officers have less time to monitor.

22. Petersilia (2003). That is not to say that such programs do not have an impact on recidivism, but that the extremely low participation rates suggest that the overall effect of such programs on abating postrelease crime is likely to be small.

The common metrics of postrelease parole failure include the rates at which parolees abscond from parole supervision, the proportion of parolees that are rearrested within given time periods of release, and the proportion of parolees returned to the custody of the state or federal prison systems for violating the terms of their parole.

Table 3 presents estimates of the rate at which parolees in California are returned to custody within six months, one year, two years, and three years of release.[23] These tabulations are based on microlevel administrative records pertaining to all prison terms beginning during the 1990s with a prison release date occurring before 1999.[24] Many of the findings from the recidivism research are evident in table 3. To start, a large share of parolees are returned to custody in California within a fairly short period. Approximately one-third of paroled offenders are rearrested and reincarcerated within six months of release, half are returned to custody within one year, while nearly two-thirds are returned to custody within three years. Nationwide, roughly two-thirds of parolees are re-arrested within three years of release, a pattern that has been consistently documented during the past thirty-five years, with roughly half returned to prison custody.[25]

The figures in table 3 show that black inmates are returned to custody at a slightly higher rate than white inmates (a difference of 3 to 4 percentage points), while Hispanic inmates are far less likely to be returned to custody than either white or black offenders. Male offenders are more likely than female offenders to serve a subsequent prison term. Although there is little relationship between age at time of release and the likelihood of being reincarcerated, the number of prior prison terms served is strongly positively correlated with the likelihood of being returned to custody. Approximately one-fifth of parolees released from their first term in prison are returned within six months, compared with more than two-fifths of offenders released from their third or higher term. Given the strong correlation between age and terms served, the strong effect of previous prison terms masks a sizable partial correlation between age at time

23. Considering that nearly all inmates in California are released to parole, the figures in the table are representative of all released inmates in the state.

24. See Raphael and Weiman (2002) for a complete description of these data and an analysis of the effects of personal characteristics and economic conditions on the likelihood that California parolees are returned to custody.

25. Petersilia (2003).

Table 3. Proportion of Prison Terms in California Where the Parolee Is Returned to Custody within Six, Twelve, Twenty-Four, and Thirty-Six Months of Release, by Offender Characteristics[a]

	Proportion of terms	Returns to prison within			
		6 months	12 months	24 months[b]	36 months[b]
All terms	1.00	0.34	0.52	0.62	0.64
Age at time of release					
18 to 20	0.02	0.30	0.50	0.61	0.64
21 to 25	0.16	0.32	0.51	0.62	0.64
26 to 30	0.23	0.34	0.52	0.63	0.65
31 to 35	0.23	0.35	0.54	0.64	0.66
36 to 40	0.18	0.35	0.54	0.63	0.65
41 plus	0.18	0.32	0.58	0.58	0.60
Male	0.90	0.34	0.53	0.63	0.65
Female	0.10	0.27	0.45	0.56	0.59
White	0.33	0.35	0.54	0.64	0.66
Black	0.34	0.38	0.57	0.68	0.70
Hispanic	0.30	0.28	0.45	0.54	0.57
Asian	0.01	0.20	0.33	0.43	0.46
Other	0.02	0.29	0.45	0.54	0.56
Offense committed					
Murder/manslaughter	0.01	0.20	0.33	0.44	0.47
Robbery	0.08	0.31	0.49	0.59	0.61
Assault	0.07	0.31	0.49	0.60	0.63
Sex crimes	0.03	0.28	0.41	0.50	0.53
Kidnapping	0.00	0.26	0.39	0.49	0.52
Burglary	0.14	0.38	0.56	0.66	0.68
Theft/fraud/other property	0.22	0.38	0.58	0.68	0.70
Drug crimes	0.36	0.33	0.51	0.61	0.63
Escape	0.00	0.50	0.66	0.74	0.76
DUI	0.04	0.20	0.34	0.44	0.46
Arson	0.00	0.31	0.46	0.55	0.58
Weapons possession	0.04	0.34	0.54	0.66	0.69
Other	0.01	0.32	0.48	0.59	0.62
Term group					
First	0.36	0.21	0.37	0.49	0.52
Second	0.21	0.34	0.54	0.65	0.67
Third or higher	0.44	0.44	0.63	0.72	0.73

a. Data refer to all terms served in California beginning during the 1990s and with an outdate occurring before 1999.
b. For this column the sample is restricted to those commitments with first terms ending prior to 1998.

of release and the likelihood of being returned to custody holding the number of previous terms constant.[26]

The differences in return rate by offense committed are large. Those inmates convicted of violent offenses (murder, rape, assault) are less likely to be returned to custody than offenders convicted of property offenses (burglary, theft). Offenders sentenced for driving under the influence or for a drug offense are also relatively less likely to serve subsequent prison terms. Again, these patterns are comparable to those documented in the research on parolee recidivism.[27]

Although these results are informative and indicative of how difficult a problem prisoner reentry is for offenders, as well as state correction officials, the commonly used measures of parole failure are at best noisy measures of criminal offending. For starters, parole failure rates are determined in part by cross-state variation in parole policies on what constitutes a parole violation and the sanctions that are meted out in the event of a violation. For example, the high rates at which parolees are returned to custody in California reflect in large part the explicit policy of the California Board of Prison Terms to revoke parole for virtually any violation, whether or not the violation constitutes a felonious act. Even among parolees returned to prison custody in California, many are returned for a technical parole violation rather than for the commission of a new felony offense.[28] This is not the case in all states, a fact reflected in state differences in overall parole failure rates.[29]

Moreover, the monitoring of parolees has a strong impact on the proportion of parolees that fail. This fact is best illustrated by an evaluation of a national demonstration program intended to assess the impact of a

26. In a more detailed analysis of these data, Raphael and Weiman (2002) find strong partial effects of age on the likelihood of being returned to custody once the number of prior terms served is taken into account. Relative to parolees that are over 40, 18- to 20-year-olds are 15 percent more likely to be returned to custody within one year, 21- to 25-year-olds are 7 percent more likely, while those that are 26 to 30 or 31 to 35 are roughly 5 percent more likely to be returned to custody after accounting for the number of prior terms served.

27. Gendreau and others (1996); Petersilia (2003).

28. Travis and Lawrence (2002). Travis (2003) estimates that in the year 2000 of the 90,000 plus California parolees returned to prison in 2000, more than 70,000 were returned for a technical parole violation rather than for a new offense.

29. In 1999 the proportion of parolees that fail to successfully complete their term of parole ranges from 17.1 percent in Massachusetts to 81.5 percent in Utah. The median state failure rate was 43.5 percent (Florida). Hughes, Wilson, and Beck (2001).

reduction in the caseloads of parole officers. Petersilia and Turner find that a reduction in the ratio of cases to parole officers causes an increase in the parolee recidivism rate, as parole officers have more time to closely scrutinize the behavior of parolees.[30] Finally, gauging the amount of crime committed by paroled inmates from arrest and parole violation statistics misses all crime that is undetected by parole authorities, as well as crime committed by those who are released unconditionally. Hence common measures of parolee failure rates are poor metrics of the amount of crime committed by recently released inmates.

In 2002 the Bureau of Justice Statistics released an analysis of prisoner recidivism that presents a more direct assessment of the amount of crime committed by released prisoners. The BJS analysis focused on a sample of all prisoners released in 1994 from fifteen state prison systems, linking prisoner release records to arrest records from the fifteen corresponding state criminal history repositories.[31] The study uses this linked sample to present various estimates of recidivism. For our purposes, the most useful calculations are the proportions of arrests for felony offenses in 1994 that are accounted for by prisoners released.

The BJS finds that released inmates account for a disproportionately large share of felony arrests in the fifteen states under study (11 percent of homicide arrests, 10 percent of robbery arrests, 12 percent of burglary arrests, and roughly 10 percent of those arrested for motor vehicle theft). Given that recent prison releases account for less than one half of 1 percent of the noninstitutionalized population, these figures suggest a very high rate of offending among released prisoners. The 180,000 released offenders rearrested within three years (roughly 68 percent of releases) racked up 744,480 new felony charges, an average of four new crimes for each offender. More than 100,000 of these charges were violent offenses.

To be sure, the BJS figures are flawed measures of the proportional contribution of parolees to crime. For one, the authors measure the number of charges filed against former prisoners rather than the number of crimes for which former prisoners are convicted. Since parolees and other releases are likely to be among the first suspects investigated and

---

30. Petersilia and Turner (1993).

31. For the direct assessment see Langan and Levin (2002). The states included in this analysis are Arizona, California, Delaware, Florida, Illinois, Maryland, Michigan, Minnesota, New Jersey, New York, North Carolina, Ohio, Oregon, Texas, and Virginia.

perhaps charged by authorities, one might argue that a total count of charges is likely to overstate the criminality of releases. Alternatively, former inmates are likely to commit serious crimes for which they are never caught. Thus a count of charges may also understate the amount of crime attributable to this population. Nonetheless, these figures suggest that released prisoners commit crime at rates substantially higher than that of the average noninstitutionalized resident.

A study that presents a more direct assessment of the effect of prisoner releases on crime is Clear and others.[32] Using geocoded prisoner release and crime data for the city of Tallahassee, the authors show that an increase in resident released prisoners in one year is associated with an increase in crime in the following year.

Empirical Strategy and Data Description

We assess the contributions of recent prison releases to crime in the United States by estimating the direct effect of changes in the exoffender population on changes in the number of felony offenses reported to the police. Unlike previous recidivism research that analyzes the arrest records of released offenders, we rely on the estimated relationship between released offenders and aggregate crime rates to provide an accounting of the proportion of crime attributable to this group. The benefits of this approach are several. First, by directly estimating the effect of releases on crime, we bypass the problems associated with variation in state policy, sanctions definitions, and enforcement efforts. In addition, the estimated relationship between exinmates and the overall crime rate does not depend on whether the police apprehend the offending releasee (as the crime must simply be reported by the victim to be included in the total crime count) and will not be influenced by the erroneous arrests of exoffenders for crimes not committed.

We hypothesize that state-level crime rates are positively influenced by the population of exinmates and the population of potential offenders that have yet to serve a prison sentence. Assuming a linearly additive functional form, a simple empirical specification of state crime rates is given by the equation

32. Clear and others (2003).

$$(1) \quad Crime_{it} = \alpha_i + \beta_1 ExInmates_{it} + \beta_2 OtherOffenders_{it} + \Gamma' X_{it} + \varepsilon_{it},$$

where $i = (1, \ldots, I)$ indexes states, $t = (1, \ldots, T)$ indexes year, $Crime_{it}$ measures the number of crimes committed per 100,000 state residents, $ExInmates_{it}$ measures the number of former inmates per 100,000 state residents residing in noninstitutionalized society, $OtherOffenders_{it}$ gives the number of offenders that have yet to be incarcerated per 100,0000, X_{it} is a vector of state-level control variables that vary over time, α_i proxies a complete set of state fixed effects, β_1, β_2, and Γ are parameters to be estimated, and ε_{it} is a mean zero normally distributed error term. We allow the marginal effects of an exinmate and an offender that has never been incarcerated to differ from one another because of the considerations discussed earlier.

The principal problem that we encounter in estimating equation 1 is that neither the population of exoffenders nor the population of offenders that has yet to be incarcerated are observable. While the BJS does estimate the size of the national population of exinmates, these figures are tentative at best, computed for a small number of years, and have never been calculated at the state level.[33] And clearly a group that is nearly impossible to identify in levels is the population of other potential offenders.

Although we cannot measure the populations of exoffenders and other offenders, we can approximate changes in these populations from aggregate data on flows into and out of prison. Taking first differences of equation 1 yields,

$$(2) \quad \Delta Crime_{it} = \beta_1 \Delta ExOffenders_{it} + \beta_2 \Delta OtherOffenders_{it} + \Gamma' \Delta X_{it} + v_{it},$$

where Δ indicates the change between year t and year $t-1$, v_{it} is equal to $\varepsilon_{it} - \varepsilon_{it-1}$, and all other variables and parameters are as defined above. The change in the population of exoffenders at the state level equals prison releases in a given year less those exoffenders that are returned to prison

---

33. An alternative possibility would be to use state level parole population as estimates of the population of recently released exoffenders. In fact, this was the strategy employed in an earlier draft of this study. A major problem with this strategy concerns the fact that the proportion of offenders that are released to parole varies greatly across states and over time within states and thus is a poor gauge of the size of the population of recently released inmates.

for violating parole or for a new offense. The change in the population of other, never-incarcerated offenders will be equal to those members of this group that are incarcerated for the first time (those admitted to prison on new court commitments).[34] These flows, when cumulated, sum to the total change in the prison population and are observable for all states between 1977 and 1999.

We approximate the change in the population of exinmates at the state and year level using state-level data on total prison releases and total returns to prison of conditionally released inmates. The net change in the exoffender population is calculated by subtracting conditional returns to prison from total prison releases during a given calendar year.[35] We use new court commitments to prison as a gauge of the prison-induced change in the population of never-incarcerated offenders (that is to say, new court commitments reduce the population of noninstitutionalized offenders from this group).

To be sure, some new court commitments are attributable to former prison inmates. However, tabulations of the 1999 National Corrections Reporting System microdata indicate that new court commitments are overwhelmingly composed of never-incarcerated offenders. Approximately 8 percent of those admitted to prison on a new court commitment in 1999 have a previous felony incarceration on a previous court commitment. The comparable figure for all prison admission is 27 percent (table 1), while the comparable figure for conditional returns to prison is approximately 31 percent. Thus new court commitments are a fairly good gauge of changes in the population of never-incarcerated offenders.

Before presenting estimates of the first-differenced equation 2, several specification issues merit further discussion. First, the differencing of equation 1 eliminates state fixed effects in the crime equation. Thus all interstate fixed differences in crime fundamentals are purged from the data. We augment the specification in equation 2 by adding a full set of state fixed effects and a full set of year effects. The state fixed effects control for state-specific linear time trends in crime rates, while the time

---

34. To be sure, mortality will also contribute to changes in these populations. We are unable to observe this source of changes and thus focus on the changes in these populations driven by variation in the prison population.

35. Conditional returns to prison are given by total admissions to prison minus the number of new commitments to prison.

effect controls for year-to-year shifts in the changes in crime rates that are common to all states.

Second, as specified, the crime equations 1 and 2 restrict the marginal effects of exoffenders and never-incarcerated offenders to being constant—that is, the functional form does not allow for incapacitation effects that vary with the size of the prison population. Ideally, one would fit more flexible functional forms to the data by, for example, including quadratic or higher-order terms in equation 1. However, since we cannot observe the population of exoffenders or potential offenders in levels, this is not possible. Below, we test for heterogeneity in the marginal effects by estimating separate effects by time period. Since the prison and exoffender populations were considerably smaller during earlier time periods, cross-time period differences in the marginal crime effects provide some information on how the marginal effects of new court commitments and released offenders have changed as the prison population has increased.

Finally, in the following models we lag the key explanatory variables (the number of new court commitments and the net prison releases, both expressed per 100,000) by one year. Both variables are likely to be simultaneously determined with changes in crime rates in corresponding years. For example, an increase in new court commitments in 1977 is likely the result of crimes committed in 1977, thus inducing a spurious positive correlation between new court commitments and crime rates (that is, implying that sending people to prison increases crime). Similarly, if parole revocations result from the criminal activity of exoffenders, conditional returns to prison will be positively correlated with crime in any given year. Since we are gauging net changes in the population of exoffenders by total releases less conditional returns to prison, this will induce a spurious negative correlation between increases in the exoffender population and crime rates (implying that letting people out of prison reduces crime). To assuage this problem somewhat, we follow the lead of existing research on the relationship between incarceration and crime and lag the dependent variables by one year.[36] Thus we are primarily estimating the effect of net prison releases and new court commitments during year *t* on crimes committed in year *t+1*.

---

36. Levitt (1996).

Table 4. Descriptive Statistics for the State-Level Panel[a]

Variable	Mean	Standard deviation
Violent crimes (per 100,000)	615.62	258.38
Murder	8.37	3.49
Rape	36.68	12.08
Robbery	218.60	128.36
Assault	351.94	153.87
Property crimes (per 100,000)	4,729.79	1,146.83
Burglary	1,228.03	425.01
Larceny	2,977.33	687.79
Motor vehicle theft	524.42	227.96
Net releases per 100,000	82.22	46.95
New commits per 100,000	98.33	51.13
Unemployment rate	6.46	1.98
Poverty	0.13	0.04
Proportion black	0.12	0.08
Proportion metropolitan	0.78	0.17
Proportion under 17	0.27	0.02
Proportion 18 to 24	0.11	0.02
N	1,150	. . .

a. Figures are weighted by state-level population.

We estimate several variants of equation 2 with a state-level panel data set covering the period from 1977 to 1999. Annual data on crime comes from the Federal Bureau of Investigation Uniform Crime Reports (UCR). The UCR measures all felony offenses reported to individual police departments aggregated to the state level. We analyze the impact of exoffenders and new court commitments on overall violent crime (the sum of murder, rape, robbery, and aggravated assault), overall property crime (the sum of burglary, larceny, and auto theft), and the individual felony components of the overall violent and property crime rates. Data on new court commitments, returns to prison of the conditionally released, and total prison releases come from the Bureau of Justice Statistics. State-level demographic data (age distribution, proportion black, residing in metropolitan area, and the proportion poor) come from the U.S. Census Bureau. Finally, state unemployment rates come from the Bureau of Labor Statistics Geographic Profile data series.

Table 4 presents basic descriptive statistics of the key dependent and explanatory variables. Property crime occurs with much greater frequency than violent crime. The average property crime rate is nearly eight times the average violent crime rate. Within these aggregations, the

Table 5. State Panel Regressions of Changes in the Violent and Property Crime Rates on the Net Changes in the Population of Recently Released Inmates and New Court Commitments to State Prison[a]

Item	Change in violent crime rate		Change in property crime rate	
Net change, releases	0.21	0.16	2.95	2.21
	(0.11)	(0.09)	(0.59)	(0.46)
New commitments	−0.53	−0.30	−4.15	−2.67
	(0.11)	(0.09)	(0.57)	(0.48)
ΔUnemployment rate	2.326	−0.89	16.46	47.25
	(1.39)	(1.65)	(7.42)	(8.56)
ΔProportion poor	134.51	−38.02	955.42	980.41
	(95.33)	(78.61)	(510.27)	(406.27)
ΔProportion black	−2951.14	516.71	−7646.52	2612.27
	(1430.91)	(1297.32)	(7659.02)	(6705.02)
ΔProportion metropolitan	560.56	665.77	−223.54	1514.18
	(224.53)	(197.26)	(1201.78)	(1019.54)
ΔProportion under 17	−629.23	467.87	−5236.67	−9269.36
	(773.79)	(776.53)	(4141.74)	(4013.38)
ΔProportion 18 to 24	−4361.13	1009.02	−20552.21	−3576.35
	(903.29)	(1078.77)	(4834.91)	(5575.48)
State effects	Yes	Yes	Yes	Yes
Year effects	No	Yes	No	Yes
F test[b]	37.50	9.45	17.92	3.62
(P value)	(0.001)	(0.002)	(0.001)	(0.058)

a. Standard errors are in parentheses. All regressions include a constant term and are weighted by the state population.

b. The reported F statistics and P values come from tests of the hypothesis that the reverse incapacitation effect equals the absolute value of the incapacitation effect of new commitments.

most serious crimes are the least frequent. For example, during the 1977 to 2001 period, the average state homicide rate is 8.2 incidents per 100,000, while the average for aggravated assault is 350 per 100,000.

Results

The results are as follows.

Estimated crime effects for 1977 to 1999

Table 5 presents crime-rate regression model estimates where the dependent variable is the change in the overall violent crime rate or the change in the overall property crime rate. For each crime, the table presents estimation results for two specifications: the change equation (2) augmented with a full set of state fixed effects, and equation 2 inclusive of a full set of state fixed effects and year fixed effects. Beginning with the violent crime results, net increases in the population of exoffenders (measured by the "net change, releases" variable) positively affect crime in both specifications (significant at the 5 percent level in the first specifications and the 10 percent level in the second). A one-person increase in the number of released inmates per 100,000 residents increases the violent crime rate by approximately 0.2.

This positive effect is somewhat smaller than the absolute value of the impact of a new court commitment on violent crime. The estimation results indicate that each new court commitment to prison reduces the violent crime rate by 0.3 to 0.5 incidents (both estimates statistically significant at the 1 percent level of confidence). F tests of the hypothesis that the marginal effect of a prison release on violent crime is equal to the absolute value of the marginal effect of a new court commitment reject the null at the 1 percent level in both specifications (test results are displayed in the bottom line of the table). Thus the reverse incapacitation effect of a prison release is much smaller than the incapacitation effect of a new court commitment.

The results are somewhat similar for property crime. Prison releases increase property crime rates in both specifications (both coefficients are significant at the 1 percent level of confidence). Again, the impact on property crime of a one-person increase in the population of exinmates is somewhat smaller than the negative effect on crime of a new court commitment. The results suggest that a one-person increase in the number of exprisoners per 100,000 increases the property crime rate by between 2 and 3 incidents per 100,000. Again, the marginal effects of a release and a new court commitment are statistically distinguishable from one another.

Table 6 presents estimation results for each of the seven felony offenses that are the components of the overall violent and property crime rates. To conserve space, the table provides only the coefficients on net prison releases, new commitments, and the F tests for the equivalence of the crime effects. For each crime, we present results for the specification including state effects (specification 1) and the model including state and year effects (specification 2). With the exception of auto theft and assault, "net releases" positively and significantly affects crime rates. While the marginal effects in models controlling for state and fixed effects are somewhat smaller than the marginal effects in the model con-

Table 6. Marginal Effects of Net Changes in the Population of Recently Released Inmates and New Court Commitments on Individual Violent and Property Crimes[a]

Item	Net change, releases	New commitments	F test (P value)[b]
Δ Murder			
Specification (1)	0.011	−0.015	11.731
	(0.002)	(0.002)	(0.001)
Specification (2)	0.010	−0.014	9.691
	(0.002)	(0.002)	(0.002)
Δ Rape			
Specification (1)	0.023	−0.029	3.285
	(0.007)	(0.007)	(0.071)
Specification (2)	0.019	−0.020	0.072
	(0.007)	(0.007)	(0.797)
Δ Robbery			
Specification (1)	0.235	−0.386	30.061
	(0.057)	(0.056)	(0.001)
Specification (2)	0.179	−0.279	14.982
	(0.049)	(0.051)	(0.001)
Δ Assault			
Specification (1)	−0.061	−0.103	24.251
	(0.069)	(0.067)	(0.001)
Specification (2)	−0.051	0.011	1.524
	(0.062)	(0.065)	(0.217)
Δ Burglary			
Specification (1)	1.606	−1.972	12.554
	(0.216)	(0.209)	(0.001)
Specification (2)	1.003	−1.226	6.672
	(0.163)	(0.169)	(0.010)
Δ Larceny			
Specification (1)	1.161	−1.771	12.564
	(0.361)	(0.349)	(0.001)
Specification (2)	1.039	−1.228	1.434
	(0.298)	(0.311)	(0.232)
Δ Auto theft			
Specification (1)	0.182	−0.405	15.568
	(0.118)	(0.115)	(0.001)
Specification (2)	0.163	−0.216	0.897
	(0.107)	(0.111)	(0.345)

a. Standard errors are in parentheses. Figures correspond to the coefficients on either the net change in releases variable or the new commitments variable. Specification 1 corresponds to the first regression for each crime category in table 5 (inclusive of state fixed effects). Specification 2 corresponds to the third model estimate in table 5 (inclusive of state and year fixed effects). In all models, the dependent variable is the year-to-year change in crime rates.

b. The F statistics and P values reported in this column are from a test of the hypothesis that the reverse incapacitation effect of releasing inmates is equal to the absolute value of the incapacitation effect of new commitments.

trolling for state effects only, all coefficients are statistically significant at the 1 percent level.

With the exception of the assault rate, new court commitments reduce crime in all specifications. Again, the reverse incapacitation effects of releasing an inmate are somewhat smaller than the incapacitation effects of incarcerating a new offender. For the individual crimes, however, there are several specifications for which these effects are not statistically distinguishable from one another. For example, the positive effect of a prison release on rape is statistically identical to the absolute value of the negative effect of a new court commitment in the model with time effects. The same is true for assault, larceny, and auto theft.

To summarize the results in tables 5 and 6, releasing prison inmates is associated with increases in crime. We find positive significant effects of prison releases on the overall violent and property crime rates and for most of the individual felony offenses. However, we do find in many specifications that incapacitating those sent to prison by means of a new court commitment has a larger impact on crime than the effect of releasing prisoners. This may occur because of selective release, personal transformations while in prison, or some other mechanism that gives rise to a difference in criminality between new commitments and releases.

Is the effect of exoffenders on crime stable through time?

The results thus far demonstrate that on average, new court commitments to prison and increases in the population of exoffenders by way of prison release affect state-level crime rates during the period covered by the panel data set. One extension of the analysis of direct policy relevance to states that are considering reducing incarceration rates is to assess whether these marginal crime effects are stable across the subperiods covered by our panel. Given the large increases in prison incarceration rates during the past three decades, one might suspect that the marginal effect on crime of a new court commitment during the 1990s is likely to be smaller than the comparable effect during the 1970s, when incarceration rates were much lower.[37] This would follow if the most dangerous, criminally active offenders are incarcerated first, followed by less dangerous offenders, and so on down the line.

37. The number of prisoners per 100,000 in 1977 was 117. The comparable figure for 1999 is 450.

And given that nearly all prisoners are eventually released (many within relatively short periods), one might also suspect that more recent prison releases have a smaller effect on crime than releases during past time periods. That is, a reduction in the criminality of the offender committed on the margin will likely result in a reduction in the criminality of the offender released on the margin.

To explore the stability of these effects, we estimate separate models for three subperiods covered by the panel data set. Table 7 presents estimates of the effect of net releases and new court commitments on crime rates for three time periods: 1978 to 1984, 1985 to 1991, and 1992 to 1999. For each crime rate and each time period, the table presents the results from a regression of the change in the given crime rate on new releases, new court commitments, the other explanatory variables listed in tables 4 and 5, a complete set of state fixed effects, and a complete set of year fixed effects. To conserve space, the table only presents the coefficient estimates on net releases and new commitments.

For nearly all crime rates, the marginal effects of a prison release and a new court commitment are much larger during the late 1970s and early 1980s compared with the most recent period. For example, each one-person increase in the population of former inmates increases the violent crime rate by slightly more than one incident during the early period. During the 1990s a one-person increase in the population of exoffenders has no statistically measurable effect on the overall crime rate. We find similar patterns for property crimes and for each of the individual felony offenses. For three crime rates, there are sizable and significant effects of prison releases on crime during the 1990s. Namely, murder, robbery, and burglary are all significantly affected by prisoner releases during the latter time period.

Given the wide range of the parameter estimates presented in tables 5 though 7, and the evidence of cross-period heterogeneity in these effects, external estimates of the proportion of crime attributable to released offenders using alternative methodological approaches would be helpful for putting these results into context. The BJS recidivism study can be employed toward this end.[38] Recall that the BJS analyzed the criminal history records of offenders released from prison during 1994 and used these data to generate estimates of the proportion of arrests attributable to

38. Langan and Levin (2002).

Table 7. Regression Estimates of the Marginal Effects of Net Changes in the Population of Recently Released Inmates and New Court Commitments on Overall and Individual Crime Rates, by Time Period[a]

Item	1978–84	1985–91	1992–99
Δ Violent crime			
Net releases	1.116	−0.100	0.135
	(0.221)	(0.245)	(0.119)
New commitments	−1.259	−0.115	−0.234
	(0.268)	(0.244)	(0.141)
Δ Murder			
Net releases	0.022	0.014	0.012
	(0.007)	(0.006)	(0.003)
New commitments	−0.028	−0.016	−0.014
	(0.009)	(0.006)	(0.003)
Δ Rape			
Net releases	0.047	0.020	0.006
	(0.017)	(0.018)	(0.011)
New commitments	−0.108	−0.019	0.002
	(0.022)	(0.018)	(0.013)
Δ Robbery			
Net releases	0.929	0.111	0.168
	(0.157)	(0.119)	(0.046)
New commitments	−0.921	−0.294	−0.219
	(0.191)	(0.119)	(0.055)
Δ Assault			
Net releases	0.117	−0.246	−0.051
	(0.126)	(0.195)	(0.096)
New commitments	−0.201	0.215	−0.004
	(0.152)	(0.194)	(0.115)
Δ Property crime			
Net releases	5.847	−0.349	1.068
	(1.291)	(1.336)	(0.650)
New commitments	−6.472	−2.721	−1.117
	(1.564)	(1.331)	(0.773)
Δ Burglary			
Net releases	2.863	0.217	0.431
	(0.525)	(0.489)	(0.153)
New commitments	−2.823	−1.427	−0.703
	(0.636)	(0.860)	(0.182)
Δ Larceny			
Net releases	2.458	−0.669	0.566
	(0.821)	(0.863)	(0.443)
New commitments	−2.619	−1.017	−0.329
	(1.031)	(0.860)	(0.527)
Δ Auto theft			
Net releases	0.525	0.103	0.071
	(0.224)	(0.289)	(0.158)
New commitments	−1.029	−0.277	−0.085
	(0.271)	(0.287)	(0.187)

a. Standard errors are in parentheses. Figures correspond to the coefficients on the net change in releases variable or the new commitments variable from a regression of the change in the given crime rate on the two explanatory variables, the other explanatory variables listed in the regression in table 5, and complete sets of state and year effects. Separate regressions are estimated for each time period.

this cohort. To the extent that arrest proportions are comparable to crime proportions, these figures provide an estimate of the proportion of crime attributable to recent prison releases.

In the preceding discussion, we identified at least two factors that are likely to bias these figures as estimates of the criminality of former inmates: the fact that a large fraction of the crimes reported to the police are never cleared by arrest,[39] and the possibility that for some fraction of the recorded arrests, the suspects may be innocent of the charges filed against them. If former inmates are falsely charged in some fraction of arrests, then the BJS arrest figures will overestimate the contribution of this population to crime (holding all else constant). Crime clearance rates that are less than one will bias the BJS estimates if the proportional contribution of exinmates to crimes that are not cleared by arrest differs from the proportion of crimes that are cleared.

Despite these faults, these figures do provide a benchmark based on a labor-intensive analysis of actual arrest records that can serve as a reference point for comparison with our results. Table 8 presents this comparison. The first column of figures presents the BJS estimates of the proportion of arrests in 1994 in the fifteen analyzed states attributable to prisoners released in 1994. The second column presents our estimates of the proportion of crime in 1994 attributable to recently released offenders. These estimates are based on the estimation results from the models in table 7 (inclusive of state fixed effects and year fixed effects) for total violent and property crime and for each of the seven felony offenses.[40] The third column presents comparable results for the year 1979.

Our models suggest that exinmates released during the past year accounted for 2 percent of violent crime and 2.5 percent of property

39. A crude measure of the number of offenses cleared by arrest is given by the number of arrests for a specific type of offense divided by the number of incidents for a given calendar year. In 2001 this ratio was 0.85 for murder, 0.30 for forcible rape, 0.26 for robbery, 0.53 for assault, 0.14 for burglary, 0.16 for larceny, and 0.12 for motor vehicle theft (calculated from the *BJS Sourcebook of Criminal Justice Statistics Online, 2002*). These figures are likely to overstate clearance rates since arrests may be for incidents occurring in previous calendar years and may involve multiple offenders per incident. In fact, incident-based calculations of clearance rates for murder yield clearance rates of approximately 65 percent. Nevertheless, these figures reveal that arrests are few relative to criminal incidents.

40. To arrive at these estimates, we multiply the estimated marginal effect of a released offender (from table 7) by the number of offenders released during that year. We use the marginal effects that vary by time period in these calculations. We then divide this predicted level of crime attributable to released offenders by the actual crime rate for 1994.

Table 8. Predicted Proportion of Crime Attributable to Recent Releases, BJS Study and Predictions from Regression Models for 1980 and 1994[a]

Crime	*Bureau of Justice Statistics estimates of the proportion of 1994 arrests attributable to parolees*	*Predicted proportion of 1994 reported criminal incidents attributable to net prison releases in 1993*	*Predicted proportion of 1980 reported criminal incidents attributable to net prison releases in 1979*
Total violent	. . .	0.020	0.093
Murder	0.109	0.144	0.106
Rape	0.054	0.016	0.063
Robbery	0.099	0.074	0.184
Assault	0.044	−0.013	0.019
Total property	. . .	0.025	0.054
Burglary	0.124	0.044	0.084
Larceny	0.042	0.021	0.038
Motor vehicle theft	0.099	0.013	0.051

a. Predicted values are based on average crime rates and the number of recent releases per 100,000 for 1994 and 1980. The 1994 estimates are based on the regression coefficient from the model estimated for the time period 1992 to 1999, while the 1980 estimates are based on the regression coefficient estimated for the time period 1978 to 1984 (see table 7). The BJS estimates of the proportion of arrests attributable to parolees are based on analysis of the arrest records of parolees released in 1994 in Arizona, California, Delaware, Florida, Illinois, Maryland, Michigan, Minnesota, New Jersey, New York, North Carolina, Ohio, Oregon, Texas, and Virginia.

crime in 1994. For the individual offenses, our estimates of the proportion of crimes committed by recent releases are fairly close to the BJS estimates for murder and robbery, yet are somewhat smaller for the other offenses.[41] Our estimates suggest that recently released offenders accounted for roughly 14 percent of murder and 7 percent of robbery. The BJS estimates indicate that recently released offenders account for 11 percent of homicide arrests and 10 percent of robbery arrests. Although these are small portions of total crime, the amount of crime attributable to recent releases is large relative to their proportional representation in the general population.[42]

To be sure, our estimates are lower-bound estimates of the contribution of former inmates to crime. The figures in table 8 are for the proportions of crime attributable to the change in the population of exoffenders during the year and do not account for the larger subpopulation of former prison inmates released in previous years who are likely to be criminally active. For instance, in 1999 net releases from prison totaled to slightly

41. The BJS study does not provide overall tabulations for total violent and property crime.

42. Net prison releases in 1999 amount to one-tenth of 1 percent of the U.S. population.

more than 300,000 persons. In the same year, approximately 640,000 noninstitutionalized former inmates were under parole supervision (most were inmates released within the preceding three years). Given that roughly 75 percent of released inmates in 1999 were conditionally released, the population of noninstitutionalized offenders recently released from prison is likely to be about 850,000 people.[43] This is roughly 2.8 times the size of the net increase in the population of exoffenders in 1999.

Whether these unaccounted-for former inmates are more or less criminally active than the most recent releases is a difficult question to answer. Our time-specific estimates suggest that past releases are more criminally active than current releases, although those released during the late 1970s are unlikely to be substantial contributors to current crime rates. However, former inmates that have survived more than a year out of prison are likely to be a negatively selected lot with respect to their criminal propensities (that is to say, they are less likely to offend than others by virtue of the fact that they have not been reincarcerated). As a benchmark, it is probably safe to assume that the proportion of crime attributable to all former inmates is likely to be at least double the amount attributable to those released during the past year. Based on our estimates in table 8, this would suggest 4 percent of violent and 5 percent of property crime.

The Role of Parole Boards

The results presented thus far suggest that while former inmates commit a small portion of crime overall, they commit crime at a rate far out of proportion to their representation in the general population. Moreover, for the serious offenses of murder and robbery, both our estimates, as well as the BJS estimate, indicate that a sizable fraction of crime is attributable to former inmates.

The postrelease criminal behavior of released offenders is likely to be

43. We calculate this figure by dividing the parole population by the proportion of releases in 1999 that are conditional. Given that most parolees have been released in the past three years, we interpret this population estimate as a ballpark estimate of the number of offenders that have been released in the past three years that continue to be noninstitutionalized.

influenced by the correction policies pursued by individual states. For example, there is variation across states in the discretion granted to correction authorities in determining whom to release from prison and when. Under indeterminate sentencing regimes, parole boards often have nearly complete discretion over release and parole decisions and demand evidence of rehabilitation before paroling a convicted felon into the community. In contrast, in states that have limited the discretion of parole boards, or eliminated parole boards, release and parole decisions are made formulaically.

Critics of determinate sentencing tend to argue that under discretionary regimes, the expectation that one shape up before being released renders release a personal goal rather than an administrative eventuality and thus provides an incentive for positive behavioral change. In addition, by retaining discretion over parole decisions, correction officials are able to sustain the incarceration of those offenders most likely to reoffend on release. However, critics of indeterminate sentencing argue that offenders serve too small a portion of their sentence, reducing the ultimate incapacitation effect of a prison term as well as the deterrent effect associated with the likelihood of being apprehended and convicted.[44]

We now explore whether the impact of released inmates on state-level crime rate varies by whether the state operates under a determinate or indeterminate sentencing regime. We estimate separate crime models for two groups of states: states where as of the year 2003 parole boards retained full discretion over parole decisions and states where the decisionmaking power of parole boards has been curtailed or parole boards have been abolished.[45] States in the first category correspond most closely with traditional indeterminate sentencing systems, while states in the latter category correspond to regimes where parole is largely mandatory and parole decisions are made by administrative rules.

Table 9 presents these results for the overall violent and property crime rates and for the seven individual felony offenses. The table presents the coefficient estimates on the net release and new commitment

44. See Petersilia (2003) for a thorough discussion of these arguments.
45. This breakdown of states is based on the classification presented in Petersilia (2003). States with powerful parole boards include Alabama, Alaska, Colorado, Idaho, Kentucky, Montana, Nevada, New Jersey, North Dakota, Oklahoma, Pennsylvania, Rhode Island, South Carolina, Utah, Vermont, and Wyoming.

**Table 9. Comparisons of the Marginal Effects of Net Changes in the Population
of Recently Released Inmates and New Court Commitments for States
with Strong Parole Boards and States with No or Weakened Parole Boards[a]**

Item	States where parole board has full release power	States that have abolished, or limited the discretion of, parole boards
Δ Violent crime		
Net releases	−0.103	0.177
	(0.207)	(0.104)
New commitments	−0.203	−0.307
	(0.222)	(0.107)
Δ Murder		
Net releases	0.016	0.009
	(0.006)	(0.003)
New commitments	−0.015	−0.014
	(0.006)	(0.003)
Δ Rape		
Net releases	0.051	0.018
	(0.019)	(0.007)
New commitments	−0.061	−0.017
	(0.021)	(0.008)
Δ Robbery		
Net releases	0.034	0.173
	(0.082)	(0.060)
New commitments	−0.134	−0.279
	(0.088)	(0.062)
Δ Assault		
Net releases	−0.203	−0.023
	(0.174)	(0.069)
New commitments	0.007	0.003
	(0.186)	(0.072)
Δ Property crime		
Net releases	−0.434	2.425
	(1.075)	(0.543)
New commitments	−1.672	−2.794
	(1.152)	(0.561)
Δ Burglary		
Net releases	−0.057	1.094
	(0.378)	(0.193)
New commitments	−0.594	−1.287
	(0.405)	(0.199)
Δ Larceny		
Net releases	−0.358	1.169
	(0.744)	(0.346)
New commitments	−0.666	−1.294
	(0.797)	(0.358)
Δ Auto theft		
Net releases	−0.019	0.162
	(0.211)	(0.129)
New commitments	−0.412	−0.212
	(0.225)	(0.134)

a. Standard errors are in parentheses. Figures correspond to the coefficients on the net change in releases variable or the new commitments variable from a regression of the change in the given crime rate on the two explanatory variables, the other explanatory variables listed in the regression in table 5, and complete sets of state and year effects. States with powerful parole boards include Alabama, Alaska, Colorado, Idaho, Kentucky, Montana, Nevada, New Jersey, North Dakota, Oklahoma, Pennsylvania, Rhode Island, South Carolina, Utah, Vermont, and Wyoming.

variables from a regression of the change in the crime rate on these two variables, the control variables in table 5, and complete sets of state and year fixed effects. We estimate separate models for strong parole board and weak parole board states. Starting with the overall violent and property crime rates, the marginal effect of a prison release is larger in states with weak parole boards in both equations. Although the difference is small relative to the standard errors of the parameter estimates for violent crime, there is a notably large difference in the marginal effect for property crime rates. Indeed, net releases do not exert statistically significant effects on violent or property crime in states with strong parole boards. However, for states with weakened or no parole boards, releases have a large and strongly significant effect on property crime and a modest and marginally significant effect on violent crime.

The results for individual offenses are mixed. Although the impact of releases on murder and rape is slightly larger in states with strong parole boards, these differences are small and for the most part statistically insignificant. However, the effect of releases on robbery, burglary, and larceny (the crimes for which exoffenders exhibit the greatest recidivism as noted in the discussion of table 3) are considerably larger in states with weakened parole boards. In summary, the results suggest that strong parole systems in which state boards have discretion over whom to release and when are likely to be an effective policy tool in limiting the postrelease criminal activity of former inmates.

Conclusion

The results of our analysis indicate that a small portion of crime is attributable to former inmates. We find statistically significant positive effects of net increase in the population of former inmates on nearly all felony offenses measured by the FBI. While the proportional contribution of the most recently released offenders to overall crime is small (2 percent of violent crime and 2.5 percent of property crime), our results indicate that former offenders contribute significantly to the serious violent offenses of murder and robbery. Moreover, we believe that our estimates are lower-bound estimates of the proportion of crime attributable to all former inmates, given that the population of exoffenders is many times larger than the increase in this population in a given year.

Our analysis shows that the increase in crime caused by a one-person increase in the exoffender population is smaller than the absolute value of the reduction in crime caused by a one-person increase in the rate of new court commitments. These results suggest that the average inmate released from prison is less criminally inclined than the average new court commitment, or that being incarcerated totally removes opportunities for criminal activities while the conditional supervision exercised over most freed inmates suppresses criminal activity. Our analysis suggests that much of this pattern is explained by the incapacitation effect of imprisonment on criminal activity since average personal and other relevant characteristics of recent releases and prison admits are quite similar.

We also find some evidence that the impact of prison releases on crime differs in states with different parole systems. We find that the effect of former inmates is weaker in states where parole boards retain full discretion over parole decisions compared with states where the decisionmaking power of parole boards has been curtailed or abolished. Although these results are not definite proof of the effect of parole systems on crime, they do suggest that discretionary parole boards may play a positive role in releasing prisoners who are more prepared for reintegration.

Certainly, many have criticized centralized parole systems, arguing that parole decisions are arbitrary and that factors such as race and gender may affect the timing and likelihood of release or that released offenders serve too small a portion of their sentence. Whether these problems are permanent features of discretionary parole boards or rather problems of implementation or practice that can be remedied remains uncertain. Nonetheless, our results suggest that the potential benefits of discretionary parole boards in reducing crime committed by parolees should be included in debates about the relative merits of different parole systems.

In either case, the results of this study highlight in stark form society's interests in the successful reentry of former prison inmates. Nearly all inmates in state and federal prison will eventually be released and confronted with negotiating the noninstitutionalized world as exconvicts, whether or not this reentry occurs in states with discretionary parole boards. And our results suggest that the failure of released inmates to do so will generate new crime that is out of proportion to their numbers in the general population.

We find that prisoner releases currently have much smaller impacts on serious crime when compared with the similar effects in decades past. These smaller effects probably reflect the fact that at the currently high incarceration rate, the marginal prison inmate is much less criminally inclined than the marginal inmate of decades past. This fact, and our findings on the effectiveness of parole boards, leads us to believe that states could indeed reduce their steady-state prison populations in a targeted fashion without deleterious impacts on crime.

However, such a reduction should be carried out in a cautious and deliberate manner. We find that in all time periods, released offenders have significant effects on very serious felony offenses, such as homicide and robbery, and thus state correction departments should carefully think through changes in sentencing, parole policy, and other actions intended to reduce incarceration rates. Several strategies can be pursued to minimize the impacts of releases on crime. To start, correction departments could devote more resources toward systematically assessing the risk of recidivism and potential danger to the community and place more weight on these assessments in deciding whom to release and, if possible, whom to divert from a prison sentence all together. Presumably, this is precisely the activity of a centralized parole board. Such efforts can be augmented with the targeting of reentry services (such as employment assistance and housing search assistance) toward the newly released prisoners that have proved in the past to be the most responsive to positive incentives.

To be sure, there are certainly some former inmates who must simply be monitored closely. Most state correction departments rate the risks associated with each parolee and graduate the degree of parole officer involvement accordingly. Perhaps augmenting support services and providing positive incentives for those that do not fall into this category of exoffenders may eventually reduce the criminal activity of high-risk offenders, as parole officers may be more free to concentrate their surveillance efforts on the high-risk group. At a minimum, a better understanding of the relative efficacy of various prerelease and postrelease programs is needed. Given the high costs of criminal victimization, even modest effects of such programs on crime reductions are likely to pass a cost-benefit test.

Comments

Mark Duggan: During the past two decades, the U.S. prison population increased by a factor of four, with 1.36 million individuals in state and federal prisons by the end of 2002. An additional 0.80 million were held in local jails, juvenile facilities, and other correctional institutions during that same year.[46] One consequence of this growth has been a steady rise in the number of individuals released from prison in each year. For example, approximately 550,000 individuals were released from state prisons in 1999, nearly half the number residing in state prisons at the end of the year. If, as previous studies suggest, these individuals are significantly more likely than the average person to commit crimes, it is plausible that the release of these prisoners has a substantial impact on area-level crime rates.

Despite the obvious importance of this issue, no previous study has tackled this question head on. Most research has instead explored whether recently released prisoners violate the terms of their parole and are returned to custody within a certain time after release.[47] While these studies have contributed a number of important findings, they cannot be used to estimate the effect of recently released prisoners on area-level crime rates for three reasons. First, individuals released from prison may commit a crime and yet not be caught by the authorities, which tends to understate their effect on crime. Or those released from prison may be targeted by authorities and arrested for crimes that they did not commit, thus to some extent overstating their contribution to crime rates. And

46. Harrison and Beck (2003).
47. Gendreau and others (1996); Petersilia (2003).

finally, a person released from prison may commit a significant number of crimes before being caught. Thus the outcome variables used in previous studies are clearly an imperfect measure of total criminal activity among recently released prisoners.

In the current study, Steven Raphael and Michael Stoll address the research question outlined by estimating the contribution of recently released prisoners to state-level crime rates. To do this, the authors utilize a data set from the Bureau of Justice Statistics that includes the number of individuals released from prison and the number newly committed to prison in each state and in each year from 1977 to 1999.[48] Combining these data with crime data from the FBI, demographic information from the U.S. Census Bureau, and unemployment data from the Bureau of Labor Statistics, the authors investigate the hypothesis that crime increases in response to an increase in the number released from prison and declines when the number newly committed to prison increases. In essence, the authors are testing a reverse incapacitation effect in the first case and a pure incapacitation effect in the second case.

There are several important findings in this study. First, the authors convincingly demonstrate that years in which states release a relatively high number of prisoners are followed by significant increases in crime while the opposite is true for the number imprisoned for the first time. Additionally, the authors find that the magnitude of these two effects is not equal—a person who is imprisoned appears to reduce crime by more than a person released from prison increases it. This is consistent with a number of possible hypotheses that predict criminal tendencies decline following imprisonment, including a positive effect of prison programs on earnings potential or a negative effect of parole supervision on the propensity to commit crime. Raphael and Stoll also find that the impact of prison releases was substantially greater early in the period (1978–84), suggesting that the person released from prison today is much less criminally active than his or her counterpart from two decades ago when prison populations were much lower. Finally, the authors demonstrate that prison releases are not significantly related to changes in crime in those states with powerful parole boards, perhaps because these states can selectively release those individuals who are least likely to commit crimes in the future.

---

48. Harrison and Beck (2003).

The findings in this study suggest several avenues for future research. First, it would be interesting to investigate whether the state of the economy influences the effect of prison releases on crime. The fact that the estimated effect was so much greater 1978–84, a time that included the deepest recession in the postwar period, suggests that some of the heterogeneity over time may be caused by economic factors. By extending the time period to include the most recent recession, one could test whether the sensitivity of crime to prison release is greater now than in the recent past. This may be all the more relevant given that many states—in response to fiscal distress—are speeding up the release of prisoners.

Another direction for future research would investigate the source of state and time variation in the number of prisoners released and the number newly imprisoned. As previous authors have noted, changes in prison populations may be caused by changes in current or expected future crime rates.[49] For example, a state may release relatively many prisoners when the crime rate is increasing, and these increases may persist from one year to the next. Given that approximately half of all states are at or above the capacity of their prison systems, it is possible that this is important. To surmount this possible source of bias, one could investigate whether policies that led to sharp increases or declines in the number released from prison or newly admitted to prison yield similar estimates.

Although the data may not be available for the entire time period considered, one could also utilize information on releases from and admissions to other types of correctional institutions. In the 2002 calendar year, more than 37 percent of incarcerated individuals were in local jails, juvenile facilities, or similar institutions. To the extent that changes in state-level entry and exit rates to these facilities may be correlated with the corresponding changes in state prison systems, it may be useful to control for these factors as well.

One final avenue for future research would consider the optimality of current prison policy. Given their effect on future crime rates, individuals released from prison may impose substantial costs on society in the future. These costs must then be weighed against the costs to taxpayers of incarceration. To the extent that those states with strong parole boards have managed to reduce these costs below what they otherwise would be, it may be possible to speed the entry of certain prisoners into society

49. Levitt (1996).

while having little impact on the crime rate. But this benefit of strong parole boards must be weighed against the costs of having a less transparent sentencing system that may be more open to abuse.

Anne Morrison Piehl: Public attention to the prison population has traditionally emphasized the number of inmates in state and federal prison facilities, recording annual changes as the population continually increased over more than thirty years. Recently the flow of inmates, especially the flow out, has captured the interest of researchers, policymakers, and others. The federal government's $100 million Going Home grant in 2002 and the president's announcement during the State of the Union address of another $300 million in prisoner reentry funding are but two indicators of the high level of current policy interest in inmate release.

It is well documented that those being released from the nation's jails and prisons are quite disadvantaged in education, employment prospects, housing, social supports, substance abuse, and physical and mental health. Given these deficits, the limited social services available (particularly for those with criminal records), and inmates' criminal histories, concerns have arisen about the criminal behavior of these former inmates. Raphael and Stoll's research provides a timely contribution to the literature by measuring the contribution of released offenders to state crime rates.

No matter how one measures it, criminal offending is highly concentrated within the population, so it would certainly be surprising if exinmates did not contribute appreciably to crime. To the extent that the various actions of the many actors in the criminal justice system function to allocate punishment to those particularly responsible for criminal activity, the prisons and jails will contain high-rate offenders disproportionately to the general population and even relative to the population of offenders. (Imagine a random technology, punishing each offense with equal probability. Then, those with higher offending rates will have higher rates of punishment.) Unless the period of incarceration provides substantial rehabilitation or time for maturation, upon release these offenders may commit further crimes when they rejoin free society.

With interest high in this phenomenon, Raphael and Stoll provide magnitudes of these effects to help guide the debate and, furthermore, provide some policy advice. As discussed, a number of institutional details must be considered to make these assessments.

Characterizing the Flows

Each year approximately 600,000 people leave state or federal prisons (and a similar number enter). This flow represents nearly 45 percent of the number of inmates incarcerated at any point in time (which was 1.4 million at year-end 2002). All of these figures would be much higher if they included the nation's jails, which hold another 650,000 people awaiting trial or serving short sentences. These flows are considerable.

The research design used by Raphael and Stoll compares the flow into prison to the flow out. The flow out of prison may differ substantially from the flow into prison for several reasons. Obviously, the composition of the groups will be greatly affected by the length of the terms of incarceration—the exit cohort is overrepresented by those with short stays. There are two groups among those with short stays: people sentenced to short terms of incarceration and people who have been released previously who violated the terms of release (parole revocations). Beck and Blumstein have documented that the flow out of prison is increasingly composed of rereleases, that is, people who have been released under their current criminal sentence at least once before.[50] Some call this cycling in and out of prison "churning."[51]

Table 1 shows that among prison admissions, 60 percent have a new court commitment; the rest are admitted due to "failure" while under some other sanction such as parole or probation. Although there are state differences in the meaning of these statuses, a failure on parole usually means that the person served time in prison in the fairly recent past. And of course, many of the 60 percent with new court commitments may have served time in the past, whether in state prison or a locally run jail. Although one's status at entry to prison conveys something about one's criminal history, it is far from complete.

From the comparison of characteristics of those entering prison to those leaving, Raphael and Stoll conclude that the populations are quite similar except for age and criminal history. In light of their other research on labor demand that documents employers' resistance to hiring people

50. Beck and Blumstein (2003).
51. See, for example, Lynch and Sabol (2001).

with criminal records, they note that just 27 percent of those released had a prior felony incarceration before the current term. They then suggest that worsening employment prospects may mark an important difference between these flows, as those leaving prison have worse records than when they entered. However, more than half of all felony convictions do not result in incarceration, so this variable likely greatly overstates the difference of these populations on this score.[52]

Although the characteristics of the flows into and out of prison look quite similar and in fact the populations even overlap, one aspect of the flow that may matter to crime rates is the flow itself. That is, there may be an independent contribution to crime of changing status. When an offender is released, he or she generally must secure housing, employment, and whatever social supports are required. That the flow matters and not just the characteristics of the flow population is suggested by the universal finding that recidivism rates are highest in the months just following release.

Is Recidivism or Crime the Right Outcome?

One approach to assessing the magnitude of the impact of prison release on crime rates is to measure the recidivism of those released from prison and compare it with the overall crime rate. Another is the approach taken in the current paper, relating cross-state variation to crime rates. There is a long-standing debate about which is a preferable outcome, recidivism or crime.

It is common to assess the connection between incarceration and criminal activity by measuring recidivism following release. In fact, the federal government recently released microdata on releases from fifteen states (covering two-thirds of prison releases) along with three years of follow-up information on arrests, convictions, and subsequent incarceration. One strength of this approach is that information on offending is linked to those released from prison, not inferred from aggregate relationships. A weakness is that there may be much criminal activity that goes undetected.

Furthermore, as highlighted by Raphael and Stoll, if the wrong outcome measure is used, one might capture more information about crimi-

52. In 2000, 40 percent of felony convictions in state courts involved a sentence to prison (www.ojp.usdoj.gov/bjs/abstract/fssc00.htm).

nal justice policy than about criminal activity. Some offenders are released under the supervision of criminal justice authorities (such as parole) with requirements that they comply with various conditions under the threat of sanctions including reincarceration. As a result of the punishment of so-called technical violations, supervision may lead to outcomes such as reincarceration even without further criminal activity. This may happen because parole is operating appropriately, conditions of supervision are onerous, or supervising agencies are overly zealous.[53]

There is tremendous variation across states in the extent to which inmates are subject to conditions following release, ranging from under one-quarter of the population to nearly 100 percent. In addition, states (and offices within states) vary in their policies toward revocations versus second and third chances following violations. This variation will, in some way or another, be in the background of every calculation of criminality among released inmates.

The Bureau of Justice Statistics reports that those released from prison in 1994 were responsible for approximately 10 percent of the arrests for serious violent offenses such as homicide and robbery and about 5 percent of aggravated assault and larceny in the year of release. This percentage varies a great deal across states.[54] As crime rates have declined appreciably and the number of released offenders has increased, it is likely that the proportion of arrests that is attributable to newly released offenders has grown since then.[55]

Raphael and Stoll dismiss these estimates because arrest may be biased against known offenders. But one could use the raw data to recalculate, using conviction to see if an appreciably different picture emerges. Another critique of the recidivism approach is that it misses any chaos introduced by the flow of offenders out of prison. That is, if exinmates seek to regain their "turf," this might generate criminal activity by others, leading recidivism studies to underestimate the effect of inmate release on local or regional crime rates.

Crime, regardless of who commits it, is certainly a compelling outcome measure. Raphael and Stoll study changes in crime in relation to

---

53. For more details on postincarceration supervision, especially on difficulties in evaluating its effectiveness, see Piehl and LoBuglio (2003).

54. Rosenfeld and others (2003).

55. This will be true in an almost mechanical way unless the characteristics of released inmates have changed greatly during the past few years. No evidence suggests they have.

state-level prison flows, measuring the change in the exinmate population as the difference between the number of releases and the number returned to prison for violations of conditional supervision and measuring the change in the "other offender" population as the number of new court commitments. The more essential distinction between the usual recidivism study and the current paper is the use of flows in the estimation. The flow is used for convenience (as information on the stock is just not available), but it also means that the resulting estimates emphasize marginal rather than average effects.

Notably, the state differences in how conditional supervision is assigned and used will influence the measure of the change in the ex-inmate population. That is, for states with large numbers of people under conditional supervision, the flow back to prison is more likely to come in the form of conditional returns than as new commitments. Perhaps these differences are adequately accounted for by the state fixed effects in the regressions. Although the authors hope to "bypass the problems associated with variation in state policy," it appears to be impossible to do so in this field of study.

The Pool of Potential Offenders

Their estimation method is to estimate the relationship between the changes in state crime rates and these flows. Of course they would prefer to have appropriate measures of the stocks so they could calculate changes rather than relying on these measures, but no one collects the necessary data on former inmates. The most frustrating aspect of empirical work in criminal justice is the perpetual absence of reliable data from sources other than administrative ones. We are generally missing information on people without a current relationship to criminal justice authorities.

In analyzing flows, it is crucial to consider whether there are any other relevant flows into or out of the pool of potential offenders. Unfortunately, the literature does not provide sufficiently detailed guidance on the entry of people into this pool or out of it. Current research in criminology works to categorize types of offending patterns, but this is insufficient for understanding how the flow measures used in this paper may or may not be correlated with other important features of the population.

Raphael and Stoll's effort to compare net releases to those entering prison is intriguing, especially in light of the substantial amount of churning noted earlier. There are two important cautions, however, to their comparison of the magnitudes of the estimated effects. First, "net releases" is defined as the number of releases in a year minus the number of conditional returns. For many of these conditional returns, the subsequent time served is likely to be very short, especially compared with the expected time served for those with new court commitments. My calculations from the 2000 release cohort from the National Corrections Reporting program database confirm this: the median time served for new commitments was fourteen months, while the median time served for those with revoked parole was less than half as long, six months.

Second, states that rely heavily on the use of conditional supervision following incarceration will have relatively more conditional returns and relatively fewer new commitments, inducing a positive correlation between the two key independent variables. That these variables are measured in changes alleviates some of the concern with cross-state differences in policy, but an accounting of changes in policy (such as abolishing parole) would be more reassuring. For this reason, the models that include state fixed effects are preferred because they account for linear state-specific time trends. It would also be interesting to see estimates based on only the gross flows, so one could see the separate magnitudes for those conditionally returned.

Policy Concerns

In the end, one might not care too much about whether the role of exoffenders in crime is measured by recidivism or by crime rates. Those most affected by crime, and those most affected by the release of prison inmates, live in the country's urban centers. If the purpose is to document a problem associated with prison release, then high rates of recidivism among released inmates is perhaps sufficient. (Another approach to this question, which I have not seen reported, would be to sample arrests and match them with criminal history records.)

The more important distinction between the rest of the literature and the current contribution is that the approach taken by Raphael and Stoll is likely to do a better job of estimating marginal effects, which will be more useful for making particular policy recommendations. If this is the goal, then it is necessary to make a full accounting of the policy issues underlying the identifying variation. The proxies for the flows utilized in this paper work best at distinguishing the flows of exinmates from other offenders in states where there is substantial availability and use of parole supervision. For other policy questions, one might care to distinguish between flows in and flows out, regardless of changes in exinmate status. Given that there is a complex interaction between measures and policies that cannot be avoided in this field of study, perhaps it is more advantageous to take this task on rather than try to avoid it.

References

Beck, Allen, and Al Blumstein. 2003. "Reentry as a Transient State between Liberty and Recommitment." Unpublished paper. Washington: Bureau of Justice Statistics.

Bonczar, Thomas P. 2003. "Prevalence of Imprisonment in the U.S. Population, 1974–2001." NCJ 197976. Bureau of Justice Statistics. Department of Justice.

Clear, Todd R., Dina R. Rose, Elin Waring, and Kristen Scully. 2003. "Coercive Mobility and Crime: A Preliminary Examination of Concentrated Incarceration and Social Disorganization." *Justice Quarterly* 20(1): 33–64.

Gendreau, Paul, Tracy Little, and Claire Goggin. 1996. "A Meta-Analysis of Adult Offender Recidivism: What Works?" *Criminology* 34 (4): 575–607.

Glaze, Lauren E. 2002. *Probation and Parole in the United States, 2001.* Washington: Bureau of Justice Statistics.

Greenberg, David F. 1985. "Age, Crime, and Social Explanation." *American Journal of Sociology* 91: 1–21.

Harrison, Paige, and Allen Beck. 2003. "Prisoners in 2002." *Bureau of Justice Statistics Bulletin.* Department of Justice, Office of Justice Programs.

Holzer, Harry J., Steven Raphael, and Michael A. Stoll. 2001. "Will Employers Hire Ex-Offenders? Employer Preferences, Background Checks, and Their Determinants," forthcoming in *The Impact of Incarceration on Families and Communities,* edited by Mary Patillo-McCoy, David Weiman and Bruce Western. New York: Russell Sage Foundation.

———. 2003. "Employer Demand for Ex-Offenders: Recent Evidence from Los Angeles." Unpublished manuscript.

Hughes, Timothy A., Doris J. Wilson, and Allen J. Beck. 2001. *Trends in State Parole, 1990-2000.* Washington: Bureau of Justice Statistics.

Langan, Patrick A., and David J. Levin. 2002. *Recidivism of Prisoners Released in 1994.* Washington: Washington: Bureau of Justice Statistics.

Levitt, Steven D. 1996. "The Effect of Prison Population Size on Crime Rates: Evidence from Prison Overcrowding Litigation." *Quarterly Journal of Economics* 111(2): 319–51.

———. 2003. "Understanding Why Crime Fell in the 1990s: Four Factors that Explain the Decline and Six Factors that Do Not." University of Chicago. Unpublished.

Levitt, Steven D., and Sudhir Alladi Venkatesh. 2000. "An Economic Analysis of a Drug-Selling Gang's Finances." *Quarterly Journal of Economics* 115(3): 755–90.

Lynch, James P., and William J. Sabol. 2001. "Prisoner Reentry in Perspective." *Crime Policy Report,* vol. 3. Washington: Urban Institute.

Marvell, Thomas, and Carlisle Moody. 1995. "The Impact of Enhanced Prison Terms for Felonies Committed With Guns." *Criminology* 33(2): 247–81.

Petersilia, Joan. 2003. *When Prisoners Come Home: Parole and Prisoner Reentry.* Oxford University Press.

Petersilia, Joan, and Susan Turner. 1993. "Intensive Probation and Parole." In *Crime and Justice: An Annual Review of Research*, edited by Michael Tonry, vol. 17, 281–335. University of Chicago Press.

Piehl, Anne Morrison, and Stefan F. LoBuglio. 2003. "Does Supervision Matter?" Unpublished paper. Harvard University (September).

Raphael, Steven, and Jens Ludwig. 2002. "Prison Sentence Enhancements: The Case of Project Exile." In *Evaluating Gun Policy: Effects on Crime and Violence*, edited by Jens Ludwig and Philip J. Cook. Brookings.

Raphael, Steven, and David Weiman. 2002. "The Impact of Local Labor Market Conditions on the Likelihood that Parolees are Returned to Custody." University of California, Berkeley. Unpublished manuscript.

Rennison, Callie. 2003. *Criminal Victimization 2001: Changes 2000–01 with Trends 1993–2001*. NCJ 194610. Washington: Bureau of Justice Statistics.

Rose, Dina R., and Todd R. Clear. 1998. "Who Doesn't Know Someone in Jail? The Impact of Exposure to Prison on Attitudes of Public and Informal Control." Paper presented at the Southern Sociological Society annual meeting. Atlanta.

Rosenfeld, Richard, Joel Wallman, and Robert Fernango. 2003. "The Contribution of Ex-Prisoners to Crime Rates." Unpublished paper. University of Missouri, St. Louis (July).

Travis, Jeremy. 2003. *Parole in California, 1980–2000: Implications for Reform*. Washington: Urban Institute Justice Policy Center.

Travis, Jeremy, and Sarah Lawrence. 2002. *California's Parole Experiment*. Washington: Urban Institute Justice Policy Center.

JOEL WALDFOGEL
University of Pennsylvania

Who Benefits Whom in Local Television Markets?

URBAN ECONOMISTS have recently devoted substantial attention to exploring the production-side benefits of cities.[1] The consumption-side benefits of agglomeration have received far less attention.[2] Separately, empirical studies of entry in industrial organization tend to use geographic markets as observations. These studies, such as Bresnahan and Reiss, make use of the relationship between market size and the number of firms operating to draw inferences about the effects of entry on pricing behavior.[3] These studies show, incidentally, that larger markets tend to have more firms. When consumption data are available, studies often show that in larger markets, a higher fraction of the population consumes a product in the industry being studied. Other studies have begun to document the relationship between market size and the distribution of product qualities offered.[4]

Although they were not originally directed at urban economists, these studies' results may be of interest to urban economics. They show empir-

This research has been supported by the Ford Foundation. I am grateful to Bob Cohen of Scarborough Research for allowing me access to their data and to Jim Collins for patiently explaining the data to me. All errors are my own.

1. See, for example, Ciccone and Hall (1996); Holmes (2002); or Rosenthal and Strange (forthcoming).

2. Some studies have begun to fill this gap. See, for example, Glaeser, Kolko, and Saiz (2001).

3. Bresnahan and Reiss (1990).

4. See Berry and Waldfogel (1999, 2003), respectively, for studies documenting (a) a positive relationship between radio listening and market size and (b) the relationship between market size and product quality.

257

ically that when production carries substantial fixed costs, larger markets can offer more, more varied, and sometimes higher-quality products. Ensuing broader product options can increase consumer welfare by offering more types of consumers options they prefer; and product variety can draw a higher share of residents to consumption. In this sense people can benefit one another, by agglomeration into local product markets, in their capacity as fellow product consumers.

But consumers need not benefit one another equally. A final strand of recent industrial economic research of possible interest to urban economists asks "who benefits whom" in differentiated product markets. This research examines the relationship between the distribution of product-preferring consumers in the market and the mix of products offered. Using local media markets as examples, this strand documents that consumers will benefit one another only to the extent that they bring forth products that also appeal to others, which, in turn, will occur only if they share similar preferences. Again, this research uses geographic markets as a means of observing multiple markets. In so doing, however, the work documents results of possible importance for urban economics by showing starkly different within-group and across-group distribution of agglomeration benefits through product markets. This paper continues this line by examining effects of white and minority consumers on each other in local television markets.

Blacks and whites (and Hispanics and non-Hispanics) have substantially different preferences in media products. The radio formats attracting two-thirds of black listeners collectively attract less than 5 percent of white listeners.[5] In markets with two daily papers, black readership tends to be heavily concentrated in only one of them.[6] Local markets with larger black populations have more black-targeted radio stations and daily papers that cater more heavily to black consumers' tastes. Moreover, blacks are more likely to consume local radio and daily newspaper products in markets with more heavily black populations. As a consequence, blacks and whites are better off, in their capacity as local media consumers, as their markets have larger black and white populations, respectively.

The scope for these sorts of effects to operate in markets is larger, the higher fixed costs are relative to market size. This is why black and white

---

5. Waldfogel (2003); Siegelman and Waldfogel (1998).
6. George and Waldfogel (2003).

consumers affect one another more significantly in daily newspaper markets, which have only a handful of products per market, than in local radio markets, averaging twenty-five stations per market.

Unlike daily papers and radio, which are predominantly local media, television is a mixed local-national medium. Much programming, including network prime time and almost all cable channels, is uniform across place. However, outside of prime time, local broadcast stations, including both independent stations and affiliates of networks (such as ABC, CBS, or Fox), determine much of their programming locally. The latter set of programming decisions allows a mechanism for television consumers to affect their fellow local residents. Yet, given widespread availability of a large number of specialized national cable (and satellite) channels, it is not clear whether local viewers' welfare depends on local programming decisions. Rather, specialized national channels may satisfy diverse tastes, leaving little scope for local programming decisions to incrementally affect consumption or, by extension, welfare. This is relevant to an ongoing debate about the benefits of localism in broadcasting.[7] Given the wealth of nonlocal programming options, it is not clear whether local programming incrementally affects viewer welfare. Moreover, distributional effects in television, which is perhaps the most influential news, information, and entertainment medium in the United States, remain to be studied. Americans spend on average more time with television than with other media, and a much higher share of households watch television than read local newspapers.

This paper examines the effects of the size and racial composition of local populations on the types of local programming offered and on the viewing behavior of various types of television audiences. In that sense the paper is part of a small but growing body of research on the consumption benefits of urban agglomeration. I find that, as in other media, preferences in television programming differ sharply between blacks and nonblacks and between Hispanics and non-Hispanics. I show that the targeting of local programming to minority viewers is much greater in markets with larger minority populations, whereas prime-time and national cable programming are, by definition, insensitive to local preference distributions. This paper documents that the quantity of locally controlled minority-targeted television draws minority audience to viewing.

7. For example, the FCC recently created a localism task force (www.fcc.gov/localism/).

Together, these relationships suggest that blacks and Hispanics are better off, in their capacity as television viewers, in markets with larger black and Hispanic populations.

In local media markets, the welfare of consumers in each preference group depends on the distribution of product-preferring types in the market. This is interesting by itself and also because it casts doubt on the prevailing belief in a clear distinction between market and collective choice allocation schemes. Friedman has eloquently argued that markets avoid the tyrannies of the majority endemic to allocation through collective choice. Mounting evidence that the welfare of minority consumers depends on local minority population in local media markets indicates that, for this industry at least, the difference between market and collective choice allocation is a matter of degree, not kind. The relationship between demographic composition of markets and the targeting of programming content is important because related research documents a relationship between the presence of black-targeted media and the tendency for blacks to vote.[8]

Population Composition and Groups' Welfare

Which products do markets bring forth when products are imperfect substitutes and each product carries some fixed costs? This is a difficult question to answer. Dixit and Stiglitz present a model in which products are symmetrically substitutable, reducing the problem to "how many products." Their model allows them to examine whether markets bring forth adequate or excessive variety; but their treatment of substitution abstracts away most important features of firms' decisions (as well as the preference landscape of a heterogeneous society). Spence lays out the "product selection" problem, pointing out the distinction between market and optimal mixes of products that are made available. As a positive matter, it is not clear what determines the mix of products available in differentiated product contexts with fixed costs, and this line of research, documenting the determinants of product mixes, is an attempt to fill that void.[9]

The product selection problem in this context has two parts. First, the market must determine how much programming to air, that is, how many

8. Friedman (1962); Oberholzer-Gee and Waldfogel (2001).
9. Dixit and Stiglitz (1977); Spence (1976a, b).

local broadcast stations will operate in a market, and how many channels of cable programming local cable operators will carry. Because local broadcast facilities have fixed costs, larger markets will support more of them. This is the familiar relationship between market size and firms and products from the entry literature.[10]

The second part of the problem is the mix of programming to air. The general economic problem facing a station is the decision about which program to air in each of the time slots it controls. At least three features of the firm's environment affect its decisionmaking. First, the program preferences of the station's potential audience affect the desirability of airing particular programs. Second, the audience appeal of a program in a time slot depends on the programs simultaneously aired by competing outlets. Third, program choice might be influenced by a "carryover effect," or tendency for viewers to continue watching a station during consecutive time slots. One can imagine a formal problem in which each firm's profits depend on its programming choices, as well as its competitors' choices. Finding an equilibrium for such a context is a dauntingly complex prospect. Goettler and Shachar have made strides in this direction. While I recognize the richness of the firm's problem in choosing its programming mix, as well as the complexity of attempts to model such a context, this paper pursues the more modest goal of describing how the available mix relates to the distribution of persons, by preference type, in the population.[11]

Even in this descriptive characterization, how "product selection" affects welfare is different in television, radio, and newspapers, and the way I view the product affects how I view its determinants. In radio, each station typically chooses which one of roughly fifty formats to broadcast, then broadcasts it all the time.[12] Markets of different size have different numbers of radio stations on the dial. Hence, the quantity of programming targeting any particular group depends on the absolute size of the targeted group locally. For example, the *absolute size* of the local black population is a useful variable for explaining the quantity of black-targeted radio programming available. Unlike the situation for radio, larger markets do not have many more newspapers. Rather, as Berry and

10. See Bresnahan and Reiss (1990, 1991) for general studies of entry and Berry and Waldfogel (1999) for a (radio) broadcasting example.
11. Goettler and Shachar (2001).
12. See Waldfogel (2003) for lists of radio broadcast formats.

Waldfogel document, they have larger newspapers.[13] Further, newspapers contain scores of articles each day and arguably are a more complicated product than radio programming. It is helpful simplification to imagine that newspapers choose a point along a one-dimensional white-to-black-targeted spectrum. In the case of daily newspapers, it is more fruitful to examine the relationship between the *fraction* black in the market and the appeal of the one or few products to black consumers.[14] The television problem is something of a hybrid between the radio (*"how many stations?"*) and newspaper (*"what mix of content?"*) examples. Larger markets have more local television stations, and this is true even across the 66 large U.S. markets in our sample. Although all of the markets have ABC, CBS, NBC, Fox, and PBS affiliates, only 60 have WB, and 56 have UPN, affiliates. Affiliates of Hispanic-targeted Telemundo and Univision are even rarer, with 15 and 23 of 66 sample markets covered. Thus some variation in the amount of content targeting various groups is driven by factors determining the total amount of programming available in the market. Beyond that, there is also substantial variation in the *fraction* targeted to each group. In the empirical descriptions of program targeting that follow I allow the local quantity of minority-targeted programming to depend on both the local fraction black (or Hispanic), as well as the absolute population sizes.

Programming decisions can affect viewer welfare by allowing viewers access to more preferred programming options. For example, if black and white preferences for content are different, then black viewers will derive more satisfaction in markets with more black-targeted programming. Although one cannot observe satisfaction, one can draw at least suggestive inferences about satisfaction from the tendency to watch television. This is the path pursued in the following pages.

Data

Data for this study are drawn from two sources, Scarborough Research and the census. The Scarborough Prime Next data set has information on the media and product consumption patterns for each of roughly180,000 individuals surveyed in the latter half of 1999 and the first half of 2000 in

13. Berry and Waldfogel (2003).
14. See George and Waldfogel (2003) for evidence on this point.

66 large U.S. markets.[15] Of particular interest are the following variables: race, Hispanic status, and detailed television viewing data, especially for broadcast television. Respondents are asked to report all of the television half hours (between 6:00 a.m. and 1:00 a.m.) they watch during a seven-day period on affiliates of each of the following ten networks: ABC, CBS, FOX, NBC, PAX, PBS, TEL, UNI, UPN, and WB, as well as on independent stations (IND). This viewing is called "network affiliate viewing." Cable information is more rudimentary in this version of the Scarborough data. Survey respondents indicate dichotomously whether they regularly watch each of about 70 cable channels.

With thirty-eight half hours in a day, seven days in a week, and eleven channel choices, there are 2,926 individual program viewing variables, and each one represents a particular product choice. Our ultimate interest is in the relationship between viewers' satisfaction and the local population distribution, as determined by the availability of suitable programs. Because there is no scope, by construction, for prime-time program options to depend on the local distribution of types, it is important to disaggregate viewing measure into separate prime-time and locally controlled measures.[16] The basic measure of television viewing is the number of program half hours that a person reports having watched. The average person in the sample watches 11.0 evening prime-time half hours per week and 24.5 other (largely locally controlled) half hours, for a total of 35.5 half hours per week. Table 1 shows how total viewing (of the networks for which detailed viewing data are available) is distributed across networks for each group. ABC, CBS, and NBC attract the largest viewership for all groups, except Hispanics, for whom Univision is the largest draw.

With the network viewing data I can create measures of channel availability and measures of the quantity of black- or Hispanic-targeted programming on the air in each market. I calculate the number of broadcast stations in each market as the number of the eleven local channel types (ten network plus independent) receiving viewers in each market. Our markets have between 6.0 and 11.0 local broadcast stations by this mea-

---

15. See www.scarborough.com/primenext/.

16. In eastern and Pacific time zones, prime time runs from 8:00 p.m. to 11:00 p.m., Monday-Saturday, and 7:00 p.m. to 11:00 p.m. on Sunday. Prime time begins and ends one hour earlier in central and mountain time zones. We treat this as prime time for all networks, even though not all networks air national programming during the same hours.

Table 1. Weekly Half Hours Viewed, by Race and Hispanic Status

Network	Markets with affiliate	Nonblack	Black	Non-Hispanic	Hispanic
ABC	66	8.40	8.71	8.70	6.57
CBS	66	8.97	10.43	9.43	7.52
Fox	66	3.58	4.88	3.82	3.62
IND	41	0.74	1.20	0.79	0.75
NBC	66	8.51	8.41	8.72	6.89
PAX	56	0.51	0.66	0.54	0.51
PBS	66	1.42	1.13	1.42	1.17
TELEMUNDO	15	0.59	0.53	0.06	2.39
UNIVISION	23	2.12	2.37	0.15	10.11
UPN	56	1.18	2.89	1.43	1.50
WB	60	1.22	2.56	1.40	1.49

Source: See text for U.S. census data and Scarborough Prime Next data set for tables 1 through 13.

sure, and the markets average 8.8.[17] I calculate the number of cable channels similarly. Markets average 48.8 cable stations and from 45.0 to 57.0 across sample markets.

I calculate the numbers of black- and Hispanic-targeted shows as follows. If, for example, more than 90 (or 75 and so on) percent of its local audience is black, I deem the show "black targeted." The quantity of black-targeted programming in a locale is simply the number of shows that are so deemed black targeted. This measure is affected by the composition of local population. For example, if a locale were 100 percent black, then all shows attracting viewers would appear to be black targeted. Because prime time is targeted the same way everywhere, I can use differences in this measure's quantity of black-targeted programming in prime time across locales to normalize the measure of the quantity of black-targeted local programming.

Do Program Preferences Differ by Group?

Research on other media indicates that programming preferences in radio and newspapers differ sharply by race and Hispanic status. Journal-

17. This measure of local broadcast stations slightly understates the true number because it allows for only one independent station. However, calculations using more comprehensive BIA data confirm the positive relationship between market size and local broadcast stations.

istic evidence suggests that these differences extend to television.[18] The Scarborough data allow direct testing of how television preferences differ by race.

The strategy for investigating whether television program preferences differ by group is to examine whether blacks, whites, and Hispanics, when faced with multiple options, choose differently. The wider the range of options facing viewers, the more we can learn about the extent of differences in preferences. That is, if there were only three similar viewing options at a point in time (such as prime-time network television in the 1960s), we might not see much difference in the tendency to view different types of programming. However, if groups with different preferences face many options, including some apparently targeted at black or Hispanic viewers, we can see the extent of differences in preferences.

The data give us essentially three separate "experiments" for testing how much preferences differ across viewers. First, viewers in all markets face the same prime-time national programming options. Second, viewers in all markets face similar sets of national cable options. Finally, *within* each market, viewers face the range of locally controlled programs.

Table 2 shows the percent of blacks and Hispanics (and nonblacks and non-Hispanics) watching television between 8:00 p.m. and 11:00 p.m. (eastern time) on Thursday evenings during the 1999–2000 television season on six major national networks. For example, 2.5 percent of black persons watched ABC from 8:00 p.m. to 8:30 p.m., compared with 4.2 percent of nonblacks. During the same time slot, 4.7 percent of black households watched UPN, while only 1.6 percent of nonblacks watched UPN. That is, blacks have roughly three times the tendency to watch that (and other UPN shows), compared with nonblacks. Similarly, Hispanics have roughly double the tendency to watch UPN shows compared with non-Hispanics.

Table 3 displays the data differently, to show the percentage of Thursday prime-time audiences that are black and Hispanic. Given that blacks and Hispanics each make up small fractions of the U.S. population, their greater tendencies to watch particular programs are not high enough to make them large shares of national shows' audiences. For example, the audience for the UPN 8:00 p.m. to 8:30 p.m. time slot, which blacks are three times as likely as whites to watch, was only 26.7 percent black. The

18. Waldfogel (2003); George and Waldfogel (2003); James Sterngold, "A Racial Divide Widens on Network TV," *New York Times,* December 29, 1998, p. A1.

Table 2. Tendency to View Thursday Prime-Time Shows, by Group, 1999–2000 Season

Percent

Time	ABC	CBS	Fox	NBC	UPN	WBX
Blacks						
8:00-8:30 p.m.	2.5	5.8	2.5	5.1	4.7	2.0
8:30-9:00 p.m.	2.8	5.4	2.7	3.1	4.7	2.0
9:00-9:30 p.m.	4.7	4.3	2.8	4.6	4.7	3.2
9:30-10:00 p.m.	4.8	4.2	2.8	3.1	4.6	3.2
10:00-10:30 p.m.	3.3	3.6	4.6	7.8	2.8	2.3
10:30-11:00 p.m.	3.3	3.5	4.1	7.6	2.2	2.1
Nonblacks						
8:00-8:30 p.m.	4.2	6.3	1.8	10.4	1.6	0.7
8:30-9:00 p.m.	5.1	6.1	1.9	6.3	1.7	0.8
9:00-9:30 p.m.	8.9	4.6	1.8	9.0	1.7	1.7
9:30-10:00 p.m.	9.2	4.6	1.8	5.5	1.7	1.7
10:00-10:30 p.m.	4.5	4.1	3.5	11.5	1.1	1.2
10:30-11:00 p.m.	4.3	4.0	2.9	11.2	0.9	1.0
Hispanics						
8:00-8:30 p.m.	2.2	2.9	1.5	8.0	3.2	1.2
8:30-9:00 p.m.	2.8	2.6	1.7	4.8	3.2	1.2
9:00-9:30 p.m.	4.5	2.1	1.6	5.5	3.2	2.7
9:30-10:00 p.m.	4.5	2.0	1.6	3.6	3.3	2.8
10:00-10:30 p.m.	2.4	2.2	3.0	7.1	1.6	1.6
10:30-11:00 p.m.	2.3	2.2	2.7	6.8	1.2	1.2
Non-Hispanics						
8:00-8:30 p.m.	4.2	6.6	1.9	10.0	1.8	0.8
8:30-9:00 p.m.	5.1	6.4	2.1	6.1	1.9	0.9
9:00-9:30 p.m.	8.9	4.8	1.9	8.9	1.9	1.7
9:30-10:00 p.m.	9.2	4.8	1.9	5.4	1.9	1.8
10:00-10:30 p.m.	4.6	4.2	3.6	11.5	1.3	1.3
10:30-11:00 p.m.	4.4	4.1	3.0	11.2	1.1	1.1

Note: Percent of each group watching the time slot on that network. The 8:00-8:30 p.m. time slot contains shows aired at 8 p.m. in the eastern and Pacific time zones and at 7:00 p.m. in other time zones.

audience for the ABC 8:00 p.m. to 8:30 p.m.time slot was only 6.8 percent black, by contrast.

On Thursdays, NBC had the audiences with the largest white share (roughly 94 percent nonblack), followed closely by ABC (roughly 93 percent), CBS (about 90 percent nonblack), and Fox (85 percent nonblack). The UPN and WB network shows have audiences with the smallest white shares, at 75-80 percent nonblack. The patterns for Hispanics are similar, with FOX, WB, and UPN attracting audiences with the

Table 3. Black and Hispanic Shares of Thursday Prime-Time Audience, 1999–2000 Season

Percent

Time	ABC	CBS	Fox	NBC	UPN	WBX
Black						
8:00-8:30 p.m.	6.8	10.3	14.4	5.7	26.7	25.3
8:30-9:00 p.m.	6.3	10.0	14.6	5.8	26.0	23.6
9:00-9:30 p.m.	6.2	10.3	16.7	6.0	25.3	19.1
9:30-10:00 p.m.	6.1	10.2	16.2	6.5	24.8	18.7
10:00-10:30 p.m.	8.2	9.9	14.3	7.8	23.4	20.1
10:30-11:00 p.m.	8.6	10.0	15.0	7.8	22.1	21.3
Hispanic						
8:00-8:30 p.m.	5.3	4.5	7.9	7.9	16.1	13.0
8:30-9:00 p.m.	5.5	4.1	8.3	7.8	15.7	13.1
9:00-9:30 p.m.	5.1	4.4	8.2	6.3	15.4	14.3
9:30-10:00 p.m.	5.0	4.3	8.0	6.6	15.3	14.1
10:00-10:30 p.m.	5.2	5.3	8.2	6.2	11.8	11.7
10:30-11:00 p.m.	5.3	5.3	8.7	6.1	10.8	10.7

Note: The 8:00-8:30 p.m. time slot contains shows aired at 8:00 p.m. in the eastern and Pacific time zones and at 7:00 p.m. in other time zones.

largest Hispanic shares, although those audiences have smaller Hispanic than black shares.

Although the network prime-time data indicate that different groups tend to choose different programming, the choices on the national networks may not be broad enough to reveal the extent of differences in preferences. The data contain information about whether persons in the sample regularly watch each of 70 cable networks, presumably including a broader range of variation than on prime time in the broadcast networks. Table 4 displays the tendencies to watch (the percent of the sample regularly watching the cable channel) and distributions of audiences, by race and Hispanic status.

Blacks make up 11.1 percent of the sample but 60.8 percent of the persons regularly watching BET (Black Entertainment Television). The networks with the next-highest black audience shares are premium movie channels: Showtime (22.0), Cinemax (19.7), HBO (18.4), and the Movie Channel (18.1). That is, BET is the only black-targeted cable network, and as table 4 shows, 41.8 percent of black persons regularly watch it, compared with 3.4 percent of whites.

The cable data are somewhat misleading for Hispanics because two Spanish-language networks (Univision and Telemundo) appear in the

Table 4. Cable Channel Viewing Tendencies, by Race and Hispanic Status
Percent

	Tendency to watch					Audience share	
	Hispanic	Non-Hispanic	Black	Non-black	Overall	Hispanic	Black
A & E	24.8	40.8	33.2	40.0	78.4	6.1	9.4
American Movie Classics	3.2	3.6	2.5	3.7	7.1	8.9	7.7
Animal Planet	17.7	17.6	15.9	17.8	35.2	9.8	10.0
BET	8.9	7.5	41.8	3.4	15.2	11.3	60.8
BRAVO	1.2	1.1	0.8	1.2	2.2	10.2	7.5
Cartoon Network	21.2	14.6	23.9	14.2	30.5	13.5	17.4
Cinemax	15.1	11.2	20.5	10.4	23.1	12.7	19.7
CMT (Country Music Television)	6.1	10.6	3.9	10.9	20.3	5.9	4.3
CNBC	12.7	20.6	15.0	20.4	39.7	6.2	8.4
CNN	23.8	36.5	29.4	36.0	70.6	6.5	9.2
Comedy Central	17.2	18.5	18.6	18.4	36.8	9.1	11.2
Court TV	9.4	10.9	20.7	9.5	21.5	8.5	21.4
C-SPAN	0.4	0.9	1.4	0.8	1.8	4.3	17.2
E!	15.3	15.8	14.9	15.9	31.6	9.4	10.4
Encore	1.3	0.7	1.1	0.7	1.5	17.4	16.2
ESPN	21.5	30.7	26.9	30.2	59.7	7.0	10.0
ESPN Classic Sports Network	0.3	0.4	0.6	0.3	0.7	9.3	17.2
ESPN2	14.2	19.8	16.2	19.7	38.5	7.2	9.3
Florida News Channel	0.4	0.4	0.6	0.4	0.9	9.8	15.6
Food Network	9.3	11.1	12.1	10.8	21.9	8.3	12.2
Fox Family Channel	23.9	28.7	31.7	27.8	56.4	8.2	12.4
Fox News Channel	11.8	16.4	19.2	15.6	32.0	7.1	13.3
Fox Sports Espanol	3.2	0.2	0.8	0.5	1.0	60.1	16.9
Fox Sports Net	9.7	11.4	10.4	11.3	22.4	8.4	10.3
Fox Sports Ohio	3.2	0.2	0.8	0.5	1.0	60.1	16.9
Fox Sports World	3.0	2.6	3.6	2.5	5.2	11.3	15.4
Fox Sports World Espanol	1.8	0.1	0.3	0.2	0.5	72.2	13.8
FX	7.9	9.5	8.9	9.4	18.7	8.1	10.5
FXM	0.3	0.4	0.5	0.3	0.7	8.1	16.7
Galavision	9.9	0.2	1.2	1.1	2.3	84.7	11.7
GEMS	1.6	0.1	0.4	0.2	0.5	64.3	17.2
HBO	27.9	23.6	39.9	22.0	48.0	11.3	18.4
Headline News	11.7	18.3	17.3	17.7	35.3	6.4	10.8
HGTV	6.8	12.4	7.9	12.4	23.8	5.6	7.4
Home Shopping Network	5.3	6.4	9.1	5.9	12.5	8.2	16.1
Home Team Sports (HTS)	0.3	1.0	1.7	0.9	1.9	3.2	18.9
Lifetime Television	19.7	25.5	34.7	23.7	49.9	7.7	15.4
MSG (Madison Square Garden Network)	1.4	1.4	1.7	1.4	2.9	9.2	12.8

continued on next page

Table 4. Cable Channel Viewing Tendencies, by Race and Hispanic Status (continued)
Percent

	Tendency to watch					Audience share	
	Hispanic	Non-Hispanic	Black	Non-black	Overall	Hispanic	Black
MSNBC	7.2	12.0	8.2	11.9	23.1	6.1	7.9
MTV	21.3	15.5	20.7	15.5	32.1	12.9	14.3
NECN (New England Cable News)	0.3	0.6	0.3	0.6	1.1	5.7	6.9
NESN (New England Sports Network)	0.2	0.5	0.2	0.5	1.0	5.0	3.7
Nick at Nite	11.0	12.5	16.4	11.8	24.7	8.7	14.7
Nickelodeon	17.1	13.5	19.8	13.1	27.6	12.0	15.8
None	23.6	18.4	18.3	19.0	37.9	12.1	10.7
Other cable network/ service	14.8	13.1	14.3	13.2	26.6	10.8	11.9
Outdoor Life	0.3	0.3	0.2	0.3	0.6	8.3	8.0
QVC	3.4	5.8	5.8	5.5	11.1	6.0	11.5
Sci-Fi	12.5	13.7	18.0	13.1	27.2	8.9	14.6
Showtime	13.1	10.3	21.0	9.3	21.2	12.0	22.0
Speedvision	0.1	0.1	0.1	0.1	0.2	10.8	14.8
SportsChannel Florida	0.8	0.6	0.6	0.6	1.2	13.0	12.4
STARZ!	1.5	1.4	2.2	1.3	2.7	10.5	17.8
Sunshine Network	0.8	0.8	0.8	0.8	1.5	10.5	11.7
TBS	20.1	27.9	30.3	26.8	54.4	7.2	12.3
The Discovery Channel	36.9	40.8	33.6	41.2	80.8	8.9	9.2
The Disney Channel	21.4	18.3	19.9	18.4	37.2	11.2	11.9
The Golf Channel	1.9	4.1	2.8	4.0	7.7	4.7	8.0
The History Channel	17.9	26.2	20.9	26.0	50.9	6.8	9.1
The Learning Channel (TLC)	16.6	19.8	17.7	19.7	39.0	8.3	10.1
The Movie Channel	11.7	11.0	18.0	10.2	22.1	10.3	18.1
The Weather Channel	24.1	40.1	32.6	39.3	77.0	6.1	9.4
TNN	10.6	18.8	12.6	18.6	35.9	5.7	7.7
TNT	24.7	30.5	34.9	29.3	59.8	8.0	12.9
Travel Channel	6.2	7.5	5.8	7.6	14.8	8.2	8.7
TV Guide Channel	5.1	3.4	4.5	3.4	7.0	14.1	14.1
TVLand	4.5	7.5	9.5	7.0	14.5	6.1	14.5
USA Network	22.8	28.6	30.5	27.8	56.2	7.9	12.0
VH1	17.1	14.6	15.1	14.9	29.8	11.1	11.2
WGN	0.8	0.6	0.7	0.6	1.3	12.8	12.8

Table 5. Black-Targeted Half Hours on Local and Network Television

		Local shows with black audience percent greater than				Prime-time shows with local black audience percent greater than			
		50	66	75	90	50	66	75	90
ABC	Mean	10.27	5.48	3.55	1.97	0.11	0.02	0.02	0.00
66	Max	137	102	64	19	3	1	1	0
CBS	Mean	10.44	3.70	2.52	1.29	0.02	0.00	0.00	0.00
66	Max	73	25	21	11	1	0	0	0
Fox	Mean	27.20	16.41	12.26	7.68	0.62	0.18	0.08	0.00
66	Max	200	159	123	64	18	5	4	0
NBC	Mean	9.02	4.11	2.79	1.36	0.00	0.00	0.00	0.00
66	Max	64	33	23	13	0	0	0	0
PAX	Mean	11.34	7.16	5.96	4.04	1.68	0.55	0.38	0.13
56	Max	59	47	45	38	17	9	7	2
PBS	Mean	14.52	9.36	7.95	6.11	0.18	0.00	0.00	0.00
66	Max	82	66	66	45	3	0	0	0
TEL	Mean	1.80	1.00	0.80	0.80	0.13	0.13	0.13	0.13
15	Max	6	5	4	4	1	1	1	1
UNI	Mean	1.78	0.39	0.22	0.22	0.43	0.17	0.00	0.00
23	Max	20	5	3	3	6	4	0	0
UPN	Mean	43.23	30.91	25.18	16.93	7.38	4.95	3.80	2.13
56	Max	149	121	107	80	40	28	18	14
WB	Mean	37.88	26.60	22.55	15.43	5.80	3.73	2.78	1.48
60	Max	149	138	130	88	24	21	13	9
IND	Mean	16.83	10.61	8.39	6.44	1.85	0.8	0.44	0.34
41	Max	91	47	34	31	22	7	4	4

network data. Both have overwhelmingly Hispanic audiences. The Hispanic tendencies to watch TEL and UNI are 15.1 and 31.4 percent, respectively. TEL and UNI audiences are 90.1 and 91.5 percent Hispanic, respectively. At least two additional cable networks are Hispanic targeted. For example, Fox Sports Espanol and Galavision have substantial audiences that are more than half Hispanic.

Locally controlled television programming provides a third avenue of insight into how preferences differ across consumers. The 66 locales in these data vary between 0.9 and 40.5 percent black and between 0.4 and 47.4 percent Hispanic. I can calculate the share of the audience of each affiliate's half-hour time slot that is black. Table 5 describes these data. The top row indicates that ABC affiliates air an average of 10.27 (1.97) non-prime-time half hours with audiences at least 50 (90) percent black. By all of these metrics, UPN, WB, and Fox air the largest numbers of black-targeted half hours among the 10 covered networks. For example,

WB affiliates average 15.43 half hours with audiences that are more than 90 percent black. One market has 88 WB half hours outside evening prime time with such overwhelmingly black audiences.

The second half of the table does the same exercise for prime-time shows. These shows are, by construction, not locally controlled nor are they extremely black targeted. That prime-time shows appear black targeted in some markets and not others is an artifact of different fractions black in the various markets' populations. Indeed, this is a potential shortcoming of the measure. However, the absolute size of the problem is small: on UPN and WB affiliates, I deem roughly 10-15 percent as many evening prime-time shows black as I deem locally controlled slots black targeted. That is, the vast majority of the variation in the number of black-targeted local shows in the measure is real, not an artifact of the way the measure was created.

Table 6 does the same exercise for Hispanic-targeted shows. With the important exception of Univision and Telemundo affiliates, network affiliates carry relatively few Hispanic-targeted shows.

The estimates in tables 5 and 6 indicate that local markets have substantial numbers of shows with overwhelmingly minority audiences. Whereas prime-time programming attracts, at most, national audiences that are about a third black, much local programming is clearly aimed at blacks. The eleven networks air 2,926 sample half hours per week. An average sample member lives in a market with 57 shows that have more than 90 percent black local audiences and 197 shows with majority-black local audiences.

The local data indicate, to a greater extent than the national prime-time or cable data, the distance between black and white preferences and the fact that local programming, far more than national programming, caters to those preferences.[19]

Does the Mix of Programming Vary with the Local Audience?

Clearly, locally controlled programming varies more than nationally controlled programming in the extent of its black targeting. Hence the

---

19. It remains to be seen whether particular half hours on national cable networks appeal particularly to black audiences.

Table 6. Hispanic-Targeted Half Hours on Local and Network Television

		Local shows with Hispanic audience percent greater than				*Prime-time shows with local Hispanic audience percent greater than*			
		50	66	75	90	50	66	75	90
ABC	Mean	1.98	0.67	0.56	0.39	0.03	0.00	0.00	0.00
66	Max	36	14	13	10	2	0	0	0
CBS	Mean	2.08	0.95	0.71	0.36	0.00	0.00	0.00	0.00
66	Max	25	14	10	5	0	0	0	0
Fox	Mean	7.92	4.47	3.61	2.26	0.39	0.03	0.00	0.00
66	Max	100	60	45	22	17	1	0	0
NBC	Mean	2.15	0.86	0.64	0.30	0.03	0.00	0.00	0.00
66	Max	37	12	10	4	1	0	0	0
PAX	Mean	4.46	2.95	2.38	1.57	0.75	0.34	0.27	0.14
56	Max	52	36	32	14	7	5	5	4
PBS	Mean	8.21	5.17	4.15	3.20	0.35	0.05	0.03	0.02
66	Max	53	41	34	28	8	1	1	1
TEL	Mean	111.13	108.67	105.80	91.53	32.60	32.20	31.33	27.20
15	Max	214	214	209	174	44	44	44	43
UNI	Mean	175.87	172.13	168.91	147.00	41.65	41.26	39.96	32.13
23	Max	235	234	234	228	44	44	44	44
UPN	Mean	9.86	5.41	4.45	3.07	1.34	0.61	0.43	0.27
56	Max	55	38	33	26	13	7	7	7
WB	Mean	11.25	7.08	5.92	3.55	1.37	0.50	0.32	0.10
60	Max	105	79	65	45	20	9	8	4
IND	Mean	9.15	4.68	3.17	2.00	1.12	0.44	0.34	0.22
41	Max	67	33	17	16	9	5	5	5

wider dispersion in the minority content of audiences. Does the amount of black-targeted local programming vary across place according to demographic composition?

The quantity of black- and Hispanic-targeted programming available in each locale depends on the total amount of programming and the fraction that is group targeted. I begin by characterizing the relationship between the total quantity of available programming and market size. Table 7 reports results of regressions of the numbers of broadcast, cable, and total (broadcast + cable) channels and market population, in levels and logs. The results confirm what intuition would suggest: larger markets have more programming options.

The relationships bear some discussion. Across these large markets (ranging in size from 243,000 to 18 million people) there is proportionally more variation in local broadcast facilities than in cable stations.

Table 7. Market Size and Channel Availability

	1	2	3	4	5	6
	Number of broadcast channels	*Number of cable channels*	*Total channels*	*Log # total channels*	*Log # cable channels*	*Log # total channels*
Population '90 (millions)	0.230 (0.053)**	0.379 (0.081)**	0.609 (0.116)**			
Log population '90				0.114 (0.019)**	0.024 (0.006)**	0.037 (0.007)**
Constant	8.305 (0.193)**	47.984 (0.296)**	56.288 (0.425)**	0.555 (0.273)*	3.543 (0.080)**	3.522 (0.093)**
Observations	66	66	66	66	66	66
R squared	0.23	0.25	0.30	0.35	0.23	0.34

Note: Standard errors in parentheses.
*Significant at 5 percent.
** Significant at 1 percent.

This situation presumably reflects the real fixed costs of adding another broadcast facility. Almost exclusively, the cable stations are national, while the broadcast affiliates have some locally originating or locally controlled programming. Thus the amount of "local" programming is fairly sensitive to the size of the local market, while the amount of nonlocal programming is less sensitive, especially proportionally.

I can also use the station-level data to ask whether targeted presence varies with group population. While there are no wholly black-targeted networks, WB and UPN carry substantial black-targeted programming, while Univision and Telemumdo, which broadcast in Spanish, are Hispanic targeted. Table 8 reports probit estimates of the presence of these group-targeted affiliates on group sizes. The Spanish-language stations are much more likely to be present as markets have larger Hispanic populations. WB and UPN are driven more by overall market size. I cannot reject the hypothesis that black and nonblack population coefficients are equal in columns 1 and 2. Particularly for Hispanics, then, there will be more group-targeted programming because there are more Spanish-language stations.

An analysis of the programming, rather than the station, is also needed. As already documented, the total quantity of programming depends on market size, so I allow the quantity of black-targeted programming, for example, to depend on the absolute size of local black population and on the share of local population that is black. Because four commercial networks are ubiquitous in the sample, it is possible to

Table 8. Affiliate Presence and Group Size

	1 WB present	2 UPN present	3 Telemundo present	4 Univision present
Black population (millions)	−1.312	1.397		
	(2.791)	(1.961)		
Nonblack population (millions)	4.417	0.571		
	(1.780)*	(0.436)		
Hispanic population (millions)			11.755	87.033
			(3.214)**	(32.063)**
Non-Hispanic population (millions)			−0.920	−3.248
			(0.515)	(1.308)*
Constant	−1.509	0.188	−1.251	−1.658
	(0.991)	(0.403)	(0.479)**	(0.759)*
Observations	66	66	66	66

Note: Probits on whether network's affiliate is present in the market. Standard errors in parentheses.
*Significant at 5 percent.
**Significant at 1 percent.

perform scale-independent analyses of the quantities of group-targeted programming aired on these affiliates. For these analyses, only the shares should matter.

Figures A-1 and A-2, in the appendix to this chapter, show the relationships between the percent of local population that is black (or Hispanic) and the number of half hours with local audiences in excess of 90 percent black (Hispanic). Each figure shows prime-time shows, as well as non-prime-time shows. Because the amount of prime-time programming targeting minorities cannot vary across place by construction, I include this figure to show that the local programming local population composition relationship is not an artifact of the way the measure is calculated.

Both figures show striking positive relationships: locales with higher fractions black or Hispanic have substantially more black- or Hispanic-targeted programming outside of prime time (on the 11 networks). Memphis and New Orleans, for example, with black populations of more than a third of their totals, each air more than 200 local half hours with audiences at least 90 percent black. Similarly, San Antonio, nearly half Hispanic, has about 400 local half-hour shows with audiences at least 90 percent Hispanic. Both of these relationships run through the origin; that is, markets with no blacks or Hispanics have no black or Hispanic-targeted programming.

Table 9. Group-Targeted Programming and Local Group Population

	A. Blacks			
	1	*2*	*3*	*4*
	Local black-targeted programming	*Local black-targeted programming on ubiq. 4*	*Local black-targeted programming*	*Local black-targeted programming on ubiq. 4*
Percent black	464.354	112.740	457.015	118.443
	(49.190)**	(16.137)**	(52.271)**	(17.027)**
Black population			4.480	–3.481
(millions)			(10.244)	(3.337)
Constant	–7.130	–2.656	–7.489	–2.377
	(7.884)	(2.586)	(7.977)	(2.599)
Observations	66	66	66	66
R squared	0.58	0.43	0.58	0.44
	B. Hispanics			
	1	*2*	*3*	*4*
	Local Hispanic-targeted programming	*Local Hispanic-targeted programming on ubiq. 4*	*Local Hispanic-targeted programming*	*Local Hispanic-targeted programming on ubiq. 4*
Percent Hispanic	1,148.043	34.734	982.285	45.404
	(84.663)**	(5.222)**	(91.670)**	(5.605)**
Hispanic population			4.709	–0.303
(millions)			(1.359)**	(0.083)**
Constant	4.590	0.826	5.036	0.797
	(10.459)	(0.645)	(9.662)	(0.591)
Observations	66	66	66	66
R squared	0.74	0.41	0.78	0.51

Note: Dependent variable is number of nonevening prime-time half hours with audiences more than 90 percent Hispanic. "Ubiquitous 4" networks (ABC, NBC, CBS, and Fox) are present in all 66 sample markets. Standard errors in parentheses.
*Significant at 5 percent.
**Significant at 1 percent.

Table 9 documents the responsiveness of local program targeting to black and Hispanic population share, respectively, overall and for the four ubiquitous networks. The top panel shows results for blacks. The quantity of non-prime-time black-targeted programming on network affiliates is larger in markets with higher black concentration. Column 2 shows that the relationship, though smaller in magnitude, holds for the four ubiquitous networks, as well as overall. That is, at least part of the effect is pure positioning. Columns 3 and 4 show the quantity of black-targeted programming is not sensitive to the absolute size of black population (after controlling for the black share of population).[20] Hence, the quantity of black-targeted programming seems determined primarily through positioning rather than entry, at least across these large markets.

Results for Hispanics are somewhat different from results for blacks. Here, as column 3 shows, the absolute size of the Hispanic population matters, confirming the finding in table 8 that the number of Hispanic-targeted broadcast affiliates depends on Hispanic market size. Differences in the quantity of Hispanic-targeted programming across markets are driven by entry as well as positioning.

Do Viewers Value Group-Targeted Programming?

There is more minority-targeted programming in places with larger minority shares (and populations for Hispanics), but the deeper question is whether the greater quantity of programming brings additional benefits to the target audiences. In one sense, this is obvious. I have already documented that, when confronted by variation in programming, different groups choose different options. Still, if broader options benefit people, we should see a greater tendency for people to view options targeted at them.[21]

Table 10 examines the relationship between the black and Hispanic tendencies to watch network (and network affiliate) television and the numbers of group-targeted local half hours. Columns 1-3 examine blacks, and columns 4-6 examine Hispanics. The first (fourth) column employs an OLS specification. In the second (fifth) column, the local programming variable is instrumented with the share of local population that is black (Hispanic). The third (sixth) column employs market fixed effects. Thus the effect of black programming on the black viewing tendency is identified as the relationship between the extent of black local

20. When we replace black population with total population in columns 3 and 4 total population, like black population, is statistically insignificant. Although entry increases black-targeted programming—recall table A-1—the entry effects are swamped in magnitude by positioning effects.

21. Because network television viewing is unpriced, viewing information shows only where the demand curve intersects the quantity axis, not at what slope. Without price information, formal inferences about welfare are not possible. Throughout this paper I draw suggestive inferences about welfare under the maintained assumption that higher consumption reflects higher welfare (from television viewing).

Table 10. Do Minority Viewers Value Minority-Targeted Programming?

	1 Black OLS	2 Black IV	3 Black MSA FE	4 Hispanic OLS	5 Hispanic IV	6 Hispanic MSA FE
Black-targeted local	0.016	0.026				
segment	(0.009)	(0.009)**				
Hispanic-targeted local				0.013	0.007	
segment				(0.003)**	(0.004)	
Black dummy			7.860			
			(0.305)**			
Hispanic dummy						1.044
						(0.374)**
Black * 90 percent			0.023			
black segment			(0.003)**			
Hispanic * 90 percent						0.014
Hispanic segment						(0.001)**
Constant	21.735	20.909	15.147	16.026	17.347	15.837
	(1.192)**	(1.270)**	(0.270)**	(1.351)**	(1.612)**	(0.273)**
Observations	19,793	19,793	178,784	17,348	17,348	178,784
R squared	0.06	0.05	0.10	0.04	0.04	0.09

Note: Robust standard errors in parentheses (clustered on CMSA in columns 1, 2, 4, and 5). Black- and Hispanic-targeted local segments are ones with audiences that are at least 90 percent black or Hispanic, respectively.
*Significant at 5 percent.
**Significant at 1 percent.

programming and the gap between the black and white viewing tendencies. In all of the specifications, blacks view more television in places with more black-targeted programming. The pattern for Hispanics is similar, although the IV estimate (column 5) is not significant.

The Bottom Line: Preference Externalities in Local Television Programming

Blacks and whites, and Hispanics and non-Hispanics, prefer different television programming. Markets with higher minority shares have larger amounts of minority-targeted programming. Minorities derive more satisfaction from television—inferred from their greater tendency to watch—in markets with more minority-targeted programming. Hence, one can infer that raising the black or Hispanic share of local population will raise the welfare of local blacks, in their capacity as local television consumers.

Broadly, there are two ways of examining the relationship between population composition and welfare (as implied by viewing). First, one can examine the relationships between each group's viewing and population composition. I call this the "simple cross section approach." Thus, for example, one can examine the cross-market relationship between black viewing and the share of local population that is black. A possible shortcoming of that approach is that some unobserved characteristic of the market may be correlated with both the population composition and the tendency for persons to watch television.[22] Because there are data on both black and nonblack tendencies to watch television, one can circumvent this problem by pooling black and nonblack observations together and including market fixed effects in the regressions. In this "MSA fixed effects" approach, the effect of, say, the percent black on the tendency for blacks to watch television is identified from the relationship between the percent black and the gap between black and nonblack television viewing.

First the simple cross section approach. Table 11 reports regressions of black and nonblack viewing on black and nonblack population and on the black population share. I separately estimate these models on prime-time and local viewing hours. For example, columns 1 and 2 show that black viewing outside of prime time increases in the local black population and decreases in the local nonblack population. Nonblack viewing does not vary with black and nonblack populations. Columns 3 and 4 reexamine these relationships during prime-time hours. Black prime-time viewing increases in local black population, but the size of the effect is less than a quarter of the size of the local effect.

Columns 5 through 9 of the table are estimated with the black population share. Black viewing increases with the share black. Isolated blacks watch roughly 20 half hours outside of prime time per week. Blacks in markets that are, say, 50 percent black watch roughly 28 half hours. White viewing is invariant with respect to the local fraction black.[23]

---

22. An illustrative, although not necessarily plausible, example is weather. If blacks are concentrated in some regions with different weather, and if the nature of the weather affects the appeal of being indoors (and therefore watching television), then the fraction black and the tendency for blacks to watch television will be related for reasons unrelated to the mechanism outlined in this chapter.

23. Recall from the discussion of figure A-1 that the market with the most black-targeted local programming (New Orleans) had about 235 half hours per week, out of a total of nearly 3,000. Although whites face fewer white-targeted segments in heavily black markets, they nonetheless face a large amount of white-targeted programming.

Table 11. Direct Evidence of Preference Externalities in Local Television (Blacks)

Half hours viewed

	1 Local Nonblack	2 Local Black	3 Prime-time Nonblack	4 Prime-time Black	5 Local Nonblack	6 Local Black	7 Prime-time Nonblack	8 Prime-time Black
Black population (millions)	-0.451	4.548	0.367	0.948				
	(0.822)	(1.049)**	(0.247)	(0.445)*				
Nonblack population (millions)	0.026	-0.640	0.064	-0.054				
	(0.159)	(0.178)**	(0.032)	(0.069)				
Percent black in CMSA					-1.667	15.599	-0.147	0.275
					(3.004)	(5.319)**	(1.352)	(2.006)
Observations	158,991	19,793	158,991	19,793	158,991	19,793	158,991	19,793
R squared	0.10	0.06	0.05	0.01	0.10	0.06	0.05	0.01

Note: Robust standard errors in parentheses (cluster on CMSA). All specifications include age and sex dummies.
*Significant at 5 percent.
**Significant at 1 percent.

Table 12 revisits the question using the simple cross section approach for Hispanics. Here the relationships are insignificant. That is, there is no evidence that Hispanics watch more noncable television in markets with absolutely or proportionately more Hispanic residents.

Table 13 examines both blacks (relative to nonblacks) and Hispanics (relative to non-Hispanics) using the MSA fixed effects approach. Each of the regressions includes group-specific age and gender dummies, as well as MSA fixed effects. These results confirm that blacks benefit blacks (relative to their effect on whites). Moreover, Hispanics benefit Hispanics (relative to their effects on non-Hispanics) in these specifications. Effects are larger for blacks than for Hispanics.

As in other media, the welfare of minority television viewers with distinct preferences depends on their neighbors. The presence of a substantial variety of cable channels makes this dependence of local residents' welfare on their neighbors surprising. If cable did not exist, one might expect stronger dependence of minority viewers' welfare on their neighbors' preferences. Although I cannot examine a world without cable, I can ask whether this dependence is stronger for viewers without cable. I explored this possibility and found no stronger dependence of group viewing on population composition among those without cable connections. Of course, given the endogeneity of cable connection, it is not entirely clear what one might make of such regressions.

Conclusion

A growing body of evidence shows that, when preferences differ across audience groups, the satisfaction of local media consumers depends on the size of their groups' local populations. This relationship has been documented in prior research for local radio and daily newspaper markets. This chapter documents that this relationship holds, particularly for blacks, in local television markets. Findings are as follows:

—Television programming preferences differ sharply between blacks and nonblacks, and between Hispanics and non-Hispanics;

—The quantity of group-targeted programming is larger in markets with more minorities (proportionately more for blacks, absolutely and proportionately more for Hispanics);

Table 12. **Direct Evidence of Preference Externalities in Local Television (Hispanics and non-Hispanics)**
Half hours viewed

	1 Local non-Hispanic	2 Local Hispanic	3 Prime-time non-Hispanic	4 Prime-time Hispanic	5 Local non-Hispanic	6 Local Hispanic	7 Prime-time non-Hispanic	8 Prime-time Hispanic
Hispanic population (millions)	-0.238 (0.193)	0.021 (0.271)	-0.044 (0.102)	-0.075 (0.076)				
Non-Hispanic population (millions)	-0.040 (0.072)	0.265 (0.119)*	0.134 (0.044)**	0.151 (0.031)**				
Percent Hispanic in CMSA					-3.337 (3.035)	6.719 (4.256)	4.005 (1.091)**	1.829 (0.989)
Constant	16.192 (0.477)**	18.092 (1.245)**	7.460 (0.200)**	8.043 (0.469)**	16.226 (0.455)**	18.056 (1.388)**	7.509 (0.214)**	8.285 (0.516)**
Observations	161,436	17,348	161,436	17,348	161,436	17,348	161,436	17,348
R squared	0.10	0.04	0.05	0.02	0.10	0.03	0.05	0.02

Notes: Robust standard errors in parentheses (cluster on CMSA). All specifications include age and sex dummies.
*Significant at 5 percent.
**Significant at 1 percent.

Table 13. Direct Evidence of Preference Externalities, MSA Fixed Effects Estimates

	Half hours viewed outside prime time			
	1	*2*	*3*	*4*
Black dummy	3.817	6.429		
	(0.805)**	(0.000)		
Black dummy * percent black	21.936			
	(2.131)**			
Black dummy * black population		5.758		
		(0.538)**		
Black dummy * nonblack population		−0.787		
		(0.097)**		
Hispanic dummy			2.462	1.902
			(0.742)**	(0.718)**
Hispanic dummy * percent Hispanic			7.018	
			(1.569)**	
Hispanic dummy * Hispanic population				0.099
				(0.208)
Hispanic dummy * non-Hispanic population				0.372
				(0.072)**
Number of CMSAs	66	66	66	66
Observations	178,784	178,784	178,784	178,784
R squared	0.10	0.10	0.09	0.09

Note: All equations include MSA fixed effects, as well as group-specific age and gender dummies. Standard errors in parentheses. Population is measured in millions.
*Significant at 5 percent.
**Significant at 1 percent.

—Minority viewing of network affiliates increases with their quantity of minority-targeted programming; and

—Minority viewing (and, one might plausibly infer, viewer welfare) depends on the distribution of one's neighbors' tastes.

These results have practical and theoretical interest. First, the theoretical: in this context, with large fixed costs and preferences that differ sharply across groups of consumers, consumer satisfaction depends on the distribution of program-preferring types in the local market. Here, as in other local broadcasting contexts, the dichotomy between market and collective choice allocation suggested by Friedman does not hold.[24] Second, the practical: despite the large number of national cable channels widely available in the 66 large markets examined in this study, local television exerts an effect on local viewers' welfare. Policymakers might bear this in mind as they consider rules that give advantage to national

24. Friedman (1962).

broadcast programming at the expense of local programming. Finally, although agglomeration provides a consumption rationale for cities, at least for media markets, the consumption benefits of agglomeration are not the same for all sorts of consumers.

As with most studies, caveats are in order. First, although my study documents welfare benefits of agglomerating with people sharing similar preferences, I offer no evidence on the importance of the benefits of, say, media products, in comparison with the importance of other aspects of the quality of life such as school quality or safe neighborhoods. That remains a topic for future research.

Appendix

Figure A-1. Black Population Share and Black-Targeted Shows

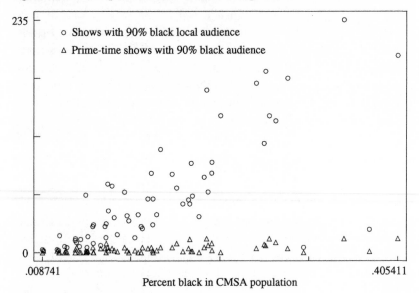

Figure A-2. Hispanic Population Share and Hispanic-Targeted Shows

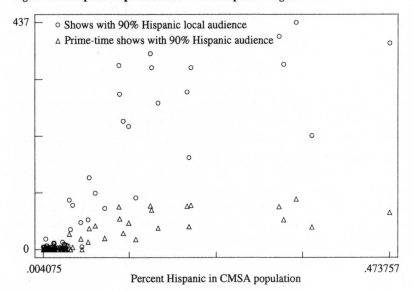

Comments

Thomas J. Holmes: This paper is the third installment of the "Whom Benefits Whom?" series by Joel Waldfogel and his coauthors.[25] It is now well understood that when scale economies and product differentiation are important, individuals can benefit from having more people live nearby—the increased demand can make it economically feasible to make locally available a large variety of products. The big idea of Waldfogel's research project is that when individuals have different preferences, it matters who these additional neighbors are. If additional neighbors to individual x have different preferences than individual x, the additional neighbors may not help the individual get access to more of the kinds that he or she likes. In fact, adding more people with different preferences might even hurt individual x. Waldfogel focuses on media markets, but the idea is more general. If a small town has a minor league baseball team, and if a bunch of people who like hockey move in, the increased scale of demand may make it possible for the town to get a hockey team. If the hockey team takes some of the baseball team's market away, leading to the exit of the baseball team, the addition of the hockey fans has hurt the baseball fans.

The earlier papers in the series examined how the sizes of racial and ethnic groups affected the newspaper market.[26] These are very interesting papers. They make a compelling case that different demographic groups have quite different tastes and that product variety targeted at a particular

25. George and Waldfogel (2003); Waldfogel (2003).
26. George and Waldfogel (2003); Waldfogel (2003).

group is closely linked to size of that demographic group in the market. The work also shows that consumption behavior is affected, suggesting that this increased variety has welfare effects. For example, a black person living in an area with a large black population is more likely to listen to the radio. The presumption is that this change in behavior results from the larger variety of black-targeted radio found in areas with larger black populations.

The current installment of the series conducts the same kind of exercises with local television markets. Given the size of the television industry, it is an important one to look at, and the paper makes a useful addition to the series. My discussion just raises one concern about a data limitation that arises with this project, which was not as much of an issue in the earlier work. This limitation makes it difficult to cleanly measure the link between variety and market size.

Data Limitation

To examine the relationship between the number of products targeted at a particular ethnic group and its market size, one needs some way of classifying the degree to which a product is targeted at a particular ethnic group. In Waldfogel's article "Preference Externalities," information comes as part of the raw data. Radio stations are classified in the data as, for example, "black-gospel," "black-talk," and so on.[27] It is then straightforward to examine the link between the number of black-gospel stations in an area and the size of the black population.

The data on television viewing considered are rich in many ways. For each half-hour time slot for each station, there is demographic information about who is watching the show. However, there is no information about what the program is that people are watching. There is no information that the show is *Baywatch* or *Friends*. There is no analog to the classification of a program as "black-gospel" in the radio data. To get around this issue, Waldfogel attempts to infer something about the degree of targeting of a program, based on who is watching the program. A difficulty is that markets with larger black populations will naturally have larger black audiences, even if the programming remains the same.

---

27. Waldfogel (2003).

Some formal notation helps make the point. Let i index a half-hour slot for a particular local station. Let $t_i \in [-1,1]$ represent the degree to which programming in the time slot is targeted to a black audience. Suppose that the per capita viewing by race follows a simple mechanical statistical model,

$$q_i^B = \varepsilon_i^B + t_i$$
$$q_i^W = \varepsilon_i^W - t_i$$

for blacks and whites (which for simplicity are assumed to be the only ethnic groups). At $t_i = 0$, there is no targeting. As t_i increases, per capita viewing by blacks increases and by whites decreases.

Suppose β is the population share of blacks in the local market. Then the share of the audience of time slot i that is black is

$$s_i = \frac{\beta q_i^B}{\beta q_i^B + (1-\beta) q_i^W} = \frac{\beta(\varepsilon_i^B + t_i)}{\beta(\varepsilon_i^B + t_i) + (1-\beta)(\varepsilon_i^W - t_i)}.$$

The paper defines a program i as "black targeted" if its audience share s_i is above a given threshold, for example, $s_i \geq .90$. The problem is that the audience share s_i increases in the population share β, everything else held fixed. Hence we would expect to see a positive correlation between programs defined as targeting blacks and the black population share, even if the programming did not change.

Waldfogel is aware that this is an issue and looks at the difference between prime-time programming and non-prime-time programming to get a handle on its significance. The idea is that prime-time programming is determined at the national level and is the same for all stations in a given network. It does not vary across cities with different black populations. Non-prime-time programming is determined at the local level and might vary with black population. Since the black population makes up a relatively small share of the total at the national level, but can be large in certain cities, we might expect to find black targeting in certain local markets but find very little at the national level. To speak to this issue, table 5 reports that the mean number of national programs defined as black targeted (at the .90 threshold) for the WB network is 1.5 per week across the various WB affiliates, while the mean number of black-targeted local shows across the affiliates is 15.4. For the UPN network, the corresponding means are 2.1 and 17.0. That the number of targeted programming slots at the national level is much smaller (about 10 to 15 percent) than the number of targeted slots at the local level is interpreted as evidence of two things: that targeting is much less prevalent at the national level and that the concern raised about the targeting measure is not important. One problem I have with this discussion is that it ignores that there are only three hours of prime time in a day compared with up to twenty-one hours of non-prime-time programming in a day. For that reason, we would expect counts of targeted slots to be significantly lower for prime-time programming compared with non-prime time, even if the average level of targeting was the same.

My bottom line is that it is tricky to measure the extent of black targeting based on the approach used in Waldfogel's paper in this volume. To get a cleaner handle on this measurement for future work, more structure in the modeling of the problem or obtaining more data would be useful. The additional structure might include formal modeling of consumer choice behavior. The additional data that might be helpful would include detailed information about what the programs are and viewing information about particular programs across markets.

The preceding discussion is relevant only for the part of the paper that links product variety to size of ethnic group. The part of the paper that relates individual television-viewing behavior to market size does not require a measure of product variety, so concerns about how to measure variety do not arise.

Roger G. Noll: Joel Waldfogel's paper has two purposes. The first is to demonstrate that theoretical and empirical research on the effects of entry in product-differentiated markets has useful implications for understanding the effect of city size on economic welfare. Waldfogel argues that consumer welfare is likely to increase with the size of the local market because of increasing product variety, creating a positive externality of population growth. The second is to illustrate this point by showing that larger cities with a greater proportion of minorities produce more television programming that, to use Waldfogel's term, is targeted at minority audiences.

Waldfogel's second point provides a rationale for "localism" in television, whereby the Federal Communications Commission (FCC) allocates stations with relatively low power to provide service to small geographic areas for the purpose of putting programming decisions in the hands of local entrepreneurs who, arguably, will tailor program schedules to local tastes. Waldfogel's analysis can be interpreted as justifying the FCC's historical spectrum allocation policy in broadcasting. The alternative policies are to allow market transactions in spectrum to determine the geographic area that is served by a single station (as with radio telephony), to use an administrative process to create some number of more powerful regional stations (as with radio broadcasting), or to move broadcasting increasingly to cable and satellite distribution, with growing displacement of local broadcasting by national cable and satellite networks, which has been happening since the FCC ended its freeze on cable television development in 1972.

This comment focuses primarily on the second point, although the findings have application to the welfare economics of the first point. Waldfogel's empirical work finds that as the number and proportion of minorities in a metropolitan area grow, the number of programs that attract a primarily minority audience increases. This empirical observation no doubt is correct. Waldfogel then concludes that this phenomenon reflects, first, significant differences in preferences among racial and ethnic groups, and, second, decisions by local stations to target programs to minorities in a fashion that would not be expected of national television networks (or, by implication, more powerful regional stations). These conclusions imply a justification for localism and other policies that protect off-air broadcasting against competition from cable and satellite systems that deliver national channels.

As this comment shows, Waldfogel's inferences from his empirical work are not consistent with actual program schedules, and the specification of his empirical model is not the most appropriate one for finding the effect that he seeks. The summary explanation is simple. Television stations do not engage in significant local program production or variation in the type of syndicated programs that they broadcast and so exhibit no actual targeting behavior. Moreover, affiliates of secondary networks—PAX, UPN, and WB—face different constraints and incentives than affiliates of the four major networks—ABC, CBS, Fox, and NBC—or independent stations. Like independents, they produce almost no local programs, and their program schedules do not vary significantly across cities. Thus variation in the number of programs that are viewed primarily by minorities cannot be for the reason advanced by Waldfogel, and localism is not producing the effect he observes.

The Theory of Program Selection

The conceptual model underlying Waldfogel's analysis is the Steiner model, which in turn is an application of Hotelling's theory of spatial competition. Steiner's original model dealt with radio, but it clearly applies to television as well, as was illustrated in subsequent work by Noll, Peck, and McGowan and Owen, Beebe, and Manning.[28] While Hotelling imagined competition among products for which attributes varied continuously, Steiner assumed that the product (programs) is divisible into discrete types and asked how product variety and consumer welfare were affected by the number of producers. In Waldfogel's version, the types are categories of programs that are oriented toward racial and ethnic groups.

The basic mechanics of the Steiner-Waldfogel model are revealed in a simple example. Suppose that there are three types of programs: M ("mass audience" appealing to everyone), W (appealing mainly to whites), and B (appealing mainly to blacks). The fourth option is N (not watching television). Suppose that the percentage of the population that is white is N_w and black is N_b, where $N_w > N_b$. Assume that all citizens have one of the following three preference orderings: P_1: M>W>B>N; P_2: W>N>M>B; and P_3: B>N>M>W.[29] Note that this structure of preferences implies that total viewing increases as new types of programs enter the market. Let the number of blacks and whites with each preference, expressed as a percentage of the total populations, be N_{b1}, N_{b2}, N_{b3}, N_{w1}, N_{w2}, and N_{w3}, where $N_{b1} + N_{w1} > N_{b2} + N_{w2} > N_{b3} + N_{w3}$. Assume further that the percentage breakdown of the six types of viewers is as follows:

Type of viewer	N_w	N_b	N_{b1}	N_{b2}	N_{b3}	N_{w1}	N_{w2}	N_{w3}
Percent of population	83	17	11	.5	5.5	55	27.5	.5

28. Steiner (1952); Hotelling (1929); Noll, Peck, and McGowan (1973); Owen, Beebe, and Manning (1974).

29. Although the number of possible preference orderings is 24, the essence of the Steiner model is captured in this simpler version. The crucial assumptions is that the audiences with minority tastes will not watch anything other than their favored type.

These assumptions imply that most blacks and whites prefer type M, about one-third of each group will watch only programs that cater to their ethnicity, and a tiny proportion of each group will watch only programs that cater to the other ethnicity. All of these assumptions are broadly consistent with the facts about viewership reported by Waldfogel except the assumption that no viewers of types W or B switch from other types when their favored type is offered. Ignoring this fact makes the model more transparent, but it does affect the qualitative results.

Commercial broadcasting stations seek viewers for the purpose of selling advertising, while public broadcasting stations seek audiences for the purpose of generating contributions. For simplicity, assume that revenues from advertisers and contributors do not depend on demographics so that revenues are proportional to audience. If so, the first broadcast entrant will pick program type M, which will attract 66 percent of all viewers. Steiner assumed that consumers are indifferent across programs of the same type and so divide themselves randomly among these programs. Under this assumption, a second station expects to attract 33 percent of the population if it broadcasts type M, 28 percent if it shows type W, and 6 percent if it selects type B. Thus the second station also will broadcast type M. The third station will select type W for 28 percent rather than M for 22 percent. Following this same logic, the equilibrium programming configurations for one to sixteen stations are shown in table 14. After fourteen stations have entered, the next can obtain one-eleventh of the M audience of 66 for 6.0 percent of the audience, one-fifth of the W audience of 28 for a 5.6 share, or all of the B audience for a 6.0 percent share. Thus either the fifteenth or the sixteenth station will enter as a B.

The preceding exercise demonstrates important features of the Steiner-Waldfogel model and shows that some of Waldfogel's inferences from his data are not warranted.

When the B station finally emerges, it is "black targeted" in Waldfogel's terminology in that its audience is more than 90 percent black (black share is 5.5 to 6.0 percent). Yet most blacks (68 percent) do not watch black-targeted programs. Qualitatively, this finding is reported by Waldfogel. Waldfogel's empirical observations about stations' program decisions indicate, at most, targeting to a minority of a minority. The programs that are "black targeted" in the sense that they attract the largest

Table 14. The Effect of Station Entry on Programming Diversity

	Number of stations by program type		
Total stations	M	W	B
1	1	0	0
2	2	0	0
3	2	1	0
4	3	1	0
5	4	1	0
6	4	2	0
7	5	2	0
8	6	2	0
9	7	2	0
10	7	3	0
11	8	3	0
12	9	3	0
13	9	4	0
14	10	4	0
15	11	4	0
16	11	4	1

Note: Based on assumptions explained in the text.

black audiences generally do not have overwhelmingly large shares of black viewers.

Another feature of the model is that the optimal market structure is monopoly, not competition, which was the main point of Steiner's original paper.[30] After the first firm enters offering M, another M station can not improve welfare. This feature of the Steiner model leads to Waldfogel's conclusion that black-targeted programs increase welfare because they increase the size of the audience (by adding more black viewers). If a monopolist controlled all stations, the program shown on the second channel would be W, causing the total audience to increase from 66 to 94 percent of the population, and the monopolist's third station would show B, expanding viewing to 100 percent of the total. Thus local competition reduces welfare relative to monopoly because it requires more stations to serve the entire audience. Of course, this finding is perfectly general for all differentiated product goods: monopolists will add more product variety to the extent that it increases *net* sales but will not add varieties that do no more than divide the same customers across more separate products. Put this way, however, the problem with Waldfogel's conclusion is

30. Steiner (1952).

clear—the issue is not just numbers of purchasers but willingness to pay for more variety.

To resurrect the idea that broadcasting competition is beneficial requires more categories of programs and more preference orderings. If type M programs subdivide into a large number of categories, and some viewers prefer each category, welfare can be enhanced by competitive entry into the M type. But once subdivisions of the M type are introduced, the welfare economics is ambiguous because station revenues are not based on prices that measure the preference intensity of viewers.

In the example, the twelfth M-type program will draw an audience of 5.5 compared with an audience of 6.0 for the first B-type station. If the willingness to pay of each viewer of the twelfth M channel is $7, and the willingness to pay of the B-type viewers is $1, the twelfth M-type program will generate more than six times as much welfare as the first B type. Indeed, if the audience for the twelfth M type is distributed among blacks and whites according to their proportion of the population (17 percent black), the surplus generated just for blacks by the twelfth M-type program exceeds the surplus generated for blacks by the first B-type program ($.17 \times 5.5 \times \$7 = 6.5 > 5.5 \times \$1 = 5.5$).

These examples illustrate a fundamental point about the theory of consumer demand for television. One cannot draw conclusions about viewer welfare from observations about changes in total audience. The surplus that is related to this measure is for advertisers and broadcasters. Waldfogel's conclusion about the relationship between the size of the black audience and the number of programs that are watched mostly by blacks requires that at least one of the following is true: a large proportion of blacks will switch to black-targeted programming if it is offered, in which case a revealed-preference argument can be invoked; or the willingness to pay for additional programs of other types is small compared with the willingness to pay for B-type programs, even though the audience for marginal programs in each type is roughly the same.

The Nature of Program Choice by Stations

The validity of Waldfogel's concept of black-targeted programs hinges on two assumptions. The first is that stations select programs outside of prime time, while networks select programs in prime time. Waldfogel compares prime-time programs and other programs and shows that targeting is more prevalent outside of prime time. Waldfogel infers from this fact that local stations are more responsive to black preferences than networks are. The second assumption is that programs for which the audience is mostly black are different from other programs. Obviously, if the same program is "black targeted" in one city and "white targeted" in another, the data on the share of programs watched mostly by blacks convey no meaningful information about differences in tastes by race, programming decisions by networks, or black welfare by type of station.

Most scholarly research on television concludes that localism is inefficient because "local" programming is not, in fact, local. Program content is a pure public good in that the cost of producing a program does not depend on how many stations broadcast it or how many viewers watch it. Because the average cost of a program per station and per viewer falls as more stations elect to show it, programs that are nationally distributed have an enormous cost advantage over programs that are locally produced or even programs that are shown on only a few stations. To compete effectively with a program that is broadcast on one hundred or more stations, a locally produced program must be very inexpensive or very popular. For this reason, most television stations produce almost no local programs, the local programs that they do produce have low production costs and feature mostly talking heads (news, sports), and most of their programs are distributed nationally to stations in many markets. The main exceptions to this generalization are stations with unusually large audiences, which for the most part are *network affiliates of the Big Four networks in large cities*, not independents or affiliates of minor networks.

Station programming behavior is also strongly influenced by policy constraints. Entry by television stations is hardly free. The FCC decides how many stations are assigned to a market, and this relationship is only loosely related to population.[31] Localism requires that stations in nearby cities do not interfere with one another. In regions where large cities are close together, such as the Atlantic seaboard from Washington, D.C., to Portland, Maine, nearly all cities, even very large ones, have few stations, while in sparsely settled areas, like the Mountain West, even small markets sometimes have many stations. This fact explains the low explanatory power of Waldfogel's regression of the number of stations on the

31. Nelson and Noll (1985).

population of a city. The significance of this fact is that the extent to which program diversification is likely to take place, in accordance with the Steiner model, depends on the number of stations in relation to the size of the population. Truly local programming is most likely in large cities with a *small* number of stations (because it can draw a larger audience and so have a lower cost per viewer). To the extent that minorities prefer unique forms of local productions, such as local news, these programs are *less* likely as the number of stations increases.

Another important constraint is the "prime-time access rule." The four major networks must not operate during six prime-time hours per week.[32] The four major networks have chosen not to operate from 7:00 to 8:00 p.m. (eastern and Pacific, and an hour earlier in central and mountain) except on Sunday. Thus network programs account for at most 80 percent of prime time, although network affiliates are free to preempt some network programs if they so choose. But the prime-time access rule does not apply to the other three networks. In principle, these networks face no limits on the fraction of a broadcast schedule that can be devoted to network programs on their affiliates.

Despite the prime-time access rule, all networks are free to offer national programming during the rest of the broadcast day. Networks can and do offer morning news magazines, daytime soap operas, news programs just before prime time, and weekend sports. Hence, the assumption that non-prime-time programming is local is not accurate.

A final important influence on station entry is the "must carry rule," which stipulates that cable television systems must carry local over-the-air broadcast stations that are "significantly viewed" in the community, which as a practical matter is interpreted by the FCC as generating an audience that is measurable within the sampling strategies of ratings entities. Thus a broadcaster with a weak UHF signal can obtain a place on local cable systems, and minor networks—PAX, UPN, and WB—have constructed a national audience from a relatively small number of affiliates by getting their affiliates onto cable systems in their regions. A station that seeks to be carried by multiple cable systems in a region faces incentives that resemble that of a network, not a local station, in choosing its programs.

32. Prime time is 7:00 to 11:00 p.m. eastern and Pacific and 6:00 p.m. to 10:00 p.m. central and mountain.

I do not have program schedules for the period that Waldfogel studied. Instead, I examined the websites of numerous television stations in a variety of markets and of the minor networks, PAX, UPN, and WB, for a week during February 2004. This period is important for stations because it is "sweeps" period—that is, when audiences are most extensively measured for the purpose of determining advertising prices. Here are some facts about their schedules.

PAX. The PAX network owns its sixty-one affiliates and provides a complete line-up of network programs from noon until midnight every day. Of these 144 weekly hours of PAX network programming, 41.5 hours are infomercials, including 34.5 of the 35.0 hours between noon and 5:00 p.m. every day.[33] The remaining programs are divided among original programs, reruns of programs originally produced for one of the Big Four networks (for example, *Diagnosis Murder, Early Edition,* and *Bonanza*), syndicated original programs that are not exclusive to PAX (for example, *Candid Camera* and *Family Feud*), and movies. PAX's original network programming accounts for six hours per week. In essence, PAX is a cooperative for acquiring movies, syndicated programs, and network reruns.

PAX affiliates can substitute other programs for the network feed, but in practice they rarely do so. For the period February 13-19, 2004, I collected the program logs for PAX affiliates in New Orleans (with the highest proportion of its population black), Washington, D.C. (a large market with many blacks), San Francisco (a large market with fewer blacks), Portland, Oregon, (a midsized market with few blacks), and Bangor, Maine (a small market with few blacks). These schedules revealed almost complete overlap in program choices among the five stations for the entire twenty-four-hour day.

For example, the Friday programming in New Orleans departs from the network feed and the program choices in the other markets. The New Orleans PAX channel runs one hour of news, while Bangor, San Francisco, and Washington each have a single half-hour news program. The D.C. affiliate runs one hour of programming about the local lottery. None

---

33. An infomercial is a complete program that is produced by an advertiser, and usually is simply one long commercial. Nearly all infomercials are distributed nationally and are broadcast on all forms of channels—network affiliates, independents, and cable networks. PAX is the only over-the-air network that incorporates infomercials into its network schedule, but several cable/satellite networks schedule infomercials.

has any additional local programming, and Portland has no local programming at all. Among the religious programs, all stations run identical programs for fourteen segments during the "nonnetwork" period. During the "network" period, the five stations drop a total of sixteen half-hour network segments (about 13 percent of the schedule). Of these, four segments are dropped for news and two for the lottery. The other segments are used for some kind of syndicated program: Bangor drops infomercials for reruns of *Beverly Hillbillies, Lassie,* and *Lone Ranger* plus a second hour of *Bonanza*, and Washington drops the network's *Bonanza* rerun to add a nationally syndicated talk show (*John Walsh*). Thus the program schedules exhibit no clear difference in programming policies.

UPN. The least active network is UPN, producing only ten hours per week of network programs. On Monday, Tuesday, and Wednesday UPN shows a total of six hours of original series. On Thursday UPN presents two hours of wrestling, and on Friday the network feed is a two-hour movie. Thus, for the remaining 158 hours per week and 18 prime-time hours, UPN affiliates are de facto independent stations, including all day Saturday and Sunday. UPN stations, theoretically, control more than 90 percent of their programming and more than 70 percent of their prime-time programming.

UPN network programs also have the highest share of blacks among the prime-time audience. Waldfogel's data show that between 8:00 and 10:00 p.m. on Thursdays, UPN's average audience share among blacks is higher than all of the major networks, and during prime time an average of seven UPN time slots have a majority black audience.[34] But during the 10:00 to 11:00 p.m. period, when UPN affiliates are in control of their programming, the UPN share of the black audience is lower than all of the Big Four, and the proportion of its audience that is black is lower. This pattern reveals that the vast majority of viewers, regardless of race and ethnicity, prefer network programs to the programs that stations select when networks are not operating. It also shows that during prime time the extent of "black targeting" is *higher* for the time controlled by the network than for the programming that affiliates control.

Because UPN has the largest audience share among blacks, its affili-

34. Waldfogel's tables include audiences for the 10:00 to 11:00 p.m. period for both UPN and WB, but during these time slots neither network shows network programs. His table 5 apparently also includes prime time on Saturday and Sunday, when UPN does not operate.

Table 15. Program Choices, by UPN Affiliates, February 13, 2004[a]

Type of program	New Orleans	Portland	San Francisco	Washington
Network	4	4	4	4
Infomercials	9	1	3	0
Religious	1	4	5	6
Syndicated	7	18	13	12
Reruns	17	11	13	16
News/local	0	0	0	0

a. Number of half-hour segments, 6:00 a.m. to 1:00 a.m.

ates are a natural place to look for "black-targeted" programs. Waldfogel finds that UPN affiliates on average have the greatest number of half-hour segments outside of prime time with both a majority black audience and a black audience exceeding 90 percent of viewers (table 5).

To examine the nature of black-targeted programs, I collected the program schedules for four UPN affiliates for February 13, 2004, and calculated the types of programs that these stations show in the periods measured by Waldfogel, 6:00 a.m. to 1:00 a.m. (eastern).[35] All four affiliates always carry the UPN network feed, so their variability in programming must arise outside the ten hours of prime-time programs offered by UPN. Table 15 shows the pattern of programming by UPN affiliates. The most striking finding is that no UPN affiliate offers any local programming. Indeed, throughout the entire week of February 13-19, 2004, no UPN affiliate offered a single news or other locally produced program. The closest things to local programs were two Saturday college basketball games on regional networks: a Virginia game in Washington and an LSU game in New Orleans. In short, the most "black- targeted" stations in the country produce exactly zero programs for their local black audience.

The selection of syndicated and rerun programs also does not have a particularly black orientation. In New Orleans, with a 40 percent black population, the network reruns are *Sabrina, Home Improvement, Roseanne, Drew Carey, King of Queens, That 70s Show, Good Times, Sanford & Sons, The Parkers,* and *Family Matters.* The last four programs feature a black cast, but only *The Parkers* (UPN) was not originally broadcast on one of the Big Four networks which, according to the data, are "white targeted" except for Fox. In Washington, which has the

35. The choice of day is unimportant, since outside of prime time most stations run the same program every weekday in the same time slot.

next highest black population, the UPN affiliate reruns are *Cops, Home Improvement, Sabrina, 3rd Rock, King of the Hill, Spin City, The Hughleys, Moesha, That 70s Show, Seinfeld, Everybody Loves Raymond,* and *Dharma and Greg.* Two of these, *Hughleys* and *Moesha,* feature black casts and were originally broadcast on UPN. The next largest black population is San Francisco, and its reruns are *The Hughleys, The Parkers, Sabrina, 3rd Rock, Simpsons, Everybody Loves Raymond, King of Queens,* and *Will and Grace.* The first two are UPN series that feature black casts. Portland's reruns are *Sabrina, Home Improvement, Dharma and Greg, Friends, Simpsons, Frasier, Just Shoot Me,* and *Cops.* None features a black cast. Thus the evidence for "black targeting" is reruns of two or three series with black casts and is just as evident in San Francisco as Washington.

The evidence for syndicated programs is even less compelling. The New Orleans station runs *Ricki Lake, Ripley's Believe It or Not, All Dogs Go to Heaven,* and *Ryan Seacrest.* None of these features a black star, although Ricki Lake's crude talk show frequently involves troubled audience members who are black. By contrast, Portland's talk show is *Montel Williams,* whose star is black. The station also shows several syndicated court programs and *Family Feud,* the game show that also is part of the PAX network lineup.

In summary, UPN affiliates, the most black-oriented group of stations in Waldfogel's sample, show programs that certainly are not more black oriented than UPN's network programs and are very similar to the non-network lineups for affiliates of other networks and independent stations. These lineups do not indicate that the tastes of black viewers differ much from those of other groups, regardless of their audience shares by race and ethnicity.

wb. The WB network is intermediate between PAX and UPN in the number of hours of programs it provides. Like UPN, WB operates for two prime-time hours per night, but unlike UPN it operates on Saturday and Sunday. In addition, WB controls the rights to several children's programs, which it offers for four hours on Saturday morning and two hours on weekday afternoons. Thus WB offers fourteen hours of prime-time programs and fourteen hours of daytime kids' programs. Of the prime-time programs, four hours are accounted for by movies and one hour is a rerun of a program shown the same week, so WB actually produces nine hours per week of original prime-time programs.

Table 16. Program Choices, by WB Affiliates, February 13, 2004[a]

Type of Program	New Orleans	Portland, Me.	Portland, Or.	San Francisco	Washington
Network	8	8	8	8	8
Infomercials	6	8	2	3	4
Religious	2	0	0	4	0
Syndicated	11	10	12	14	21
Reruns	11	11	16	9	5
News/local	0	1	0	0	0

a. Number of half-hour segments, 6:00 a.m. to 1:00 a.m.

Waldfogel's data indicate that WB is second to UPN in its appeal to black audiences, as measured by average audience share that is black and the number of programs with a majority black audience. I collected program schedules for the period February 13-19, 2004, for WB affiliates in New Orleans, Portland, Oregon, Portland, Maine, San Francisco and Washington, D.C. Table 16 shows the composition of the schedules during the 6:00 a.m. to 1:00 a.m. period for February 13, 2004.

As with the affiliates of lesser networks, WB affiliates do almost no original local programming. Only one offers a local news program; another offers a half-hour of *CNN Headline News*. The reruns and syndicated programming are conventional. The New Orleans station provides reruns of *The Littles, Fresh Prince of Bel-Air, Cosby, Simpsons, Friends,* and *the Hughleys,* three of which feature black stars but two of which (*Fresh Prince, Cosby*) were hits on major networks. Portland, Maine, airs *Sabrina, Just Shoot Me, Drew Carey, Will and Grace, King of Queens, Everybody Loves Raymond, Spin City,* and *3rd Rock,* while Portland, Oregon, shows *Roseanne, The Littles, King of the Hill, King of Queens, That 70s Show, Becker, Drew Carey,* and *Taxi.* San Francisco's reruns are *The Littles, Home Improvement, Fresh Prince, King of the Hill, Dharma and Greg,* and *Drew Carey.* Washington shows *The Parkers, Will and Grace,* and *Just Shoot Me.* The syndicated programs feature mainly court shows and talk shows. Again, there is no evidence that these stations engage in offering programs that differ much from the programs offered on other networks or independents during periods of local control.

INDEPENDENTS. To check the programming of independent stations, I consulted the TV listings of the *Washington Post* and *San Francisco Chronicle* in October 2003. The San Francisco area has nine independents. Two offer Hispanic programming, two offer programs in Asian languages in the evenings, one features religious programs, and one does not have a published program log. The six that are not Hispanic all have significant numbers of infomercials, and only two offer locally produced news. Two of the six mainly show reruns of network programs, including many of the shows listed above that are shown on affiliates of minor networks. These stations also show the full range of syndicated talk shows, including several that are also shown on affiliates of UPN and WB.

Washington, D.C., has two independent stations.[36] One of these broadcasts exclusively Russian-language programs, while the other offers an array of programs from numerous countries around the world. Neither independent shows any reruns or American syndicated programs, and neither offers locally originated programming. Not one of these programs could be construed as "black targeted" because the countries of origin of the programs are in Europe and Asia.

Waldfogel treats independents as a single unit, like a network, in his analysis of program choices and audience shares. This treatment is inconsistent with his theoretical model of station competition because the number of stations (not the number of station categories) matters for program choices that stations make. As a result, his estimations explaining the number of hours of black and Hispanic programming exclude the critical explanatory variable, which is the number of stations, perhaps categorized by whether they are independents or affiliates of the four major commercial networks, the three minor commercial networks, or PBS. This specification is necessary to detect targeting.

More important, Waldfogel's approach causes him to miss the clearest effect of a large number of stations on program diversity, which is the presence of foreign language programs. Waldfogel finds that Hispanics account for a very large proportion of the audiences of Univision and Telemundo affiliates; however, he misses the presence of a minor Hispanic network, *TeleFutura*, whose affiliates broadcast mostly Spanish-language programs, and some other independents that also broadcast in Spanish. In addition, he does not detect stations like those in Washington and San Francisco that offer programs in Asian and European languages.

For Waldfogel's findings on blacks' program choices, the question remains, Why do some programs obtain extremely high shares of a black

36. Interestingly, none is actually located in Washington. All of the stations in Washington, D.C., are affiliated with a network. The two independents are located in northern Virginia.

audience? An explanation that differs from his emerges from other studies. Goettler and Shachar studied a panel of viewers during prime time, adopting a latent variables approach to estimating simultaneously the underlying types of programs in the eyes of viewers and the determination of the distribution of viewing among program offerings (explicitly including nonviewing as an option).[37] The dimensions of program characteristics that they found significant in program choice were plot complexity, age of characters, degree of realism, and orientation toward young male urban professionals. Generally, situation comedies and crime dramas have low plot complexity, while programs based on true stories and real people have a high realism component.

Goettler and Shachar report that viewer interest among characteristics differs by demographic group. Although they did not examine race and ethnicity as a source of difference, they report that women prefer complex plots more than men, low-income and less-educated viewers exhibit greater preference for realism, and all age cohorts prefer programs with characters in their own age group (especially in situation comedies). Demographic characteristics are strongly related to whether viewers watch television in late prime time. Because blacks and whites exhibit substantial differences in the demographic characteristics that were used in their sample, one would expect that in cities with a relatively high proportion of blacks, demographic factors could lead some programs to draw predominantly black audiences. The categories of programs for which this would be expected are sit-coms and reality shows, including some of the more confrontational talk shows. These are precisely the shows that dominate the non-prime-time schedules of UPN and WB.

Conclusions

One of Waldfogel's major conclusions is that an increase in the number of minorities living in a metropolitan area creates an externality in that additional people in one racial or ethnic category increase the chance that a local channel will offer programs that are targeted to them. The preceding discussion focuses on Waldfogel's findings about black audiences and shows that his inferences from his empirical findings are not consistent with the programming shown on the stations that are said to have the most black targeting, which are affiliates of UPN and WB. Judg-

37. Goettler and Shachar (2001).

ing from the programs on these channels, blacks who watch channels that have the highest black audiences have basically the same taste for mass entertainment programming as viewers who watch other stations, adjusted for demographic categories such as income, age, education, and gender.

Waldfogel's inferences are consistent with the programming that is oriented to immigrant groups for whom English is, at best, a second language. For the most part, these stations broadcast programs from the home countries of immigrant groups. These programs are by no means local, and there is no good reason that the program logs of stations in a given linguistic category need to differ very much. Whereas I have not examined the program logs for Univision and Telemundo affiliates, I suspect that they are largely overlapping, even outside of prime time.

There is no good reason why these channels must be over-the-air broadcasters. Like broadcast stations, cable systems, though most are part of large national companies, are locally managed. Because almost all cable systems have more channels than the number of television stations in even the largest markets, the Steiner model predicts that they should exhibit even more program fragmentation than local broadcasters. As a single decisionmaker deciding which channels will be on the system, a cable operator is like a broadcast monopolist in that a cable system's best strategy is to add channels that increase the number of subscribers as opposed to fragmenting further a mass audience of a given size.

The Steiner model is about the effect of the number of broadcast outlets on program diversity. In reality, English-speaking Americans reflect very little diversity in their tastes for television programs, regardless of race or ethnicity. Consequently, so-called black-targeted stations are not very different from other stations. But the Steiner model does provide a conceptual foundation for understanding the rise of foreign-language programs on independent stations and cable television channels. In this sense, Waldfogel's claim about an externality from population increase in a local area is correct—as the number of people with a particular linguistic background increases, local broadcasters and cable companies are more likely to carry programs in their native language. Moreover, because of the language barrier, these programs are likely to be viewed almost entirely by members of that linguistic group and can account for a very large portion of their viewing. In this sense, programs are targeted to an ethnic minority.

References

Berry, Steven T., and Joel Waldfogel. 1999. "Free Entry and Social Inefficiency in Radio Broadcasting." *RAND Journal of Economics* 30 (Autumn): 397–420.

———. 2003."Product Quality and Market Size." Working Paper w9675. Cambridge, Mass.: National Bureau of Economic Research (May).

Bresnahan, Timothy F., and Peter Reiss. 1990. "Entry in Monopoly Markets." *Review of Economic Studies* 57 (October): 531–53.

———. 1991. "Entry and Competition in Concentrated Markets." *Journal of Political Economy* 99 (October): 977–1009.

Ciccone, Antonio, and Robert E. Hall. 1996. "Productivity and the Density of Economic Activity." *American Economic Review* 86 (March): 54–70.

Dixit, Avinash K., and Joseph E. Stiglitz. 1977. "Monopolistic Competition and Optimum Product Diversity." *American Economic Review* 67 (June): 297–308.

Friedman, Milton.1962. *Capitalism and Freedom.* University of Chicago Press.

George, Lisa, and Joel Waldfogel. 2003. "Who Affects Whom in Daily Newspaper Markets?" *Journal of Political Economy* 111 (August): 765–84.

Glaeser, Edward L., Jed Kolko, and Albert Saiz. 2001. "Consumer City." *Journal of Economic Geography* 1 (January): 27–50.

Goettler, Ronald L., and Ron Shachar. 2001. "Spatial Competition in the Network Television Industry." *RAND Journal of Economics* 32 (Winter): 624–56.

Holmes, Thomas J. 2002. "The Role of Cities: Evidence from the Placement of Sales Offices." Staff Report 298. Federal Reserve Bank of Minneapolis (January).

Hotelling, Harold. 1929. "Stability in Competition," *Economic Journal* 39 (153): 41–57.

Nelson, Forrest, and Roger G. Noll. 1985. "The Preferences of Policy Makers for Alternative Allocations of the Broadcast Spectrum." In *Antitrust and Regulation: Essays in Memory of John J. McGowan*, edited by Franklin M. Fisher. MIT Press.

Noll, Roger G., Merton J. Peck, and John J. McGowan. 1973. *Economic Aspects of Television Regulation.* Brookings.

Oberholzer-Gee, Felix, and Joel Waldfogel. 2001. "Electoral Acceleration: The Effect of Minority Population on Minority Voter Turnout." Working Paper 8252. Cambridge, Mass.: National Bureau of Economic Research.

Owen, Bruce, Jack Beebe, and Willard Manning. 1974. *Television Economics.* Lexington Books.

Rosenthal, Stuart S., and William Strange. Forthcoming. "Evidence on the Nature and Sources of Agglomeration Economies." Vol. 4. Prepared for the *Handbook of Urban and Regional Economics.* Elsevier.

Siegelman Peter, and Joel Waldfogel. 1998. "Race and Radio: Preference Externalities, Minority Ownership, and the Provision of Programming to Minorities." University of Pennsylvania. Mimeo.

Spence, Michael. 1976a. "Product Selection, Fixed Costs, and Monopolistic Competition." *Review of Economic Studies* 43 (June): 217–35.

———. 1976b. "Product Differentiation and Welfare." *American Economic Review* 66 (May): 407–14.

Steiner, Peter O. 1952. "Program Patterns and the Workability of Competition in Radio Broadcasting." *Quarterly Journal of Economics* 66 (May): 194–222.

Waldfogel, Joel. 2003. "Preference Externalities: An Empirical Study of Who Benefits Whom in Differentiated Product Markets." *RAND Journal of Economics* 34 (Autumn): 557–68.